CW00739555

"Wesley Hill provides an intriguing argument for fundamentally reframing the questions we ask about Pauline christology and trinitarian theology. Given the exegetical care and theological consciousness on display in this well-written book, Hill's case deserves serious consideration. Along the way, the book models promising interaction between Scripture and Christian doctrine."

— DANIEL J. TREIER
Wheaton College

"In this crisply argued volume Hill demonstrates that theology and the reading of Scripture do not just belong together but need one another. Trinitarian theology, Hill convincingly shows, can provide hermeneutical resources for unlocking how Paul speaks of God the Father, the Son, and the Spirit. . . . This is theological exegesis at its finest and sharpest."

— ANGUS PADDISON
University of Winchester

"Advocates with clarity and power for a dense trinitarian reading of Paul. Hill reveals Paul's own subtle use of trinitarian categories, and he shows us how to draw on the trinitarian faith of the church to draw out the beauty and depth of Paul's vision."

— LEWIS AYRES
Durham University

Paul and the Trinity

Persons, Relations,
and the Pauline Letters

Wesley Hill

WILLIAM B. EERDMANS PUBLISHING COMPANY
GRAND RAPIDS, MICHIGAN / CAMBRIDGE, U.K.

© 2015 Wesley Hill
All rights reserved

Published 2015 by
Wm. B. Eerdmans Publishing Co.
2140 Oak Industrial Drive N.E., Grand Rapids, Michigan 49505 /
P.O. Box 163, Cambridge CB3 9PU U.K.

Printed in the United States of America

20 19 18 17 16 15   7 6 5 4 3 2 1

Library of Congress Cataloging-in-Publication Data

Hill, Wesley, 1981-
Paul and the Trinity: persons, relations, and the Pauline letters / Wesley Hill.
    pages   cm
Includes bibliographical references.
ISBN 978-0-8028-6964-7 (pbk.: alk. paper)
1. Bible. Epistles of Paul — Criticism, interpretation, etc.
2. Trinity — Biblical teaching.   I. Title.

BS2655.T75H55   2015
227′.06 — dc23
                                                    2014032506

www.eerdmans.com

For my parents,
Walter and Suzanne Hill

Contents

CONTENTS

Acknowledgements

This study grew initially from conversations with John Barclay about the character of Paul's "God-discourse." To those early talks, when I was beginning work on my M.A. dissertation at Durham University and attending Professor Barclay's "Paul and His Interpreters" module in the Michaelmas term of 2007, I owe the first stimulus for this project. (Among the most helpful pieces of advice I received from Professor Barclay was, "Go have a look at Barth's *Epistle to the Romans*." That was the start of it all.)

When it became clear that the project would attempt a serious engagement with trinitarian theologies, Professor Francis Watson stepped into the role of primary supervisor, and Professor Lewis Ayres, with his expertise in the fourth-century trinitarian controversies, became my secondary supervisor. I am deeply grateful to both of them for guiding the thesis in ways that ensured it would remain a "close" reading of Paul as well as an engagement with the *Sache* of Paul's texts; I could not have asked for better supervisors. I would also like to thank Professor Walter Moberly for many helpful informal conversations about the thesis. I would also like to thank my examiners, Angus Paddison and Mark McIntosh, for their critical engagement with the finished product and for helping me make some corrections and improvements.

My interest in Paul began as an undergraduate at Wheaton College (IL), and I would like to thank especially Dr. Scott Hafemann for his direction and encouragement as I learned Greek and began to study Paul in a serious way for the first time. A fellow student from undergraduate days, Dr. Michael Allen, has remained a uniquely encouraging friend and took time to give chapters 2-4 a careful read in the midst of his own busy schedule of teaching and research. This book could not have been written without Mike and his wife Emily's loyal, persistent encouragement, not to mention Mike's keen bibliographic instincts (where would this study have gone without his recommendation that I read Matthew Levering and Gilles Emery?). Another fellow student, this one also at Durham, Dr. Jonathan Linebaugh, read the entirety of the manuscript at least once and discussed its structure and content in detail with me at every stage. I am hugely in Jono's debt, not only for that academic assistance but also for the warm hospitality and friendship he and his family extended to me while I was in Durham. Jono and his wife Megan's daughter Callie Jane became my goddaughter the second year of my Ph.D. studies, and it was one of the bright spots of my time in the UK, to say the least.

Other fellow Durham postgraduates, especially Orrey McFarland, discussed my thesis with me in depth at virtually every turn and helped me maintain energy and good humor throughout the writing process. I am more thankful than I can say for Orrey and his wife Kristi's friendship (which began almost literally from Day One in Durham and has remained a great gift), as well as the kindness of our whole "circle" — Jon and Amelia Parker and family, Todd and Kelly Brewer, Paul and Katy Jones, Matt and Brandy Crawford, Dave and Mindy Briones, Ben and Martha Dunson, Ben and Heather Blackwell, and the whole gang at 37a N. Bailey and the other members of the New Testament Seminar.

I am grateful to Durham University for awarding me a Doctoral Fellowship which made this research possible.

I am also grateful to the members of my church in Durham, The King's Church, who opened their homes and hearts to me. Particular mention must go to Mark and Ruth Bonnington (and Ana, Gus, and Zak), Ruth Perrin, and — not least — my worship leader, next-door neighbor, theological conversation partner, and dear friend Chris Juby, his wife Hannah, and their son — my godson — Samuel Thomas. The Jubies found me a place to live before I even arrived and supported me in countless ways during our happy years together as fellow Neville Terrace dwellers.

Finally, I want to thank my family who, in the early years of my childhood, helped nurture in me a love for Scripture that, I believe, led directly to this thesis. My sister Laurie and my brother Lance have been unflagging in their commitment to me, as have my brother-in-law Justin and my new nephew Christian Michael. But above all, I am grateful to my parents, Walter and Suzanne Hill, for their love. I often say to people that my earliest childhood memories are of hearing my parents read stories from the Bible to me, including the "Arch Book" pictorial, rhyming version of Saul's encounter with the risen Lord on the road to Damascus. From those early days of "reading Paul" until my current, more sophisticated (though not necessarily wiser) reading, Dad and Mom have been my most important mentors, cheerleaders, and now friends. It is to them that I dedicate this thesis, with love.

WESLEY A. HILL

Abbreviations

AB	Anchor Bible
Ablab.	Gregory of Nyssa, *Ad Ablabium*
Adv. Eu.	Basil of Caesarea, *Adversus Eunomium;* Gregory of Nyssa, *Adversus Eunomium*
AnBib	Analecta biblica
Ant.	Josephus, *Antiquities of the Jews*
ANTC	Abingdon New Testament Commentaries
Apoc. Abr.	*Apocalypse of Abraham*
BDAG	E. W. Danker, W. Bauer, W. F. Arndt, and F. W. Gingrich, *Greek-English Lexicon of the New Testament and Other Early Christian Literature.* Chicago, 2000.
BDF	F. Blass, A. Debrunner, and R. W. Funk. *A Greek Grammar of the New Testament and Other Early Christian Literature.* Chicago, 1961.
BECNT	Baker Exegetical Commentary on the New Testament
BETL	Bibliotheca ephemeridum theologicarum lovaniensium
BHT	Beiträge zur historischen Theologie
B.J.	Josephus, *Jewish War*
BNTC	Black's New Testament Commentaries
BZ	*Biblische Zeitschrift*
BZNW	Beihefte zur *Zeitschrift für die neutestamentliche Wissenschaft*
C. Ap.	Josephus, *Contra Apionem*
C. Ar.	Athanasius, *Orationes contra Arianos*
CBQ	*Catholic Biblical Quarterly*
CCSL	Corpus Christianorum, Series graeca
CD	Dead Sea Scrolls Damascus Document

Cher.	Philo, *De Cherubim*
ConBNT	Coniectanea biblica, New Testament series
ConNT	Coniectanea neotestamentica
CSEL	Corpus scriptorum ecclesiasticorum latinorum
EKKNT	Evangelisch-katholischer Kommentar zum Neuen Testament
esp.	especially
ET	English translation
ExpTim	*Expository Times*
FS	Festschrift
GNO	Gregorii Nysseni Opera
HBT	*Horizons in Biblical Theology*
HNT	Handbuch zum Neuen Testament
HTR	*Harvard Theological Review*
HUTh	Hermeneutische Untersuchungen zur Theologie
ICC	International Critical Commentary
IJST	*International Journal of Systematic Theology*
JBL	*Journal of Biblical Literature*
JSNT	*Journal for the Study of the New Testament*
JSNTSup	*Journal for the Study of the New Testament* Supplement Series
JTI	*Journal of Theological Interpretation*
JTS	*Journal of Theological Studies*
KEK	Kritisch-exegetischer Kommentar über das Neue Testament
NIB	*New Interpreter's Bible*
NICNT	New International Commentary on the New Testament
NIGTC	New International Greek Testament Commentary
NovT	*Novum Testamentum*
NovTSup	*Novum Testamentum* Supplement Series
NPNF[2]	Nicene and Post-Nicene Fathers, series 2
NSBT	New Studies in Biblical Theology
NTD	Das Neue Testament Deutsch
NTL	New Testament Library
NTS	*New Testament Studies*
Or.	Gregory Nazianzen, *Orationes*
OTL	Old Testament Library
SBLMS	Society of Biblical Literature Monograph Series
SBLSP	*Society of Biblical Literature Seminar Papers*
SBS	Stuttgarter Bibelstudien
SC	Sources chrétiennes
SJT	*Scottish Journal of Theology*

SJTOP	*Scottish Journal of Theology* Occaisional Papers
SNTSMS	Society for New Testament Studies Monograph Series
StNT	Studien zum Neuan Testament
TDNT	*Theological Dictionary of the New Testament.* Edited by G. Kittel and G. Friedrich. Translated by G. W. Bromiley. 10 vols. Grand Rapids: Eerdmans, 1964-76.
THKNT	Theologischer Handkommentar zum Neuen Testament
TPINTC	TPI New Testament Commentaries
TynBul	*Tyndale Bulletin*
WBC	Word Biblical Commentary
WMANT	Wissenschaftliche Monographien zum Alten und Neuen Testament
WUNT	Wissenschaftliche Untersuchungen zum Neuen Testament
ZKT	*Zeitschrift für katholischen Theologie*
ZNW	*Zeitschrift für die Neutestamentliche Wissenschaft*

CHAPTER ONE

The Eclipse of Relations in the Interpretation of Pauline God-Talk

The history of interpretation of Pauline speech about God and Jesus (and, to some extent, the Spirit as well) is, among other things, the story of a replacement of one way of speaking with another. Here, before embarking on a detailed discussion of Paul himself, I want to tell the story of how Paul's interpreters opted for a newer model of "theology and christology" and rejected an older one. In what follows, I will describe the way in which the more recent theological conceptuality (a "christological" model) has replaced another (a "trinitarian" model) in several influential recent interpretations of Paul. Following that, I will articulate some of the dynamics of one element of that older, "trinitarian" model — namely, the element of the "relations" that obtain between the trinitarian "persons" — and attempt to retrieve that element as an aid for Pauline exegesis. My contention, which can only be borne out in the exegesis offered in subsequent chapters, is that Pauline interpreters ought to return to the "trinitarian" model when it comes to the task of explicating the identities of God, Jesus, and the Spirit.

For much of the history of biblical interpretation, trinitarian conceptual categories enabled readers to make sense of Paul's God-talk.[1] The

---

1. Studies of trinitarian exegesis of Paul are beginning to proliferate and achieve greater depth and subtlety as historians of doctrine give more attention to the role of exegesis in the development of doctrine; see, e.g., Craig A. Blaising, "Creedal Formulation as Hermeneutical Development: A Reexamination of Nicaea," *Pro Ecclesia* 19/4 (2010): 371-88; Lewis Ayres, *Augustine and the Trinity* (Cambridge: Cambridge University Press, 2010), esp. ch. 6; Michael A. G. Haykin, *The Spirit of God: The Exegesis of 1 and 2 Corinthians in the Pneumatomachian Controversy of the Fourth Century* (Leiden: Brill, 1994). Of course, there was significant diversity among various types of trinitarian readings of Paul's texts.

identities of God, Christ, and the Spirit[2] were explicated by means of their relations to and with one another. Interpreters were enabled, for example, to articulate who Jesus Christ was by talking about him vis-à-vis his being "sent" by the Father (e.g., in Gal 4:4), his being declared as Son according to the Spirit (Rom 1:4), and so on. What I want to try to show here is that this way of interpreting Paul has receded in prominence in much recent discussion of Paul's theology. Rather than explicating the *relations* between God, Jesus, and the Spirit in Paul's texts, many recent interpreters concerned with Paul's God-talk — or, to use the terminology more frequently employed, Paul's "monotheism" and "christology" — have focused their attention instead on the questions of whether, or to what degree, the Christian Paul continued to affirm Second Temple Jewish "monotheism" and whether, as a result, he had a "high" or "low" christology. Paul remained a believer in the one God of Israel in some sense, it is argued; hence, his task was to locate the point at which Christ belonged on the vertical axis whose most elevated pole was ontological equality with this one God and whose lowest point was creaturely subservience to God.

That one of these conceptualities or the other is right or wrong is not at issue in this first part of Chapter 1. Rather, my initial aim is simply to note the dominance of certain hermeneutical strategies and conceptual categories within recent Pauline interpretation and to show that, despite the diversity among them, the way in which their questions and conclusions are framed ensures that what we might call the "vertical plotting" of Jesus in relation to God has overshadowed other possible ways (and especially a "trinitarian" way) of describing Paul's God-talk. For my present purposes, it matters less where Jesus ends up on the vertical axis and more that this axis is the means by which his identity is construed. That Jesus belongs at

2. These terms, rather than the more traditional Father, Son, and Spirit, are preferable in discussions of Pauline theology. Paul refers to Jesus as υἱός only 15x in the seven undisputed letters, but references to "Jesus" (15x), "Jesus Christ" (20), "Christ Jesus" (44), "Lord Jesus" (18), and "Lord Jesus Christ" (32) are more plentiful. There are 23 references to God as πατήρ in the undisputed letters, but, as Paul W. Meyer, " 'The Father': The Presentation of God in the Fourth Gospel," in R. A. Culpepper and C. C. Black (eds.), *Exploring the Gospel of John* (Louisville: Westminster/John Knox, 1996), 255-73, at 263, notes, "In the undisputed letters, Paul refers to Jesus Christ as 'Son of God' or 'the Son' or 'his [sc. God's] Son' fourteen times but *never* in conjunction with any reference to God as 'Father.' He refers to God as 'the Father' (absolute) nine times (including 'the Father of mercies,' i.e., 'the merciful Father' in 2 Cor. 1:3), as the 'Father' of human beings (always 'our Father') eleven times, but as 'the Father of [our] Lord Jesus [Christ]' only three times (Rom. 15:6; 2 Cor. 1:3; 11:31), and in none of these contexts is Jesus Christ spoken of as 'Son.' "

a "high" point or a "low" point on the vertical axis is less significant than the fact that where he is placed on that axis is considered to be the crucial interpretive question.

What follows will proceed in three stages. First, I will provide a review of some representative interpreters of Paul, highlighting their concern with the relation of God and Jesus[3] in Pauline theology. These interpreters may be divided into two categories (although their points of difference and unique emphases — the ways in which they break out of a simple binary categorization — will be observed along the way): those who see Paul's christology as "high" and those who see it as "low." Second, I will offer some assessment of the varying proposals of these interpreters and note areas of agreement and disagreement before I offer my own critique and alternative proposal. Third, I will discuss the category of "relations" as explicated within some select trinitarian theologies and indicate the ways in which this category may suggest some new pathways for exegesis of Paul.

1. Pauline Monotheism and "Low"/"High" Christology

The aim of this section is to observe some trends in recent interpretation of Pauline theology and christology. A common feature of these recent discussions is the employment of "high christology" and "low christology" as shorthand ways of referring to different options for construing Paul's viewpoint.[4] Despite their frequent use, however, these terms tend to be

---

3. The Holy Spirit is notably absent from most of these discussions. Many scholars would argue that Paul is more of a binitarian than trinitarian, a judgment that will be questioned by way of exegesis in Chapter 5 below.

4. Although they are frequently employed now, the precise origin of the terms "high" and "low" christology is difficult to determine. These terms occur in English at least as far back as the mid-nineteenth century (see H. P. Liddon, *The Divinity of Our Lord and Saviour Jesus Christ: Eight Lectures Preached before the University of Oxford, in the Year 1866, on the Foundation of the Late Rev. John Bampton, M.A. Canon of Salisbury* [1866; reprint Lansing: Scholarly Publishing Office, University of Michigan Library, 2005], who uses the phrase "high Christology" [xxvi] with reference to James, whose epistle "presupposes the Christology of St. Paul" [285]; in the same context, he speaks of "so fundamental a question as the Personal Rank of Christ in the scale of being" [280]) and in German discussions dating from the same time (see I. A. Dorner, *Entwickelungsgeschichte der Lehre von der Person Christi*, 2 vols. [Stuttgart: Verlag von Samuel Gottlieb Liesching, 1845-53], ET: *History of the Development of the Doctrine of the Person of Christ* [5 vols.; Edinburgh: T&T Clark, 1861-63], and the useful introduction to Dorner's historical theological context in Claude Welch

loosely defined. According to Gordon Fee, the question of whether Paul's christology was "high" or "low" has to do with "how he viewed the relationship between Christ, as the Son of God and Lord, and the one God, as the Father of our Lord Jesus Christ, who is therefore now revealed as our Father as well."[5] For Fee, the matter turns on Jesus' preexistence:

> Although this might be considered an oversimplification, the ultimate issue has to do with the Son's preexistence; that is, does an author consider Christ to have had existence as (or with) God before coming into our history . . . ? If the answer to that question is yes, then one speaks of an author (e.g., the Gospel of John, the author of Hebrews) as having a high Christology. If the answer is either no or ambiguous at best, then the author (e.g., James) is credited with a low Christology. The ultimate question of Pauline Christology, therefore, is where Paul fits on this spectrum.[6]

In addition to the issue of Jesus' personal preexistence, there are other criteria by which the question of whether a christology is "high" or "low" is usually decided:

1. the meaning and import of the role of Christ in creation (1 Cor 8:6; cf. Col 1:16; and, outside the Pauline corpus, John 1:1-5; Heb 1:2-3, 10-12; Rev 3:14);
2. the use and meaning of the κύριος ("Lord") title for God and Christ (Phil 2:10-11; 1 Cor 8:6, among many others);[7]

[ed.], *God and Incarnation in Mid-Nineteenth Century German Theology: G. Thomasius, I. A. Dorner, A. E. Biedermann* [New York: Oxford University Press, 1965], 3-30). I am grateful to Prof. Markus Bockmuehl for alerting me to these sources.

5. Gordon Fee, *Pauline Christology: An Exegetical-Theological Study* (Peabody, MA: Hendrickson, 2007), 9.

6. Fee, *Pauline Christology*, 9-10. But compare, e.g., Raymond E. Brown, *An Introduction to New Testament Christology* (New York: Paulist Press, 1994), 4, for whom "low" and "high" christologies are not mutually exclusive categories but instead point to different aspects of Jesus' identity, so that a NT author may use "high" terminology without repudiating descriptions in "low" terminology and vice versa (e.g., "I am making no judgment that the NT writers who used low-christology terminology did not believe in Jesus' divinity. . . . Sometimes in different passages the same writer uses of Jesus terms reflecting respectively high and low christology"). From my reading of the literature, it seems that Brown's understanding is an unusual one.

7. For a list of all the relevant texts, see Richard Bauckham, "Paul's Christology of

3. the definition of "monotheism" and how radically Paul reconfigured it vis-à-vis other Jewish definitions;

4. the meaning and import of the "subjection" (ὑποτάσσειν) of Christ to God (1 Cor 15:28; cf. Phil 2:10-11).

In addition to these specific criteria, the weight interpreters give to various themes — the significance of the Adam or Wisdom backgrounds for Pauline christology, for example — functions as an indicator of how "high" or "low" interpreters consider Paul's christology.

In order to see how these criteria function, I turn now to a more thorough examination of the interpreters who identify their readings of Paul under the rubrics of either "high" or "low" christology.

i. "Low" Christology

In this section, I will concentrate on a few representative scholars, most prominently James D. G. Dunn.[8] In Dunn's reading of Pauline theology,

---

Divine Identity," in *Jesus and the God of Israel:* God Crucified *and Other Studies on the New Testament's Christology of Divine Identity* (Grand Rapids: Eerdmans, 2008), 182-232, at 186-91; David B. Capes, *Old Testament Yahweh Texts in Paul's Christology* (WUNT 2/47; Tübingen: Mohr Siebeck, 1992), ch. 3.

8. A full justification for placing Dunn's work under the rubric of " 'low' christology" must await subsequent discussion, but it is necessary at the outset to note the potentially problematic nature of this placement, since Dunn himself interprets his own conclusions as compatible with a "high" or moderately "high" christology; see, e.g., James D. G. Dunn and Maurice Wiles, "M. Wiles on *Christology in the Making* and Responses by the Author," in James D. G. Dunn, *The Christ and the Spirit;* Volume 1: *Christology* (Grand Rapids: Eerdmans, 1998), 257-69, at 258; Dunn, *The Theology of Paul the Apostle* (Grand Rapids: Eerdmans, 1998), 258: "a high christology of Jesus as highly exalted Lord"; cf. his recent characterization of himself as a "(slightly deviant) member of the Early High Christology Club" ("When Was Jesus First Worshipped? In Dialogue with Larry Hurtado's *Lord Jesus Christ: Devotion to Jesus in Earliest Christianity*," *ExpTim* 116 [2005]: 193-96, at 196). Fee (*Pauline Christology,* 13) considers Dunn's Paul to be "the 'halfway house' between an early low Christology and the full-blown high Christology of John and Hebrews." For the purposes of a typology of various viewpoints, it is important to observe the strangeness of Dunn's positive appeal to, e.g., N. T. Wright's terminology of "christological monotheism" ("Poetry and Theology in Colossians 1.15-20," in *The Climax of the Covenant: Christ and the Law in Pauline Theology* [London: T&T Clark, 1991], 99-119, at 99) when the rest of his discussion is a sustained and nuanced qualification and, in many cases, repudiation of precisely such views as Wright's. Thus, there appears to be a warrant for not taking Dunn's own

Paul's theology proper — his convictions about God — take as their start-ing point the particular form of monotheism Paul inherited from his Jewish upbringing.[9] Despite his conversion/call on the Damascus road, Paul never abandoned this Jewish heritage. The challenge for his interpreters is thus to specify the nature of the interplay between his unchanging monotheistic convictions and his newfound beliefs about the role of Jesus within God's purposes. According to Dunn, this is precisely that — a challenge — for at least two reasons. First, Paul's beliefs about God must be unearthed from beneath the surface of his discourse.[10] Paul never spelled out what he thought about God, since "it was the fundamental belief of his own [Jew-ish] tradition, the belief in which he himself had been instructed from his youth, and out of which he had lived his life for as long as he could remem-ber."[11] But, second, these convictions about God must be seen as having been changed by the revelation of Christ Paul received: "Paul's belief in Christ impacted on his theology of God."[12] The story of Jesus is, as it were, a second story superimposed on a more fundamental story — the story of the one God of Israel — by whose contours the features of the underlying story of Israel's God are to some degree reshaped.[13]

---

assessment of his work at face value but instead situating his arguments and conclusions alongside similar ones, regardless of whether their respective authors disagree about how to label them. Beyond these considerations, the broader issue, as will hopefully become clear, is the problematic nature of the rubrics "high" and "low" christologies themselves, on which, see further section 2 below.

9. Dunn, *Theology of Paul,* 18.

10. Dunn, *Theology of Paul,* 28.

11. Dunn, *Theology of Paul,* 29. As Francis Watson, "The Triune Divine Identity: Re-flections on Pauline God-language, in Disagreement with J. D. G. Dunn," *JSNT* 80 (2000): 99-124, at 104 n. 9, notes, Dunn's statements at this point resemble E. P. Sanders's famous remark: "From [Paul] we learn nothing new or remarkable about God. God is a God of wrath and mercy, who seeks to save rather than to condemn, but rejection of whom leads to death. One could, to be sure, list further statements made by Paul about God, but it is clear that Paul did not spend his time reflecting on the nature of the deity" (*Paul and Palestinian Judaism* [London: SCM, 1977], 509). This viewpoint seems prevalent in discussions of Paul's theol-ogy; in addition to Sanders, Jochen Flebbe, *Solus Deus. Untersuchungen zur Rede von Gott im Brief des Paulus an die Römer* (BZNW 158; Berlin/New York: Walter de Gruyter, 2008), 10-11, mentions W. G. Kümmel, E. Fascher, P.-G. Klumbies, A. Lindemann, K. H. Schelkle, W. Wrede, and A. Deißmann as making similar statements; cf. also J. Christiaan Beker, *Paul the Apostle: The Triumph of God in Life and Thought* (Philadelphia: Fortress, 1980), 357-58.

12. Dunn, *Theology of Paul,* 30. Cf. Paul-Gerhard Klumbies, *Die Rede von Gott bei Paulus in ihrem zeitgeschichtlichen Kontext* (Göttingen: Vandenhoeck & Ruprecht, 1992).

13. Dunn, *Theology of Paul,* 18, drawing on Richard B. Hays, *The Faith of Jesus Christ:*

If we ask in what way the "second story" alters the more basic one, Dunn's answer is that the revelation of Jesus Christ showed Paul the true depth of his Jewish convictions. As he puts it, "Paul's understanding of God's *purpose* and of God's *revelation* has been radically altered, but not his understanding of God as one and finally sovereign."[14] In other words, the Christ-event discloses the goal the God of Israel had in mind all along (inclusion of the Gentiles among his people) and the means by which God will accomplish that goal (Christ is the "vice-regent" of the one God). In Christ, the *scope* and *means of implementation* of the one God's designs have been reconfigured. But, despite this, God remains the one God he has always been, and his further self-revelation in and through Christ does not amount to a redefinition of his identity.[15]

What are Dunn's exegetical reasons for formulating his account of Pauline theology in this manner? Without attempting a full-scale reconstruction of his interpretation of numerous Pauline texts (to be discussed more fully in later chapters), I will briefly outline Dunn's key exegetical moves with regard to several representative passages in Paul's letters.

Phil 2:6-11, the so-called "Christ hymn," is often read as an instance of Paul's "high" christology, whereby Jewish monotheism is "opened up" to include Jesus, in some fashion, within its definition. For Dunn, however, this is to misread the passage. When Paul speaks of Christ Jesus "being in the form of God" (v. 6a; ἐν μορφῇ θεοῦ ὑπάρχων), he is most likely referring to Adam's creation in God's "image" (Gen 1:26 LXX; εἰκών), and the subsequent reference to Jesus' refusal to grasp "equality with God" (v. 6b; τὸ εἶναι ἴσα θεῷ) is, likewise, dependent on the account of Adam's temptation to be "like God" (Gen 3:5 LXX; ὡς θεοί).[16] On this reading, Paul spells out Jesus' identity by way of a tradition of "Adam christology." Rather than a preexistent figure occupying a space somewhere between deity and humanity after the fashion of later patristic debates, Jesus in this passage is

---

An Investigation of the Narrative Substructure of Galatians 3:1–4:11 (SBL Dissertation Series 56; Chico: Scholars Press, 1983), 5, 6.

14. Dunn, *Theology of Paul,* 255; italics added.

15. James D. G. Dunn, "Pauline Christology: Shaping the Fundamental Structures," in *The Christ and the Spirit,* Volume 1: *Christology,* 229-38, at 236.

16. James D. G. Dunn, *Christology in the Making: A New Testament Inquiry into the Origins of the Doctrine of the Incarnation* (2nd ed.; London: SCM, 1989), 115-16. Dunn's construal depends upon placing μορφή in parallelism with εἰκών, a judgment called into question by David Steenburg, "The Case against the Synonymity of Morphê and Eikôn," *JSNT* 34 (1988): 77-86.

an exalted human figure whose role is determined by a pre-formed Jewish trope wherein humanity was to fulfill an Adamic commission of submission to God and rule over creation (see, e.g., Ps 8:6).[17] Unsurprisingly, then, the final exaltation of Jesus (Phil 2:9-11a) involves Jesus' yielding up ultimate glorification to God the Father, rather than his sharing unqualifiedly in that glory himself.[18]

Dunn finds similar themes in 1 Cor 8:5-6 and 15:20-28.[19] The former passage is widely recognized as a modification of the *Shema* (Deut 6:4). Yet it does not follow that Christ is thereby identified with God as such. In a subtle formulation, Dunn suggests that Christ may share God's lordship as an expression of *God's* authority and thus remain clearly subordinate to God. Christ is the instrument of, rather than an unqualified partaker in, God's unique sovereignty.[20] The conceptuality allowing Paul to effect this attribution in 1 Cor 8:5-6 is not Adam- but rather Wisdom-christology. The split Paul introduces in the *Shema* between the creative power of God and Christ is unique in terms of the history of religion.[21] But that does not mean its appearance is entirely *de novo:* In the Jewish Wisdom traditions, the one God relates to the world through the figure of Wisdom, who personifies and enables God's immanent involvement with the world without being seen as an ontological competitor with God.[22] In Paul's formulation, what is without parallel is not that the one God operates by means of an intermediary but rather that the man *Jesus* now occupies the place given to Wisdom in Jewish traditions. But we must

17. Dunn, *Christology in the Making,* 98-100, 105-6; Dunn, "Pauline Christology: Shaping the Fundamental Structures," 231-33. For an exceptionally clear articulation of a Jewish expectation of one who would embody the role originally envisioned for Adam and its historically discrete building blocks, see N. T. Wright, "Adam, Israel and the Messiah," in *Climax of the Covenant,* 18-40, at 21-26, though Wright distances his construal from Dunn's at the point of the relation between Adam- and Wisdom-christology (19-20).

18. Dunn, *Theology of Paul,* 251-2; "Christology as an Aspect of Theology," in *The Christ and the Spirit,* Vol. 1: *Christology,* 377-87, at 380.

19. Others have noted the thematic links between these texts: e.g., Wilhelm Thüsing, *Per Christum in Deum. Das Verhältnis der Christozentrik zur Theozentrik,* vol. 1 (Münster: Aschendorff, 1965), 58, on the connection between Phil 2:10-11 and 1 Cor 15:24-28.

20. Dunn, *Christology in the Making,* 179-83; *Theology of Paul,* 253. Cf. Andreas Lindemann, "Die Rede von Gott in der paulinische Theologie," *Theologie und Glaube* 69 (1979): 357-76, at 367.

21. Dunn, *Christology in the Making,* 180.

22. For Dunn's discussion of Wisdom in pre-Christian Judaism and a listing of the relevant texts, see *Christology in the Making,* 163-76; *Theology of Paul,* 266-81.

be cautious, Dunn thinks, lest we claim too much for the exalted Jesus. Instead of Jesus' lordship redefining the one God's identity, the thought is "simply that Christ is the action of God, Christ embodies the creative power of God," which is to say, the pre-existent one is not a "being" as such but rather is "God acting wisely," with which action Jesus is now identified.[23] In Dunn's words: "By formulating the divine significance of Christ in wisdom language, Paul was able to retain the already burgeoning christology within the constraints of the Jewish monotheism that remains axiomatic for Christian theology."[24] Wisdom traditions allow Paul to attribute a high status to Jesus — but not one so high that monotheism is thereby compromised.

Likewise with regard to 1 Cor 15:20-28 — although here, as in Phil 2:6-11, Adam-christology takes precedence over Wisdom-christology. Here, too, Paul's christology is held in check by the requirement of monotheistic affirmation. Although the lordship of Christ vis-à-vis other "lords" (8:5-6) is unqualified, the relation of his lordship to that of God is not evenly balanced, as if Jesus were a second God alongside the one God.[25] Rather, Christ ultimately submits himself to God "in order that God might be all in all" (15:28).[26] This text is of particular interest to Dunn because it shows that the moment when the universality of Christ's lordship is most emphasized (via the merging of Pss 110:1 and 8:6b in 1 Cor 15:25-27) is the precise moment when Christ's subjection to God is clearly underscored — further proof that "Pauline christology again and again in its 'highest' moments shows itself to be in essence an aspect of theology."[27]

Such, in brief, is Dunn's conception of the relation between God and Christ in Pauline theology. If we compare Dunn's proposal to other interpreters who advocate a "qualified" or "low" christology, it becomes apparent that, for some, his emphasis on the subjection of Christ to God does not go far enough. Maurice Casey, for example, admits that Phil 2:6-11 "does raise Jesus to an extraordinarily high position" — a position "on the verge of deity, sufficiently close for anyone involved in Jewish culture to feel that it needed to be legitimated." Nevertheless, Casey argues that we may not infer from this text a widespread practice of worship of Jesus in

---

23. Dunn, *Christology in the Making*, 182, order slightly altered.
24. Dunn, "Pauline Christology," 236.
25. Cf. Lindemann, "Die Rede von Gott in der paulinische Theologie," 367.
26. Dunn, *Theology of Paul*, 249.
27. Dunn, "Christology as an Aspect of Theology," 382.

the Pauline churches.[28] On his reading of the evidence, Pauline christology represents a genuine development of Jewish monotheism ("a significant change") in terms of making Jesus the preeminent intermediary figure between the one God and the world. But, crucially, this development "was perceived to be within the bounds of Jewish monotheism, not beyond them"; otherwise one would find evidence of controversy in the Pauline letters over the matter of christology, but, as it is, such evidence is notably lacking.[29] For Casey, what "raised [early Christian] Christology higher" was a complex, dialectical interweaving of multiple strands: Jesus' role of bringing salvation to Gentiles, Eucharistic experience, new interpretation of that experience, which led to further experience and subsequent modification of belief, and so on.[30] In this model, Jesus is a figure *on the way* to being deified but not quite there. Early Christian, and specifically Pauline, christology is thus best understood as occupying a point on a spectrum: christology may be elevated higher and higher the more one attributes divine actions and qualities to Jesus, with Jewish monotheism providing the constraint that is gradually overcome.[31]

A recent book by James F. McGrath, *The Only True God: Early Christian Monotheism in Its Jewish Context*,[32] also finds Dunn's model insufficient, primarily because it posits too much elevation in early Christian christology too early. With regard to the focal Pauline texts — Phil 2:6-11, 1 Cor 8:6; 15:28 — McGrath sees even less christological innovation than Dunn does. Jesus has not been included *within* the Shema in 1 Cor 8:6 but instead *alongside* it:

> When the oneness of God [8:6a, "there is one God"] is coupled with another assertion of oneness [8:6b, "there is one Lord"] in this way, we must look carefully to determine whether we are indeed dealing

28. P. M. Casey, "Monotheism, Worship and Christological Developments in Pauline Churches," in C. C. Newman, J. Davila, and G. Lewis (eds.), *The Jewish Roots of Christological Monotheism: Papers from the St Andrews Conference on the Historical Origins of the Worship of Jesus* (Leiden: Brill, 1999), 214-33, at 226, 227.

29. Casey, "Monotheism, Worship and Christological Developments," 231.

30. Casey, "Monotheism, Worship and Christological Developments," 233.

31. Casey's understanding is a fully developed theory, whereby the influx of Gentiles into the early Christian movement was the catalyst that led to the drastic modification of Jewish monotheism; see Maurice Casey, *From Jewish Prophet to Gentile God: The Origins and Development of New Testament Christology* (Louisville: Westminster/John Knox, 1991).

32. Urbana and Chicago: University of Illinois Press, 2009.

with a splitting of the Shema that is without parallel, or an addition of a second clause *alongside* the Shema, which is not in fact unparalleled in Jewish literature.[33]

McGrath argues that Paul has "expanded" rather than "split" the Shema: God and Jesus together do not constitute "one God"; rather, "there is one God" *and* "there is one Lord" — both alongside one another, and yet the second occupying a subordinate, mediatorial role in relation to the first.[34] In line with typical Jewish affirmations that, since there is one God, there must also be one primary mediator of the one God's sovereignty on earth,[35] Paul too makes a similar, "unusually exalted" affirmation with regard to Jesus. "But," McGrath notes, "an exalted claim for a human being was not by definition incompatible with 'monotheism.'"[36]

Similarly, with regard to Phil 2:6-11, McGrath argues that the nuances of Paul's language must be appreciated lest the claims for a mutation in monotheistic faith be overstated. When Paul says that God has bestowed on Jesus the name that is above every name (v. 9b), it is important to observe that the divine name is *given* to Jesus (as opposed to something he possesses "by nature," for example).[37] This is fully parallel to the way some forms of first-century Judaism accorded the divine name to angelic representatives of God who were not to be identified with God ontologically. Here McGrath offers the *Apocalypse of Abraham* as an example. The name of the angel Yahoel there is comprised of two names for God, Yah(weh) and El. Nevertheless, "[t]he angel is among the worshippers of God and is not confused with God, even though as God's agent he bears the name of God himself" (see, e.g., 10.3, 8; 17.2, 7).[38] Similarly, Jesus receives the divine name not because he has somehow been "identified" with the one God (it is not clear, in any case, what that would mean) but because he

---

33. McGrath, *The Only True God,* 40.

34. Cf. Marinus de Jonge, *God's Final Envoy: Early Christology and Jesus' Own View of His Mission* (Grand Rapids: Eerdmans, 1998), 116: "early Christians were very much aware that Jesus, the exalted one, remained second to the Lord God."

35. McGrath, *The Only True God,* 42-43, adduces 1 Tim 2:5; 1 Thess 1:9-10; 2 Sam 7:22-24; and Josephus, *C. Ap.* 2.193 to show that the affirmation of one God was often seen to entail a corollary "one" entity (whether one mediator, one agent of salvation, one people, or one temple respectively).

36. McGrath, *The Only True God,* 43.

37. McGrath, *The Only True God,* 49.

38. McGrath, *The Only True God,* 49.

plays a mediatorial role not dissimilar to that of an angelic representative.[39] "Paul's application of the divine name 'Lord' and of Yahweh texts from the Hebrew Bible to Jesus is intended to present Jesus as God's agent, who shares in God's rule and authority," which becomes clearer when 1 Cor 15:27-28 is taken into consideration.[40] There Jesus is the representative man (Ps 8:6) who achieves the submission of "all things" to himself (v. 27) only to subject himself finally to God. "Monotheism is preserved not because Jesus is absorbed into God or included in the divine identity but because even though Jesus reigns over absolutely everything else on God's behalf, God himself is not subjected to Christ, but Christ is subjected to God."[41]

Describing these various interpreters and their views under the same rubric — "low christology" — and with the same terms (e.g., "monotheism") is not meant to obscure the important differences among them. What they hold in common, however, is for our present purposes of equal importance with what distinguishes them. A point of agreement for these interpreters is that Jewish monotheism serves as the axiomatic starting point, the relatively known, stable quantity against which the innovative aspects of Pauline christology are to be measured.[42] This is not to say that "monotheism" remains entirely unaffected by christological developments; but these interpreters argue that it remains basic for Paul in a way that christology does not. For Dunn, Paul rethinks the identity of Jesus from within his fundamentally intact monotheistic convictions; this leads to an astonishingly high and, by Jewish standards, extraordinary status for Jesus but one that still remains within the ambit of what would have been considered "monotheism" in first-century Judaism. For Casey, the identity of Jesus is well on its way toward becoming fully divine, but at least for Paul, the pressure of Greco-Roman conceptualities had not yet made itself felt to such a degree that Jewish monotheism had been abandoned, as it

39. McGrath, *The Only True God*, 49.
40. McGrath, *The Only True God*, 49.
41. McGrath, *The Only True God*, 50.
42. The differences between these interpreters would appear far greater if the scope of this survey were broadened beyond "Pauline christology" to include "early Christian christology." In that case, Dunn would be seen as an advocate of a "high(er) christology," since he sees a divine, incarnational christology articulated already in the Fourth Gospel (see Dunn, *Christology in the Making*, ch. 7; "The Making of Christology: Evolution or Unfolding?" in *The Christ and the Spirit*, Vol. 1: *Christology*, 388-404), whereas Casey and McGrath would be seen as operating at some remove from these conclusions, arguing for more ambiguity even in the Fourth Gospel.

later was. For McGrath, proponents of a Pauline "christological monotheism" have gone beyond what the evidence warrants. Better, instead, to construe Jesus' identity as an exceptionally high instance of an exalted divine representative who bears the divine name and mediates the divine activity but, for all that, remains subordinate to God.[43] All these interpreters are united, then, in affirming that, however high the status Paul attributes to Jesus, it does not infringe on the status of one God.[44]

I turn now to another group of interpreters also concerned with the intersection and interplay between Jewish monotheism and Pauline christology.

ii. "High" Christology

If for Dunn, Casey, and others, Paul's christology remains notably subservient to his theology, a number of interpreters who together comprise what Martin Hengel has characterized as the "new history of religion school"[45] have posited a more robust "conceptual overlap"[46] between christology and theology in Paul. In contrast to the pioneering work of Wilhelm Bousset,[47] members of this new *Schule* — Larry Hurtado[48] and Richard Bauck-

43. Cf. Thüsing, *Per Christum in Deum,* 55, for whose Paul Christ is interpreted "als dem Repräsentanten der Herrschaft Gottes."

44. Cf. Marinus de Jonge, "Monotheism and Christology," in John Barclay and John Sweet (eds.), *Early Christian Thought in Its Jewish Context* (Cambridge: Cambridge University Press, 1996), 225-37, at 231.

45. In a jacket blurb for the first American edition of Larry W. Hurtado, *One God, One Lord: Early Christian Devotion and Ancient Jewish Monotheism* (Philadelphia: Fortress, 1988). As Simon Gathercole, *The Preexistent Son: Recovering the Christologies of Matthew, Mark, and Luke* (Grand Rapids: Eerdmans, 2006), 14 n. 50 remarks, "It is an open secret that this new Schule is known, rather more informally, as the 'Early High Christology Club.' " Cf. Jarl E. Fossum, "The New Religionsgeschichtliche Schule: The Quest for Jewish Christology," in E. Lovering (ed.), *SBLSP 1991* (Atlanta: Scholars, 1991), 638-46.

46. L. Joseph Kreitzer, *Jesus and God in Paul's Eschatology* (JSNTSup 19; Sheffield: JSOT, 1987), 25.

47. Wilhelm Bousset, *Kyrios Christos. Geschichte des Christusglaubens von den Anfängen des Christentums bis Irenaeus* (Göttingen: Vandenhoeck & Ruprecht, 1913; rev. ed., 1921); ET: *Kyrios Christos: A History of the Belief in Christ from the Beginnings of Christianity to Irenaeus,* trans. J. E. Steely (Nashville: Abingdon, 1970), from the 1965 German edition.

48. See esp. Hurtado, *One God, One Lord; Lord Jesus Christ: Devotion to Jesus in Earliest Christianity* (Grand Rapids: Eerdmans, 2003); *How on Earth Did Jesus Become a God? Historical Questions about Earliest Devotion to Jesus* (Grand Rapids: Eerdmans, 2005). For a

ham,[49] to name the two most prominent interpreters — have argued that the explanation for early Christian devotion to Christ is not to be found in the Hellenization of Jewish messianic beliefs. Rather, the evidence points to this devotion having its genesis among the earliest "Palestinian" Jewish Christians, before the movement outward into the Gentile world and the changes its conceptualities introduced. Furthermore, this Christ-devotion amounted to something beyond merely exalting Jesus to the highest place in the sphere of "semi-divine intermediary figures,"[50] whether "principal angels" or "exalted patriarchs" or personified attributes or some such.[51] It entailed, instead, Jesus' reception of worship previously accorded only to the one God. This decisive step was not the culmination of a long process of christological development but happened in the oldest observable strata of the NT, so that "the highest christology of the NT is also its earliest."[52]

Hurtado has focused primarily on the behavior and religious experience in the Pauline churches — as opposed to the ideas, christological titles, or theological judgments of the apostles (merely) — that we can deduce from the evidence of Paul's letters. From the patterns of cultic devotion to Jesus among Pauline communities visible to us from the letters — including, but not limited to, prayer to him or in his name (e.g., Rom 1:8; 1 Cor 16:22; 2 Cor 1:3; 12:8; 1 Thess 3:11-13; cf. Eph 1:3; Col 1:3), invocation of his name (Rom 10:13; 1 Cor 1:2; 5:1-5; 12:3; Phil 2:11), baptism in his name (Rom 6:3; Gal 3:27; 1 Cor 6:11?), Eucharistic celebration enacted on the basis of his death (1 Cor 11:17-34) — Hurtado concludes that the place accorded to Jesus in relation to God is best described as a "mutation" in Jewish monotheism, evincing a new "binitarian" shape. The earliest Pauline Christians *worshiped* Jesus,[53] thus assigning him the

---

useful summary and critique of Hurtado's reconstruction of early christology, see Crispin Fletcher-Louis, "A New Explanation of Christological Origins: A Review of the Work of Larry W. Hurtado," *TynBul* 60/2 (2009): 161-205, and now Hurtado's response, "The Origins of Jesus-Devotion: A Response to Crispin Fletcher-Louis," *TynBul* 61/1 (2010): 1-20.

49. Bauckham's primary work on "early high christology" is now conveniently available in *Jesus and the God of Israel*.

50. Richard J. Bauckham, *God Crucified: Monotheism and Christology in the New Testament* (Grand Rapids: Eerdmans, 1998), vii.

51. See Hurtado, *One God, One Lord*, chs. 3 and 4.

52. G. B. Caird and L. D. Hurst, *New Testament Theology* (Oxford: Clarendon, 1994), 343.

53. Here lies one of the points of contention between Dunn and Hurtado. In the former's view, "If we observe the ancient distinction between 'worship' and 'veneration,' we would have to speak of the veneration of Christ, meaning by that something short of full-scale worship" (Dunn, *Theology of Paul*, 260).

closest possible relationship to God the Father without conflating the two. In Hurtado's words: "It is this accommodation of Christ as an additional figure along with God ('the Father') within a strong concern to maintain a monotheistic religious commitment that I refer to as the 'binitarian' shape of Christian worship."[54]

How do these interpreters read the relevant Pauline texts? To date, Bauckham has offered more detailed exegetical discussions of Phil 2:6-11 and 1 Cor 8:6 than Hurtado, whereas Hurtado has treated 1 Cor 15:20-28 more fully than Bauckham, who has only mentioned it in passing and largely ignored its implications for Jesus' relationship to God.[55] Since Dunn's discussion of these texts was outlined above, I will here summarize Bauckham's interpretation of Phil 2:6-11 and 1 Cor 8:6 and follow that with a brief look at Hurtado's treatment of 1 Cor 15:20-28.

For Bauckham, texts such as Phil 2:6-11 and 1 Cor 8:6 include Jesus within the divine identity. They identify Jesus by the same means by which Jewish texts distinguished the one God from all other reality. Respectively, these two texts include Jesus in both the eschatological and creational identity of God. In Phil 2:6-11, "Jesus is seen as the one who exercises God's eschatological sovereignty over all things, with a view to the coming of God's kingdom and the universal acknowledgement of God's unique deity."[56] In 1 Cor 8:6, Jesus is portrayed as the one who shares in God's creative power. This is not meant as a statement about creation *per se* or for its own sake, but rather as a way of showing that Jesus is included within the unique divine identity. "Including him precisely in the divine activity of creation is the most unequivocal way of excluding any threat to monotheism — as though Jesus were a subordinate demi-god — while redefining the unique identity of God in a way that includes Jesus."[57]

With regard to Phil 2:6-11, Bauckham begins by noting the allusions to Isa 45:23 in vv. 10 and 11 (πᾶν γόνυ κάμψῃ . . . καὶ πᾶσα γλῶσσα

---

54. Larry W. Hurtado, "The Binitarian Shape of Early Christian Worship," in *The Jewish Roots of Christological Monotheism* (n. 28 above), 187-213, at 191.

55. Hurtado discusses these texts in *Lord Jesus Christ* (121ff.) and has more recently presented an in-depth reading of Phil 2:6-11 ("A 'Case Study' in Early Christian Devotion to Jesus: Philippians 2:6-11," in *How on Earth Did Jesus Become a God?* 83-107). The second and third chapters of Bauckham's *God Crucified* contain close readings of both 1 Cor 8:6 and Phil 2:6-11. Bauckham's mention of 1 Cor 15:24-28 may be found in "The Throne of God and the Worship of Jesus," in *Jesus and the God of Israel*, 152-81, at 177.

56. Bauckham, *God Crucified*, 35.

57. Bauckham, *God Crucified*, 36.

ἐξομολογήσηται). In context, Isa 45:23 is part of a larger unit (vv. 18-25) whose repeated monotheistic assertions ("I am the Lord and there is none besides"; "I am God and there is no other besides me"; "there is none but me"; "I am God and there is no other") "make it the most insistently monotheistic passage in Isaiah 40-55."[58] It is here that the "the one Creator of all things and Sovereign over all things proves himself to be so, acknowledged as both only God and only Saviour by all the ends of the earth which turn to him in worship and for salvation."[59] In light of this function of Isa 45:23 in its original literary setting, Bauckham argues that Paul's allusions to it, when coupled with the recognition that the "name" κύριος (= YHWH) is given to Jesus (Phil 2:9, 11),[60] must be understood as elevating Jesus beyond the status of a mere servant to a full participation in the identity of God.[61] "[I]t is in the exaltation of Jesus, his identification as YHWH in YHWH's universal sovereignty, that the unique deity of the God of Israel comes to be acknowledged as such by all creation."[62]

A similar dynamic may be observed in 1 Cor 8:6. Bauckham discerns the theological import of the text from attention to its scriptural allusions. As most parties agree, Deut 6:4 with its affirmation of one Lord and God lies in the background. But Bauckham also finds evidence of another monotheistic formula, already in use in Jewish texts with which Paul would have been familiar. The formula would have read as follows, with slight variations depending on its setting: "from him and through him and to him are all things" (cf. Rom 11:36; Josephus, *B.J.* 5.218; Philo, *Cher.* 127). The primary pieces of 1 Cor 8:6 — "one God," "from whom are all things," "one Lord," "through whom are all things" — are thus preformed building blocks which Paul uses to construct a new sort of edifice. Both Deut 6:4 and the other monotheistic formula that Paul references would have been understood in Judaism as drawing the boundary between the one God as the source/sovereign over all things and all other created reality. It is notable, then, that Paul splits both affirmations and apportions their various contents to God "the Father" (1 Cor 8:6a) and

---

58. Richard Bauckham, "Paul's Christology of Divine Identity," in *Jesus and the God of Israel*, 182-232, at 192.

59. Bauckham, *God Crucified*, 52-53.

60. Bauckham, *God Crucified*, 34.

61. Richard J. Bauckham, "The Worship of Jesus in Philippians 2:9-11," in Ralph P. Martin and Brian J. Dodd (eds.), *Where Christology Began: Essays on Philippians 2* (Louisville: Westminster/John Knox, 1998), 128-39, at 134.

62. Bauckham, *God Crucified*, 53.

"Jesus Christ" (v. 6b) respectively, in such a way that "God" and "from whom are all things" become associated with "the Father," while "Lord" and "through whom are all things" become associated with "Jesus Christ." This apportioning effectively aligns Jesus with God on the side of source/sovereign over all things, rather than the other side, the created realm. In this way, Bauckham argues that Jesus is not *added to* the one God as an especially honored agent but rather *included within* the unique divine identity as inseparable from God.[63]

At first glance, 1 Cor 15:20-28 may appear to tell against this construal, since it depicts Jesus' subordination to God the Father. That the lordship of Jesus culminates in the universal reign of God the Father (v. 28) is, however, to say essentially the same thing as Phil 2:11: God exalted Jesus, so that worship of Jesus ultimately honors God. As Hurtado puts it, "Worshiping Jesus . . . was for [the early Christians] actually a requisite demonstration of their reverence for God 'the Father.'"[64] Hurtado regards this construal as differing from Dunn's, who takes Phil 2:11 to undercut any interpretation of Jesus' having "replaced" God in cultic devotion.[65] On the contrary, Hurtado thinks, "there is no indication that Paul was aware of any such an inference and was seeking to forestall it."[66] The problem with Dunn's exegesis is that it opens the door to positing some sort of development in early Christian worship, whereby Jesus was viewed increasingly highly, but not so highly in Paul's theology that Jesus had become completely identified with God. For Hurtado, there is no evidence for a transition from one sort of worship of Jesus to another, and this means that texts such as 1 Cor 15:28 are best read not as corrections of some potentially problematic tendency in devotion to Jesus but as specifying that such devotion belongs within devotion to the one God. "There is no indication in Paul's letters that among the problems he had to deal with he was ever anxious about devotion to Jesus as a possible neglect of God or threat to God's centrality."[67]

Although significant differences and points of tension remain between the interpreters surveyed in this section, all are agreed in rejecting a developmental model for early christology. The patterns of worship/

---

63. Bauckham, *God Crucified,* 35-40.

64. Hurtado, *Lord Jesus Christ,* 641; cf. Larry W. Hurtado, "Paul's Christology," in James D. G. Dunn (ed.), *The Cambridge Companion to St Paul* (Cambridge: Cambridge University Press, 2003), 185-98, at 187.

65. Dunn, *Theology of Paul,* 251-2.

66. Hurtado, "The Binitarian Shape of Early Christian Worship," 208.

67. Hurtado, "The Binitarian Shape of Early Christian Worship," 208.

cultic devotion Hurtado notes and the theological inclusion of Jesus within God's creational and eschatological sovereignty that Bauckham discusses are all traceable to the earliest strands of the New Testament. For these interpreters, there is thus no need to look for a precise sort of intermediary figure in Jewish texts to hold up as an analogy to the role Jesus plays in Paul's letters, since the worship of Jesus and the position he occupies require viewing him as *uniquely* related to God.

A second point of agreement among the interpreters considered here lies in their claim that Dunn's (and others') model of "tension" between the burgeoning early Christian christology and Jewish monotheism is flawed. In Dunn's model, monotheism and christology are conceptually separable; the former serves a limiting function, delineating the uppermost point on the vertical axis to which christology may not ascend. For Hurtado, this fails to see the conceptual overlap between monotheism and christology, whereby christology rises to the top of the axis (almost) and there intermingles and becomes enmeshed with its endpoint. Or, in Bauckham's viewpoint, Dunn's claim fails to reckon with the *lack* of rising: christology was *already* implicated from the beginning in a redefined monotheism, such that to posit a steady progression of christology higher and higher is to obscure its immediate, unparalleled genesis at the beginning of the Christian movement.

I turn now to an evaluation of these various positions and a constructive critique.

2. Pauline Monotheism and Christology: Assessment and Prospect

i. Pauline Interpreters on the Distinction between High/Low Christologies and Trinitarian Theology

All the interpreters considered above, regardless of where their conclusions fall on the spectrum of "high" and "low" christologies, share a concern to distance their reconstructions of New Testament christology from later trinitarian theology. Dunn, for example, traces a developmental line from Paul's christology, with its emphasis on Christ's exaltation and veneration, on to the Fourth Gospel's Logos christology and beyond to Nicene trinitarian theology, or "Son christology." Each of these, for Dunn, represents a further stage in the elevation of christology. In the New Testament stages, the primary question was how to understand the exalted status of Jesus within a continuing affirmation of Jewish monotheism. In Nicene theology, the question of monotheism has receded in prominence, and the question of the internal relations of divine persons was at issue. In other words, Jewish monotheism was being reconceived as something different altogether: as trinitarian monotheism.[68]

To read Paul's theology from the perspective of Nicaea, then, would be to allow an alien question (intra-trinitarian divine relations) to obscure what was at stake in Pauline christology (the exaltation of Jesus and his secondary status in relation to God). In Dunn's view, the issue of the "continuity" between the Father and the Son was established not primarily through Paul's theology but rather through the Gospel of John's Logos theology. Christology was to be seen "as an expression of Christian monotheism."[69] At Nicaea, however, the debate took a step forward. Granted that christology belongs within the ambit of monotheism, the question became one of how the relationship between Father and Son was to be specified. For Dunn, it is this question that must not be allowed to determine anachronistically the interpretation of Paul.[70]

For different reasons, Hurtado also distances his account of Pauline christology from trinitarian theology. In his major studies, he disavows a theological agenda: "I do not approach the first-century texts by reading them in light of later creedal developments and seeking to see how they might anticipate later beliefs."[71] For him, to affirm with the Christian creedal tradition that Jesus was the pre-existent divine Logos is irrelevant as far as historical investigation is concerned, which must describe the

---

68. Dunn, "M. Wiles on *Christology in the Making* and Responses by the Author," 264-65.

69. Dunn, *Christology in the Making*, xxxi.

70. Dunn, *Christology in the Making*, xxxi-xxxii. Cf. Paul A. Rainbow, "Jewish Monotheism as the Matrix for New Testament Christology: A Review Article," *NovT* 33 (1991): 78-91, at 90-91: "the adjective 'trinitarian' implies community of *substantia* or *essentia* among divine persons, and therefore more precisely describes the doctrine of the Fathers than that of the NT authors." For J. Christiaan Beker, too, theological talk of an essence shared by Father and Son obscures the fundamental asymmetry between God and Jesus in Paul's own theological grammar: "A full immanental Trinitarian hermeneutic seems to compel an interpretation of Paul's Christology in ontological rather than functional terms and thus fuses God and Christ to the detriment of the final glory of God, to which, according to Paul, Christ is subordinate and for which he lived and died" (*Paul the Apostle*, 358). To speak in trinitarian terms, then, is to depart from Pauline theology at its central point: the relation of God to Jesus.

71. Hurtado, *One God, One Lord*, viii. Cf. Hurtado, *Lord Jesus Christ*, 9.

historical particularity of the appearance of devotion to Jesus among first-century believers prior to its later flowering into Nicene orthodoxy:

> in traditional Christian faith, Jesus of Nazareth is the personal, human embodiment of the second person of the Trinity, and simply was divine from "before all time" (to use an ancient Christian creedal expression). But, whatever the validity of this traditional Christian view, the historical question remains: How did early Christians "on earth" come to see Jesus as divine and revere him as such?[72]

In the interest of answering this historical question, then, Hurtado characterizes Pauline christology as part of a "binitarian" matrix of thought, by which he means that Jesus is exalted to God's right hand, from where he mediates prayer to God, receives prayer himself, bears the divine name, and shares in divine functions. Although a resurrection-exaltation christology in its earliest articulation among Aramaic-speaking Christians remains something short of a fully incarnational theology, Hurtado thinks that we find in Paul's notion of Jesus' personal pre-existence (Phil 2:6) a move toward what would later become that theology.[73] Yet, as Crispin Fletcher-Louis notes, Hurtado's position is an unusual one when considered alongside other interpretive options.[74] On the one hand, Hurtado's reconstructed Pauline christology is "higher" than Dunn's, in that he sees more continuity between Johannine Logos christology and Pauline "incarnational" texts (e.g., in addition to Phil 2:6, 2 Cor 8:9). Thus, from the perspective of those who advocate a "low" christology, for Hurtado to label Paul's christology as "binitarian" invites the charge that Paul is more in line with trinitarian theology than his historical distance from Nicaea would lead us to expect. On the other hand, for those who see Pauline christology as being "high" or even as bearing an authentically trinitarian imprint, "binitarian" seems to be an anemic substitute for a more robust position. Hurtado, then, falls between two options: He advocates a "high" christology out of step at crucial points with more cautious positions (e.g., Dunn's), but he preserves the difference between Pauline christology and later trinitarian reflection in line with much scholarship on first-century Jewish monotheism and its early Christian mutation.

---

72. Hurtado, *How on Earth Did Jesus Become a God?* 1.
73. Hurtado, *How on Earth Did Jesus Become a God?* 102.
74. Fletcher-Louis, "A New Explanation of Christological Origins," 165.

ii. Contextualizing the Problems with Trinitarian Biblical Interpretation

The reasons Dunn, Hurtado, and others give for distancing Pauline theology from trinitarian theology may be situated within a wider frame of reference. In their reconstructions, these Pauline interpreters tap into, exemplify, and carry forward a broader phenomenon within the history of New Testament scholarship, one with deep roots in the genesis of the entire enterprise of critical biblical scholarship. I will not attempt a full survey here but simply indicate some lines of this development as a way of contextualizing the projects of Dunn, Hurtado, and other more recent interpreters.

Since at least the sixteenth century, any straightforward connection between trinitarian theology and exegesis of the New Testament has been significantly problematized. With the rise of a self-consciously critical biblical scholarship came an emphasis on the historical and conceptual gap between the early Christian writings and later trinitarian doctrine supposedly based on those writings. Appealing to the monotheistic passages in Paul such as 1 Cor 8:6 (cf. Eph 4:6) and reading these texts in accord with a particular view of reason's priority in the process of biblical interpretation, critics were able to drive a wedge between the manifestly illogical notion of a plurality of persons subsisting in a numerically one God and the allegedly clear meaning of biblical texts which lacked such a doctrine.[75] The further development of critical reading strategies continued and deepened this perspective on trinitarian doctrine, so much so that the supposed impossibility of deriving the doctrine of the trinity from the Bible in any straightforward sense becomes axiomatic even among dogmatic theologians. Biblical interpreters stressed the need for a separation between the biblical texts as they would have been understood in their original context and the dogma and theology overlaying them from a later period.[76] As Gordon Fee, Ulrich Mauser, and others have noted, this

---

75. On the Socinian handling of Pauline texts, which played a key role in the development of biblical exegetes' suspicion of trinitarian doctrine, see F. C. Baur, *Die christliche Lehre von der Dreieinigkeit und Menschwerdung Gottes in ihrer geschichtlichen Entwicklung* (Tübingen: Osiander, 1843), 165-83.

76. Johann Philipp Gabler's 1787 inaugural address at the University of Altdorf, now conveniently available in translation by J. Sandys-Wunsch and L. Eldredge, "On the Proper Distinction between Biblical and Dogmatic Theology and the Specific Objectives of Each," *SJT* 33 (1980): 133-58, is usually taken to be the classic articulation of this separation. Mention is often made, too, in this connection of William Wrede's essay, originally

demoting of trinitarian theology from a place of privilege is best understood against the backdrop of biblical theology's effort to extricate itself from the constraints of creedal and ecclesiastical formulations supposedly hindering historical investigation from continuing apace.[77] Thus, most discussions of "Paul and the trinity" — or Pauline theology and christology — usually include some appreciation of this heritage of hermeneutical critique of trinitarian theology.[78] In the words of Mauser (summarizing a position with which he does not agree),

> The historically trained New Testament scholar will today proceed with the task of interpretation without wasting a minute on the suspicion that the trinitarian confessions of later centuries might be rooted in the New Testament itself, and that the trinitarian creeds might continue to function as valuable hermeneutical sign-posts for a modern understanding.[79]

---

given as a lecture at the turn of the twentieth century, "The Task and Methods of 'New Testament Theology,'" in Robert Morgan (ed. and trans.), *The Nature of New Testament Theology* (Naperville, IL: Alec R. Allenson, 1973), 68-116, with its concern that theological judgments, such as trinitarian doctrine, not be allowed to silence or reinterpret (and thus misinterpret) the NT at those points where the NT's content differs from later dogma. For Wrede, even if trinitarian doctrine were "right," it would be unnecessary, since the task of NT theology needs no supplementation, correction, or legitimation from an external source (69-70).

77. Gordon D. Fee, *God's Empowering Presence: The Holy Spirit in the Letters of Paul* (Peabody, MA: Hendrickson, 1994), 827; Ulrich Mauser, "One God and Trinitarian Language in the Letters of Paul," *HBT* 20/2 (1998): 99-108, at 99-100. Cf. Karl P. Donfried's characterization of modern biblical scholarship's "nontrinitarian hermeneutical enterprises" ("Alien Hermeneutics and the Misappropriation of Scripture," in Carl E. Braaten and Robert W. Jenson [eds.], *Reclaiming the Bible for the Church* [Grand Rapids: Eerdmans, 1995], 19-45, at 20).

78. Gordon Fee, "Paul and the Trinity: The Experience of Christ and the Spirit for Paul's Understanding of God," in S. T. Davis, D. Kendall, and G. O'Collins (eds.), *The Trinity: An Interdisciplinary Symposium on the Trinity* (Oxford: Oxford University Press, 1999), 49-72, and Joseph Maleparampil, *The "Trinitarian" Formulae in St. Paul: An Exegetical Investigation into the Meaning and Function of Those Pauline Sayings Which Compositely Make Mention of God, Christ and the Holy Spirit* (European University Studies Series 23 Theology 546; New York and Frankfurt am Main: Peter Lang, 1995), are notable for their failure to reckon with this critique. Consequently, the crucial term of contention — "trinitarian" — is left unqualified and unreconstructed in their discussions.

79. Mauser, "One God and Trinitarian Language in the Letters of Paul," 100.

iii. *The Separation of Christology from Trinitarian Theology and the Origins of the Problematic of High/Low Christologies*

In addition to the concern to keep a historical reading of the New Testament relatively free from the anachronistic encroachments of later theological dogma, further explanations could be offered for the eclipse of trinitarian theology in Pauline interpretation.[80] Nils Dahl has highlighted certain Protestant understandings of the centrality of christology in theology and the effect these construals have had on New Testament interpretation.[81] Dahl and others trace a certain "pronounced Christocentricity" back to the influence of Ritschl in the nineteenth century, and to his precursors — the currents of anti-metaphysical theology already mentioned above in connection with Harnack and discernible also in Schleiermacher and Kant, and, arguably, in Melanchthon and the early Luther as well.[82]

The crucial point for our purposes, however, is to note the upshot of all these streams — namely, the partitioning of christology as a discrete area of inquiry from trinitarian theology more broadly conceived. Christology becomes an area of investigation in its own right, not merely as one part of the variegated matrix of trinitarian theology but rather as something discussable, in principle, in relative isolation.[83]

As we have seen above with the exemplars of both "high" and "low" christologies, one of the defining marks of current discussions of Pauline christology is how "monotheism" is taken to be the background against which Paul's christology is interpreted and evaluated. Here, too, a story could be told about the way in which a particular interpretive framework indicates a shift in approach to a set of exegetical and theological questions. If a critical recognition of the historical distance between patristic

---

80. Cf. the discussions in David S. Yeago, "The New Testament and the Nicene Dogma: A Contribution to the Recovery of Theological Exegesis," *Pro Ecclesia* 3/2 (1994): 152-64, at 152-53; Francis Watson, "Trinity and Community: A Reading of John 17," *IJST* 1/2 (1999): 168-84, at 168-69; C. Kavin Rowe, "Luke and the Trinity: An Essay in Ecclesial Biblical Theology," *SJT* 56/1 (2003): 1-26, at 1-5.

81. Nils Alstrup Dahl, "The Neglected Factor in New Testament Theology," in Donald H. Juel (ed.), *Jesus the Christ: The Historical Origins of Christological Doctrine* (Minneapolis: Fortress, 1991), 153-63, at 155-56.

82. Dahl, "The Neglected Factor in New Testament Theology," 155-56.

83. On this point, compare the interesting essays by Christoph Schwöbel: "Christology and Trinitarian Thought," in Christoph Schwöbel (ed.), *Trinitarian Theology Today: Essays on Divine Being and Act* (Edinburgh: T&T Clark, 1995), 113-46; "Christologie und trinitarische Theologie," in *Gott in Beziehung* (Tübingen: Mohr Siebeck, 2002), 257-91.

trinitarian formulations and Paul led to trinitarian doctrine being marginalized in modern Pauline interpretation, and if certain forms of theological Christocentrism contributed to this marginalization, a further factor to be considered is how a newly minted term — "monotheism" — became available to interpreters and allowed them to articulate the dynamics of Pauline christology and theology without having recourse to trinitarian categories.[84] The conceptuality of monotheism made possible the redescription of Pauline texts in ways that avoided the anachronism of importing later trinitarian doctrine into the reading of Paul, a first-century figure confronting a different set of issues and questions than the Fathers.

It is this shift that opened up the question of whether Paul's christology is to be viewed as "high" or "low." Once interpretive categories have shifted from trinitarian ones to "monotheistic" and christological ones, it becomes necessary to inquire about the potential overlap or conflict between monotheism and christology. If monotheism names the distinction between God and created reality, where does Jesus fit on the spectrum between humanity, angelic intermediaries, and other possible figures spanning the gap between God and creation? Is he to be placed at a "low" point, alongside creatures but exalted above them in some way? Is he to be located at a "high" point, and if so, how did he come to occupy that position? The shift from the dominance of trinitarian categories to the supposedly more historical categories of monotheism and christology allows and necessitates that these sorts of questions be asked. As evidence for this assertion, one could point to the fact that the terminology of "high" versus "low" christology is relatively recent and operates at some remove from patristic discussions of Jesus' oneness with and exaltation by the Fathers.

It is now common — so much so that it can be difficult to notice, until one steps back and compares the formulations of Dunn or Hurtado to a "premodern" or self-consciously "trinitarian" reading of Paul — to describe Pauline christology with the use of vertical axis metaphors. The assumption of a wide range of interpreters, regardless of their final conclusions, is that one of the most — if not the foremost — crucial christological questions to pose when reading Paul is "the *degree* . . . of Jesus' divinity."[85]

---

84. On the origins of the term "monotheism," see Nathan MacDonald, "The Origin of 'Monotheism,'" in Loren T. Stuckenbruck and Wendy E. S. North (eds.), *Early Jewish and Christian Monotheism* (JSNTSup 263; London: T&T Clark, 2004), 204-15, and in the same volume, R. W. L. Moberly, "How Appropriate Is 'Monotheism' as a Category for Biblical Interpretation?" 216-34, at 218-22.

85. Brown, *An Introduction to New Testament Christology*, 4.

By the time Paul writes his letters, giving his own theological interpretation of Jesus' significance and also mirroring the beliefs and praxis of his churches, has Jesus risen to a high point, or the highest point, on the vertical axis whose uppermost reaches entail divinity? Or does he occupy a point beneath "God" — sharing in some of the divine functions and occupying an exceptionally exalted status vis-à-vis other divinely commissioned representatives and intermediaries but, for all that, remaining subordinate to God, on a slightly lower plane? For many readings of Paul, as we have seen, these are the questions that drive and shape discussions of Pauline christology. Asking whether Jesus is to be mapped at a "low" or "high" point is the essential thing to be determined.

I turn now to an alternative way of approaching Pauline theology, one that will determine the shape of the investigation to be pursued in subsequent chapters.

iv. The Pattern of Trinitarian Theology: The Priority of Relations

The main task of this section is to suggest a way of discussing Paul's theology and christology that does *not* begin with the "vertical" question — has Jesus been elevated all the way up the axis to God's level? — but rather with the question of *relations*. The conceptuality of a "low" or "high" christology threatens to obscure the way in which, for Paul, the identities of God, Jesus, and the Spirit are constituted by their relations with one another.

In spite of the dominance of the approaches of Dunn, Casey, Hurtado, and others, several more recent proposals have called for attention to the way Paul's christology is misconstrued if it is taken out of the matrix of relations on which it depends for its coherence. These proposals do not endorse what I have called the "vertical axis metaphor" of plotting Jesus at a "low" or "high" point on a "scale of being."[86] Rather, these alternative frameworks suggest that fruitful study of Paul's christology is better represented with the image of a *horizontal* axis, with points of connection to one another,[87] as in a two-way street — or, better still, with the metaphor of a *web* of multiply intersecting vectors.

86. Cf. Liddon, *The Divinity of Our Lord and Saviour Jesus Christ,* 280.

87. According to Robert Jenson, *The Triune Identity: God According to the Gospel* (Philadelphia: Fortress, 1982), 106, one of the achievements of "Cappadocian" trinitarian theology was to make "the [trinitarian] hypostases' mutual relations structures of the one God's life" as opposed to vertical steps from God down to humanity or from humanity up

Nils Dahl is one such representative of this minority report. Dahl proposed several decades ago, for example, that New Testament scholarship should pay attention to the relational character of christology: "In generalized terms I may say that, according to the New Testament, God the Father, Jesus Christ, and (less clearly) the Holy Spirit each have a discrete identity, and yet none of the three can be described adequately unless the *interrelationship* among them is taken into account."[88] Dahl's comments are intended to refer to the range of New Testament christologies, but I will argue that they apply especially to Paul.[89] Leander Keck's judgment is similar: "the subject-matter of christology is really the syntax of relationships or correlations" between Jesus and God, the world, and the human condition.[90]

In addition to proposing a shift in conceptual categories, Dahl explicitly invokes trinitarian theology as an explanatory lens through which to view the dynamics of New Testament christology. Early baptismal creeds, structured with reference to the triune persons, as well as the Nicene Creed, provide a model whereby the identity of Jesus is construed by way of his relations to God the Father and the Spirit.[91] In Dahl's own words:

> With few exceptions both interrogatory and declaratory creeds place the confession of faith in Jesus Christ within a trinitarian framework. I find this more relevant to the New Testament data than do most modern studies, which tend to treat New Testament Christology in isolation — whether they deal with the kerygma, or with the names

---

to God. For a critique of the language of "from above" and "from below" in christological discourse, similar to but not synonymous with the categories of "high" and "low," see the suggestive essay of Nicholas Lash, "Up and Down in Christology," in S. W. Sykes and J. D. Holmes (eds.), *New Studies in Theology,* I (London: Duckworth, 1979), 31-46.

88. Nils Alstrup Dahl, "Trinitarian Baptismal Creeds and New Testament Christology," in *Jesus the Christ* (n. 81 above), 165-86, at 181. Italics added.

89. Dahl's language, however, will be qualified in what follows: the "discrete identities" of God, Jesus, and the Spirit will not be played off against ("yet") their interrelationship but rather seen to be constituted *in* and *through* those relationships.

90. Leander E. Keck, "Toward the Renewal of New Testament Christology," *NTS* 32 (1986): 362-77, at 363, 373.

91. Cf. the comments of Paul Meyer: with regard to the Father-Son language in the Fourth Gospel, he argues "that the reader is compelled by this language to redefine the term 'Christology' itself and to recognize that in its profoundest dimension — not just in this Gospel but in all its variations throughout the diverse traditions of the New Testament — it concerns not the person of Jesus or his identity ('who he is') and the consequences of his life so much as — first, foremost, and always — his open or hidden relationship to God, and of God to him" ("The Father," 259).

and titles of Christ, or with confessional and other stereotyped christological formulas. Until quite recently, a study of the ways in which
the New Testament authors talk about God has been neglected, and
New Testament scholars have, by and large, left it to their colleagues
in historical and systematic theology to discuss the relationship of New
Testament data to trinitarian faith and dogma. My thesis is that New
Testament Christology can be treated properly only if it is related to
faith in God, as present in the Jewish Scriptures and in contemporary
Judaism, which also had assimilated elements of Greek philosophical
monotheism. At the same time, what is said about Christ cannot be
isolated from early Christian experience of the Holy Spirit, the Spirit
of God and of Christ. Jesus is represented as the Christ of God, the
Son and agent of God, the righteous sufferer who was vindicated by
God; language used to speak about God is transferred to Jesus as well.[92]

More recently, C. Kavin Rowe has carried forward these insights of
Dahl and Keck (among others) within his own studies of New Testament
christology, primarily Lukan and also, to a lesser extent, Pauline. In his
study of the use of κύριος in the Gospel of Luke, Rowe highlights precisely
the christological problem I have noted above in relation to Dunn, Hurtado, and others' discussions of Pauline christology. Rowe's project is to
ask about the *identity* of the κύριος in Luke's Gospel. In most treatments
of Luke's use of κύριος, he contends,

> scholars have operated (if unwittingly) with a rather simple, if not sim-
> plistic, concept of identity in which the assumption that governs the
> thought about the identity of Jesus or God (or any other character) is
> what we may call static — as opposed to narrative or dynamic — in
> its structure. Identity in this sense is conceptualized as a static entity
> which can, in turn, be related to other static entities (with, for example,
> an = or ≈ or ≠ sign).[93]

Rowe's point is that discussions of the κύριος title operate with similar assumptions to the ones I have sketched above in relation to Dunn,

---

92. Dahl, "Trinitarian Baptismal Creeds and New Testament Christology," 179-80.
Cf. the comments in C. F. D. Moule, "The New Testament and the Doctrine of the Trinity:
A Short Report on an Old Theme," *ExpTim* 88 (1976): 16-20, at 19.
93. C. Kavin Rowe, *Early Narrative Christology: The Lord in the Gospel of Luke* (Grand
Rapids: Baker Academic, 2009), 17.

Hurtado, and others: that God stands at one level and Jesus at another, and the question, consequently, is how far or to what degree Jesus may rise to God's level in the worship, praxis, and theology of various early Christian communities. It is this sort of analysis which Rowe characterizes as a "static" conceptuality and which I have called a "vertical axis" conceptuality. Likewise, Rowe observes that in much Lukan scholarship κύριος

> is related to God and Jesus in terms of "levels," with God on one level and Jesus on another. The use of κύριος somehow raises Jesus to God's level, which then supposedly allows for (rather vague) conclusions about Jesus' status ("transcendent," "other," etc.). Κύριος is thus the ≈ sign that stands between the God-level and the Jesus-level and relates them to one another. In this way, the title is, as such, independent of God and of Jesus, non-constitutive for their identity and their relation, a word that functions as a mere interface between the different levels of status.[94]

For Rowe, this neglects alternative ways of conceiving identity, and the rest of his project is a sustained effort to show the strength of one such (narratival) approach.

Rowe has attempted a complementary analysis, albeit in much more cursory fashion, of some Pauline texts (Rom 8:9-11; 10:13; 2 Cor 3:17a; Gal 4:4-6).[95] Rather than inquire into the degree of equality between Jesus and God — which might be conceived in rather static terms — Rowe highlights the significance of relationality for grasping the dynamics of Pauline theology and christology (and pneumatology) in, for example, his exegesis of Gal 4:4-6:

---

94. Rowe, *Early Narrative Christology*, 18. Here Rowe alludes to the view of Joseph A. Fitzmyer, *The Gospel according to Luke* (2 vols.; AB 28-28A; Garden City, NY: Doubleday, 1981, 1985), 1:202, worth quoting here for its striking similarity to the views of many of the Pauline scholars discussed above: "[In] using *kyrios* of both Yahweh and Jesus in his writings Luke continues the sense of the title already being used in the early Christian community, which in some sense regarded Jesus as on a level with Yahweh. This is not yet to be regarded as an expression of divinity, but it speaks at least of his otherness, his transcendent character."

95. In two articles: C. Kavin Rowe, "Romans 10:13: What Is the Name of the Lord?" *HBT* 22/2 (2000): 135-73; "Biblical Pressure and Trinitarian Hermeneutics," *Pro Ecclesia* 11 (2002): 295-312.

God the Father (*theos* is always the Father in Galatians) exists in relation to his Son as well as in relation to the Spirit of his Son. The Spirit of the Father's Son, in turn, testifies (in the hearts of believers) to the Father of the Son. This relationship between the Father, his Son, and the Spirit of the Father's Son is mutually constitutive, which is to say that the economy of the one God, the creator of the world, is here spoken of in a way in which each of the three "persons" are immediately interrelated: the Father is the Father of his Son; the Son is, obviously, the Son of his Father; and the Spirit is the Spirit of the Son of the Father.[96]

This relational mutuality implies a dynamic understanding of the interplay between christology, theology, and pneumatology. By way of exegesis of Paul, then, Rowe thus calls for renewed attention not simply to the textual data of the New Testament but to the underlying concepts and assumptions whereby New Testament interpreters attempt to articulate the trajectories and implications of the texts they study.

Finally, mention may be made here of the work of Francis Watson.[97] Framed as a reply to Dunn's *Theology of Paul,* Watson's essay "The Triune Divine Identity" proposes that any approach to Pauline *theo*logy proper (i.e., Paul's "God-talk") which assumes that God's identity is the relatively fixed point and the real interpretive task is thus to determine where Jesus fits in relation to it has neatly inverted a core Pauline concern:

> Far from merely assuming or reproducing pre-Christian Jewish views of God, Paul's texts everywhere assert or assume a distinctively Christian view of God. Traditional Jewish God-language is relocated within a framework in which the word "God" is misunderstood and misused if it is not always and everywhere accompanied by reference to Jesus and to his Spirit.[98]

Watson goes on to spell out what the phrase "accompanied by" entails: "God [is] *defined* in relation to Jesus."[99] Or, more fully, "Jesus is integral to God's own identity, and that is a statement both about who God is and about who Jesus is. Paul's understanding of deity is . . . relational in form,"[100]

96. Rowe, "Biblical Pressure and Trinitarian Hermeneutics," 304.
97. Watson, "The Triune Divine Identity."
98. Watson, "The Triune Divine Identity," 104-5.
99. Watson, "The Triune Divine Identity," 111. Italics added.
100. Watson, "The Triune Divine Identity," 111-12.

just as his understanding of christology is equally relational in form. The task of determining the identity of Jesus in Paul is best served not by inquiring after Jesus' usurping (or else preserving) "monotheism" — the uniqueness of "God," considered as already known apart from Jesus[101] — but rather by asking how Jesus' *relations* with and to God the Father and the Spirit are internal to his, and thus also their, identities. In this account, "monotheism" is not so much preserved as completely reworked in light of, or indeed *as,* the relations between God, Jesus, and their Spirit.[102]

Taken together, these various proposals (i.e., in Rowe, Dahl, Keck, and Watson) coalesce quite strikingly. However, a survey of even the most recent work on Pauline christology does not show much engagement with their appeals. Scholars continue to pursue Pauline christology in disregard for the kind of relational and correlative considerations urged by the interpreters mentioned here.[103] In light of this neglect, I will take up the challenge posed by these discussions and seek to adopt it as a working framework with which to reread Paul.

3. Contemporary Trinitarian Theologies as a Resource for Pauline Interpretation: Persons and Relations

The previous section noted a "minority report" among New Testament scholars with regard to Pauline christology and its relationship to Pauline theology proper. Whereas several leading interpreters in the field have adopted one framework ("high" versus "low") as a way of discussing Pauline christology, other interpreters have advocated a significant remapping of Paul's theology, christology, and pneumatology in a direction that emphasizes the mutually conditioning, mutually constitutive relations between

---

101. Cf. N. T. Wright, *The New Testament and the People of God* (Christian Origins and the Question of God 1; Minneapolis: Fortress, 1992), xv: "The christological question, as to whether the statement 'Jesus is God' is true, and if so in what sense, is often asked as though 'God' were the known and 'Jesus' the unknown; this, I suggest, is manifestly mistaken. If anything, the matter stands the other way around."

102. Donald H. Juel, "The Trinity in the New Testament," *Theology Today* 54/3 (1997): 312-24, at 314: "Speaking about 'God' requires speaking about a relationship between 'Father' and 'Son.'"

103. Neil Richardson, *Paul's Language about God* (JSNTSup 99; Sheffield: Sheffield Academic Press, 1994) is a partial exception to this trend (see especially his conclusions on pp. 306-7).

these categories/"persons." Major voices within New Testament studies have explicitly argued for keeping Pauline christology and theology at some distance from trinitarian theology, but the interpreters surveyed in the previous section take the opposite tack and plead for a rereading of Paul's theology that treats the concepts and categories of trinitarian theology as hermeneutical resources rather than as liabilities. My aim in what follows is to undertake some of the work that must be done to further that exegetical task. But in order to do so, I need to clarify in what ways the grammar of trinitarian theology will and will not be invoked, and to specify the methodological safeguards that will protect my exegesis from devolving into an exercise in imaginative theologizing.

In this section my goal is twofold: first, to provide a typology of some contemporary trinitarian theologies, limited in scope by its attention to the theme of "relations" within these theologies. Since, as we have seen, the relational character of christology has been neglected in Pauline interpretation, and since I have proposed a trinitarian retooling of christological discussions by way of the mutual relations between God, Jesus, and the Spirit, therefore this term — "relations" — and its correlatives ("relationality," "relatedness," "persons," "mutually constituting," "identity/ies") will need to be carefully parsed if they are to serve as exegetical aids. Second, I will briefly discuss issues of interpretive method and describe, in light of the foregoing, the ways in which the grammar of these trinitarian theologies will and will not be employed in my exegesis of Paul.

i. Persons in/as Relations? Understanding a Conceptual Category of Trinitarian Discourse

For Francis Watson, the key insight of trinitarian theology that is relevant for Pauline interpretation — seen above all in the father-son terminology used of God and Jesus — is that "God and Jesus are identified by their relation to each other, and have no existence apart from that relation."[104] Here Watson reiterates a theological commonplace, found throughout the tradition of trinitarian theology, that made its first entrance into the discourse in the early years of the Arian controversy. Prior to the Council of Nicaea, Arius contended that the Son is not to be understood as co-eternal with the Father: "He did not exist at the same time as the Father,

---

104. Watson, "The Triune Divine Identity," 115.

as some have said in speaking of 'relatives.' "[105] The precise identity of the "some" to whom Arius refers is not entirely clear, but their argument may be reconstructed through an examination of their terminology which Arius repeats. The "relatives" mentioned refer to the "pro-Nicene"[106] explanation of the inherently relational character of father-son language: One cannot be a father without a son and vice versa.[107] By the late 350s, this argument was made with recourse to Aristotelian categories that described relative beings as simultaneous. As Gilles Emery characterizes it: "if 'Father' and 'Son' are indeed mutually related names, then whenever there was a Father, there must have been a Son."[108]

Although Athanasius was the first to exploit the mutuality of the father-son names for thinking about the eternal being of God, it is "the Cappadocians" — Basil of Caesarea, Gregory of Nyssa, and Gregory of Nazianzus — who are usually credited as being the first to develop this line of reasoning in a genuinely creative direction and fully appropriate it for subsequent trinitarian discourse. Distinguishing between those designations which refer to an entity's reality considered in itself and those terms which specify an entity's relation to another, Basil of Caesarea considered the father-son pairing an instance of the latter and used it to demonstrate the eternal coexistence of the Father and the Son.[109] For Basil, a person may be described both with the language of a generic essence (οὐσία) and of individuating properties (ἰδιώματα or ἰδιότητες). The apostle Paul, for example, may be described as a human being with regard to his essence

---

105. Athanasius, C. Ar. 1.29 (cf. 3.6; 14.34). Recent scholarship on the fourth-century theological debates, however, has focused "on Arius as a catalyst for a controversy within which his particular theology rapidly becomes marginal" (Lewis Ayres, Nicaea and Its Legacy: An Approach to Fourth-Century Trinitarian Theology [Oxford: Oxford University Press, 2004], 12 n. 3). Arius kicked off the extended debates, but, as Ayres comments, summarizing the post-1960s scholarly consensus, "No clear party sought to preserve Arius' theology" (13).

106. The term "pro-Nicene" is used here in line with Lewis Ayres's effort to name the "culture" of pre- and post-Nicaea discussions whose basic contours are in harmony with the official creedal pronouncements (Nicaea and Its Legacy, ch. 9).

107. In Athanasius's words: "that the Son is co-eternal with the Father the very nature of the relation proves. For no one is father of a son until that son exists" (C. Ar. 3.6).

108. Gilles Emery, O.P., The Trinitarian Theology of St. Thomas Aquinas (trans. Francesca Aran Murphy; Oxford: Oxford University Press, 2007), 80, referencing Aristotle, Categories 7 (7 b15). Cf. Emery, Trinity, Church, and the Human Person: Thomistic Essays (Naples, FL: Sapientia Press, 2007), 17-18.

109. Basil of Caesarea, Adv. Eu. For discussion, see Ayres, Nicaea and Its Legacy, 198-204.

(οὐσία) and as a particular person by reference to the qualities which mark him out as such (the ἰδιώματα or ἰδιότητες of being a Jew, a man from Tarsus, etc.).[110] In the case of the divine persons, the personal names — e.g., "Father," "Son" — indicate not the divine nature or essence (οὐσία) but the relations (σχέσις) that obtain between the persons.[111] In Emery's description, "There are therefore two kinds of names, substantial and relative. Correspondingly there will be two levels in our knowledge of God the Trinity: that of *substance* and that of the relative *properties* of hypostases."[112] Trinitarian language about God operates through the "combination" or "redoublement" of these modes of discourse.[113]

This way of speaking about the relations among the trinitarian persons came to include the Spirit as well as Father and Son. However, unlike "Father" and "Son," the personal name itself — "Spirit" — was not immediately recognizable as a relational term, and so interpretive work had to be done to demonstrate that "the identity of God and of Jesus is bound up with a third party, the Holy Spirit, who is both the Spirit of God and the Spirit of Christ."[114] It was obvious that "Father" implies a corresponding "Son," and vice versa, but it was not so apparent how the Spirit belonged integrally within that same relational matrix. Athanasius and the Cappadocians argued backward from the triadic unity of God's saving action to the mutuality of the intra-divine life and thus secured a place for the Spirit within the triune relations.[115] But within this divine life, it became necessary to find a deeper basis for the difference between the persons of

---

110. Basil, *Adv. Eu.,* 2.4. For discussion of this point, see Sarah Coakley, "'Persons' in the 'Social' Doctrine of the Trinity: Current Analytic Discussion and 'Cappadocian' Theology," in *Powers and Submissions: Spirituality, Philosophy and Gender* (Challenges in Contemporary Theology; Oxford: Blackwell, 2002), 109-29.

111. Ayres, *Nicaea and Its Legacy,* 201-2.

112. Emery, *Trinity, Church, and the Human Person,* 18.

113. Emery, *Trinity, Church, and the Human Person,* 18; "Essentialism or Personalism in the Treatise on God in Saint Thomas Aquinas?" *The Thomist* 64 (2000): 521-64; cf. Matthew Levering, *Scripture and Metaphysics: Aquinas and the Renewal of Trinitarian Theology* (Challenges in Contemporary Theology; Oxford: Blackwell, 2004), 214-16.

114. Watson, "The Triune Divine Identity," 119, slightly altered.

115. For my purposes, it is unnecessary at this point to draw fine distinctions between the various (sometimes strikingly differing) ways Athanasius and the Cappadocians articulated their pneumatologies; on the differences, see Ayres, *Nicaea and Its Legacy,* 211-18, and Christopher A. Beeley, *Gregory of Nazianzus on the Trinity and the Knowledge of God: In Your Light We Shall See Light* (Oxford Studies in Historical Theology; New York: Oxford University Press, 2008), 277-84.

Son and Spirit in the "generation" of the Son and the "procession" of the Spirit, since a shared divine activity was not enough to undergird both the ontological oneness of the divine persons and also their non-identity with one another. This theological trajectory does not need to be narrated in full here; the crucial point is to observe that the divine persons eventually came to be distinguished by their relations of origin.[116] It became important to show that the Spirit's manner of proceeding differed from the Son's generation, and only thus were they to be distinguished. What the difference between generation and procession amounted to remained finally unknowable, and intentionally so.[117] The crucial point was that there was a difference, regardless of its inability to be rationally comprehended or adequately set forth with terminological precision.[118]

This basic conceptual scheme for understanding trinitarian relations dominated the discourse of medieval theology primarily because of Augustine's influence. Like the Cappadocians, Augustine maintained the twofold way of speaking of God. Trinitarian theology might refer, on the one hand, to God's unity or essence as well as, on the other hand, to the internal divine relations, but the personal names — "Father," "Son," and "Spirit" — should be construed not as referring to the divine essence *simpliciter* but, in a "redoubled" way, to the relations which distinguish and thus constitute the persons qua persons. In Augustine's words:

> If . . . what is called Father were called so with reference to itself and not to the Son, and what is called Son were called so with reference to itself and not to the Father, the one would be called Father and the other Son with regard to substance [*ad se*]. But since the Father is only called so because he has a Son, and the Son is only called so because he has a Father, these things are not said with regard to substance,

116. Gregory of Nyssa, *Adv. Eu.*, 1.227, 278-80; *Ablab.* 117, 135; Gregory Nazianzen, *Or.* 31.9.

117. Gregory Nazianzen, *Or.* 5.8; John of Damascus, *Expositio fidei*, 8.191-93.

118. Richard of St. Victor, *De Trinitate* 3, argues from the nature of love for the necessity of the Father and Son's mutual relationship implying a third, the Spirit. In Sarah Coakley's summary: "perfect love must occur in a *relationship* of perfect equality (requiring two persons) but also . . . such a relationship (*if* perfect) must necessarily be outgoing, overflowing to at least one other as a shared communitarian benefit (and so the 'third' is needed)" ("Why Three? Some Further Reflections on the Origins of the Doctrine of the Trinity," in Sarah Coakley and David Pailin [eds.], *The Making and Remaking of Christian Doctrine* [FS Maurice Wiles; Oxford: Clarendon Press, 1993], 29-56, at 36). Coakley's entire essay is an effort to explore the problem of the hypostatization of the Spirit.

as neither is said with reference to itself but only with reference to the other. . . . Therefore, although being Father is different from being Son, there is no difference of substance, because they are not called these things with regard to substance but with regard to relationship [*ad aliquid*]. . . .[119]

This Cappadocian-Augustinian account of relations owes its prominence in Western trinitarian theologies mainly to Thomas Aquinas. Through him it became rooted in medieval and Reformation scholastic traditions and from there, as we will see, underwent significant critique in the hands of post-Hegelian trinitarian "revivalists" whose work continues to determine the shape and agenda of much current constructive trinitarian discussion.

According to Emery, "Thomas' original contribution consisted in systematically deepening the patristic legacy. His innovation was to extend this theological tradition [toward the notion of] the constitution of the divine persons through relation, that is, the conception of subsistent relation."[120] Here Thomas built upon the twofold mode of referring to God already in play in Cappadocian and Augustinian theology: " 'Substance' and 'relation' are two aspects of, or perspectives on, God's triune being, as are 'nature' and 'person.' "[121] For Thomas, to speak of one of the divine persons with reference to the divine nature common to all three, one employs one set of terms (e.g., "substance," "nature," "being"). In this way, one could speak of the *oneness* of God by speaking of, for example, the *Son's* (one of the three person's) *essence* (which he shares with the Father and the Spirit). But to speak of the three in their relationships to one another,

---

119. Augustine, *The Trinity* (trans. E. Hill; Hyde Park, NY: New City Press, 1991), 192 (= *De Trinitate* 5.6), translation slightly modified; for the inclusion of the Spirit, see 197, 199 (= *De Trinitate* 5.12, 15; cf. 7.7). For discussion and defense of the claim that Augustine's argument here is in essential continuity with the Cappadocians', a claim often made in more recent scholarship as over against an earlier perspective which drove a wedge between Augustine's "Latin" model and an allegedly different "Eastern" one, see Lewis Ayres, "Augustine, the Trinity and Modernity," *Augustinian Studies* 26/2 (1995): 127-33; *Augustine and the Trinity* (Cambridge: Cambridge University Press, 2010), as well as the essays of Michel René Barnes, "Augustine in Contemporary Trinitarian Theology," *Theological Studies* 56/2 (1995): 237-50; "De Régnon Reconsidered," *Augustinian Studies* 26 (1995): 51-79.

120. Emery, *The Trinitarian Theology of St. Thomas Aquinas*, 84.

121. Kevin J. Vanhoozer, *Remythologizing Theology: Divine Action, Passion, and Authorship* (Cambridge Studies in Christian Doctrine; Cambridge: Cambridge University Press, 2010), 145.

one employs a different set of terms suitable to marking out the three in relation to the others but not in distinction from the one divine nature. Thus, for example, one could speak of the Son's *generation,* which points not to what he shares in common with the Father and Spirit but rather to what marks him out as one of the trinitarian persons in an "opposed" relation[122] to the Father who generates him. To say that the divine persons are "subsistent relations" is for Thomas, then, to speak *indirectly* of the divine being in which the persons "subsist," and it is to speak *directly* of how the persons are determined as three by means of their mutual relations. The persons' *identities* qua persons — each person's identity vis-à-vis the other persons' — are constituted by means of their relations.[123]

Virtually every aspect of the foregoing summary has been challenged in more recent trinitarian theologies. In order to continue to refine our understanding of the category of "relations" as it has been employed in the discourse of trinitarian theology, it is necessary to note some of these contemporary developments.

ii. "Persons-in-Relation" in Contemporary Trinitarian Theologies

If nineteenth-century Protestant trinitarian theologies shied away from discussion of personal relations in the immanent trinity, twentieth-century trinitarian theology saw a renewal of interest in "relationality" as a kind of hermeneutical key to the doctrine of the trinity.[124] However, the "relations"

122. On "relative opposition," see Emery, *The Trinitarian Theology of St. Thomas Aquinas,* 96-102.

123. Cf. Jürgen Moltmann, *The Trinity and the Kingdom* (Minneapolis: Fortress, 1993 [1981]), 173. Cf. Vanhoozer, *Remythologizing Theology,* 149: "Each of the three divine persons is fully God, has a distinct existence of his own, yet is not who he is apart from his relation to the other persons." This is, as Vanhoozer notes (144), different from the claim that each person's personhood *simpliciter* is constituted by its relations. Rather, each person's "distinct personal identity" — "who," as opposed to "what," they are — is relational; cf. Harriet A. Harris, "Should We Say That Personhood Is Relational?" *SJT* 51 (1998): 214-34, at 216-17.

124. For a useful summary as well as penetrating critique of the twentieth-century trinitarian "renewal," see Bruce D. Marshall, "Trinity," in Gareth Jones (ed.), *The Blackwell Companion to Modern Theology* (Oxford: Blackwell, 2004), 183-203. Karen Kilby, "Perichoresis and Projection: Problems with Social Doctrines of the Trinity," *New Blackfriars* 81 (2000): 432-45, at 433, characterizes the more recent "social" or "relational" understanding of the trinity as the "new orthodoxy" in trinitarian discourse. For fuller discussion of relation-

in view in this "trinitarian renewal" were as much a reaction to the historic formulations of Augustine, Thomas, and other classical figures as they were a continuation of them.

The key insight of the trinitarian renewal is now thought to be encapsulated in an axiom of Karl Rahner, often characterized as "Rahner's Rule": "The 'economic' Trinity is the 'immanent' Trinity, and conversely."[125] This axiom may imply that God's life "in himself" or *ad intra* can only be known by attending to God's self-revelation "for us" or *ad extra* — an epistemological claim — or, in a stronger interpretation, that God's being *ad intra* is the same as, or is constituted by or from, his life *ad extra*.[126] The triune God we encounter in his saving action is the same God "antecedently in himself";[127] the trinity with which we relate in the economy is the same trinity all the way back into God's eternal life.

Ironically, the figures usually identified as the heralds of the modern trinitarian renewal — Rahner and Karl Barth[128] — are viewed with suspicion by some of the renewal's most influential exemplars on account of their perceived failure to follow through with the implications of their own positions. For Rahner as for Barth, the immanent trinity revealed by the economic is best described not with the language of persons in relation but with other terminology less open to misconstrual in terms of modern notions of "personality." Barth discarded the language of "persons" to describe the trinitarian hypostases in favor of *Seinsweisen* ("modes of being").[129]

---

ality as central to much contemporary trinitarian reflection, see Ted Peters, *God as Trinity: Relationality and Temporality in Divine Life* (Louisville: Westminster/John Knox, 1993).

125. Karl Rahner, *The Trinity* (trans. J. Donceel; 2nd ed.; New York: Crossroad, 1997 [1967]), 22. The phrase "Rahner's Rule" was apparently coined by Ted Peters and Roger Olson, each of whom credits the other with the original formulation; see Fred Sanders, "Entangled in the Trinity: Economic and Immanent Trinity in Recent Theology," *Dialog: A Journal of Theology* 40/3 (2001): 175-82, at 182 n. 4.

126. "Immanent" here, in contrast to its normal pairing with "transcendent," refers not to God's nearness to creation but to God's life in himself, the "actions remaining within an agent." "Economic" and "immanent" specify two perspectives from which the one divine life and activity may be viewed simultaneously. For a useful parsing of the terminology of trinitarian theological discussion, see Fred Sanders, *The Image of the Immanent Trinity: Rahner's Rule and the Theological Interpretation of Scripture* (Issues in Systematic Theology, 12; New York and Frankfurt am Main: Peter Lang, 2005), 3-5.

127. See Karl Barth, *Church Dogmatics* I/1 (trans. G. W. Bromiley, et al.; Edinburgh: T&T Clark, 1975), 428, 466, 479-80.

128. See Karl Barth, *Church Dogmatics* (trans. G. W. Bromiley, et al.; Edinburgh: T&T Clark, 1956-75).

129. Barth, *Church Dogmatics* I/1, 355-68, esp. 359.

Rahner, likewise, settled on "distinct mode of subsistence" in an effort to avoid speaking of three separate "consciousnesses" or "centers of action."[130] Both theologians cited fears of tritheism as their rationale for these moves.

As a result, many contemporary trinitarian theologians find in Barth and/or Rahner (and/or their theological kin) a tendency toward "monism." Rather than beginning from the dynamic interaction of the three divine persons, Barth and Rahner mistakenly (according to this view) followed Augustine and the Latin West by starting from the unity of God and thus missed the "personalist" character of Eastern trinitarian theologies. Although Rahner saw clearly the danger posed to Western theology of beginning from the "one God" and only then moving to consider the three persons of the Godhead,[131] he allegedly neglected to follow this insight to its logical conclusion, and thus the task of extending his project falls to others.

What such a "personalist" correction of Rahner and Barth might entail is a question that has been pursued in a number of influential recent trinitarian theologies. Jürgen Moltmann is representative of a significant stream of contemporary reflection when he writes:

> It is impossible to say: person *is* relation; the relation constitutes the person. It is true that the Father is defined by his fatherhood to the Son, but this does not constitute his existence; it presupposes it. . . . The reduction of the concept "person" to the concept "relation" is basically modalistic, because it suggests the further reduction of the concept of relation to a self-relation on God's part. But is person merely a "concrete and really existing relation of God to himself"? If it were, then God in the three Persons would be thrice himself, and the Persons would be nothing more than the triple self-repetition of God. This modalistic view not only dissolves the trinitarian concept of person; it does away with the interpersonal concept of relation as well. Moreover the number "three" becomes incomprehensible.[132]

At issue here is what it means to say that the trinitarian persons are constituted by their mutual relations. For Moltmann, the persons must not be *reduced* to relations, which is incoherent since the category of "relation"

---

130. Rahner, *The Trinity,* 42-45, 103-15.
131. Rahner, *The Trinity,* 17.
132. Moltmann, *The Trinity and the Kingdom,* 172-73.

requires there to exist some entities logically prior to and thus able to be in relationship with one another.

Moltmann represents many contemporary trinitarian theologians who claim that "Eastern"/Orthodox trinitarian reflection avoids the problem in Western (Augustinian/Thomistic) trinitarian theology of such reductionism. Augustine and Aquinas, it is said, bequeathed to Western trinitarianism a concept of "relations" that remains deeply flawed. John Zizioulas and Colin Gunton, for example, both begin their respective trinitarian theologies with a critique of Greek philosophical and Western Christian (Augustinian/Thomistic) categories of "being." According to Zizioulas, "ancient Greek ontology . . . was fundamentally monistic," that is, marked by a preference for oneness and unity — the "general" — over multiplicity and plurality — the "particular," "the many."[133] Hence, any "differentiation" was an instance of being's corruption, since unity and sameness were the standards for measuring perfect being. Western Christian thought adopted these assumptions with minimal criticism, as is evidenced, for example, in Augustine's ecclesiology, in which the individual's reception of grace took precedence over a communal modeling of God's trinitarian life.[134] This Christian inheritance of Greek philosophical notions allegedly had disastrous consequences for the doctrine of God. The concrete actions of the three divine persons in the history of salvation were obscured by the category of the divine "being" or "oneness." In this view, "God first *is* God (His substance or nature, His being), and then exists as Trinity, that is, as persons."[135]

By contrast, Gunton and Zizioulas propose a relational ontology: the being or oneness of God is constituted by the trinitarian persons' relations to each other. For Zizioulas, the origins of this ontological revision lay with the Cappadocians, who upended Greek concepts of "being" by placing one of the trinitarian hypostases, the "person" of the Father, logically prior to the being of God.[136] As the *archē* of the trinitarian communion, the Father

---

133. John D. Zizioulas, *Being as Communion: Studies in Personhood and the Church* (Crestwood, NY: St. Vladimir's Seminary Press, 2002 [1985]), 16. Cf. Colin E. Gunton, *Act and Being: Towards a Theology of the Divine Attributes* (London: SCM, 2002), 5.

134. Colin E. Gunton, *The Promise of Trinitarian Theology* (2nd ed.; Edinburgh: T&T Clark, 1997; 1st ed., 1991), 51. The chapter cited here was originally published as an influential article, "Augustine, the Trinity, and the Theological Crisis of the West," *SJT* 43 (1994): 33-58.

135. Zizioulas, *Being as Communion,* 40.

136. Zizioulas, *Being as Communion,* 36. For this classically Eastern emphasis, cf. Vladimir Lossky, *The Mystical Theology of the Eastern Church* (London: James Clarke, 1957), 57-58.

is the source of the Son and Spirit, and together their life of communion constitutes God's "being." This "being" is not a reified fourth entity lying behind the relations between the divine persons but rather simply *is* these relations as they are "caused" by the Father.

In Gunton and Zizioulas's readings, the Western theological tradition failed to grasp this point. Rather than interpreting the trinitarian persons as "concrete particulars in relation to one another,"[137] Aquinas spoke instead of persons *as* relations.[138] For Aquinas, the divine essence cannot be constituted by the relations, since the relations are held to be identical with the essence.[139] The divine being is simple, not composite, and so not the sum of the three, but is instead a way of designating the oneness of the three persons.[140] But although they, too, wish to avoid crude notions of the divine essence as a kind of collective or committee, Gunton and Zizioulas think that on Aquinas's account, a door is opened to contemplate a divine essence that is not intrinsically relational. As Vladimir Lossky puts it,

> The hypostatic characteristics (paternity, generation, procession), find themselves more or less swallowed up in the nature or essence which, differentiated by relationships — to the Son as Father, to the Holy Spirit as Father and Son — becomes the principle of unity within the Trinity. The relationships, instead of being characteristics of the hypostases, are identified with them.[141]

For Gunton and Zizioulas, then, the classical Western tradition "is precluded from being able to make claims about the being of *particular* persons, who, because they lack distinguishable identity, tend to disappear into the all-embracing oneness of God."[142]

Others have attempted to build on these concerns of Zizioulas and

137. Gunton, *The Promise of Trinitarian Theology*, 39.

138. *Summa theologiae* I.29.4.

139. Emery, "Essentialism or Personalism in the Treatise on God in Saint Thomas Aquinas?" 534.

140. Walter Kasper, *The God of Jesus Christ* (trans. Matthew J. O'Connell; London: SCM, 1984), 281.

141. Lossky, *The Mystical Theology of the Eastern Church*, 57. Cf. Dumitru Staniloae, *The Experience of God* (Orthodox Dogmatic Theology 1; trans. and ed. Ioan Ionita and Robert Barringer; Brookline, MA: Holy Cross Orthodox Press, 1994), 245.

142. Gunton, *The Promise of Trinitarian Theology*, 41-42. In context, Gunton is speaking of Augustine.

Gunton and to extend them in a direction opened up by Hegel, Barth, Eberhard Jüngel,[143] and Wolfhart Pannenberg,[144] among others. According to the trinitarian theology of Robert Jenson, for example, "the Cappadocians acknowledged only relations of *origin* [e.g., 'being begotten', 'proceeding'] as constitutive for the divine life. Thus the *eschatological* character of God's scriptural history was suppressed."[145] If Western scholastic trinitarianism adopted Aquinas's understanding that each of the trinitarian hypostases is "a relation that itself subsists and is not merely a connection between subsistents," Jenson puts a question to this tradition: "How does this work within the narrative reality [depicted in the Bible] itself?"[146] According to him, the Western tradition's focus on the intradivine relations in the immanent trinity has obscured the biblical distinctions which necessitated the tradition's formulations in the first place. "When logically detached from the biblical triune narrative, the Nicene-Cappadocian propositions about the immanent Trinity become formulas without meaning we can know."[147] At the heart of Jenson's trinitarian theology, then, lies an attempt to interpret the trinitarian relations *historically* or eschatologically. Thus,

> the hypostases' "relations" are Jesus' historical obedience to and dependence on his "Father" and the coming of their Spirit into the believing community. "Begetting," "being begotten," "proceeding" and their variants are biblical terms for temporal structures of evangelical history, which theology then uses for relations said to be constitutive of God's life. What happens between Jesus and his Father and our future *happens in God* — that is the point.[148]

In other words, Jenson proposes that the traditional trinitarian relations are best understood not as distinctions within a timeless or pre-temporal

---

143. Eberhard Jüngel, *The Doctrine of the Trinity: God's Being Is in Becoming* (trans. Horton Harris; Edinburgh: Scottish Academic Press, 1976); *God as the Mystery of the World* (trans. Darell L. Guder; Grand Rapids: Eerdmans, 1983).

144. Wolfhart Pannenberg, *Jesus — God and Man* (Philadelphia: Westminster, 1968), 168-204; *Systematic Theology*, vol. 1 (trans. G. W. Bromiley; Grand Rapids: Eerdmans, 1991), 259-336.

145. Robert W. Jenson, *Systematic Theology* (2 vols.; Oxford: Oxford University Press, 1997), 1:108.

146. Jenson, *Systematic Theology*, 1:109.

147. Jenson, *Systematic Theology*, 1:113.

148. Jenson, *The Triune Identity*, 106.

immanent trinity but as descriptors of Jesus, his Father, and their Spirit's history as it is displayed in the gospel and the biblical narrative. "The life of God is constituted in a structure of relations, whose own referents are narrative."[149] "God is what happens between Jesus and his Father in their Spirit."[150]

This account of the trinitarian relations gains coherence within Jenson's comprehensive outline of a "revisionary metaphysics"[151] — "revisionary" in that it aims to reinterpret classic trinitarian discourse in a way that attempts an end run around its Hellenistic background and recovers its biblical grounding. For Jenson, the Spirit is the One who "witnesses" to the Son and just so "frees" the Father, thereby representing the "endless futurity" of God's triune life.[152] Where traditional trinitarian theology speaks of relations of "begetting" and "breathing" and so on, Jenson proposes to use the biblical language of "witnessing" and "freeing" to describe the relations: "The Spirit's witness to the Son, and the Son's and the Spirit's joint reality as the Openness into which the Father is freed from mere persistence in his pretemporal transcendence, are equally God-constituting with the traditional relations" of "begetting" and "spirating."[153] If the theological tradition understood God's triunity by the eternal "relations of origin," Jenson's construal locates God's triunity by the narrative, eschatological "relations of *fulfillment*."[154] God is God at and from the end. Thus, in Jenson's most succinct statement of what the relations amount to: "the Father begets the Son and freely breathes his Spirit; the Spirit liberates the Father for the Son and the Son from and for the Father; the Son is begotten and liberated, and so reconciles the Father with the future his Spirit is."[155]

From this brief survey, we can see that, despite a vast variety of approaches and emphases, trinitarian theologies share a concern to specify how the identities of the trinitarian persons are constituted in, by, or through their relations to one another. Such an analysis is not meant as a "lowest common denominator" judgment, as though noting commonali-

149. Jenson, *Systematic Theology*, 1:218.

150. Jenson, *Systematic Theology*, 1:221.

151. Robert W. Jenson, "A Reply" [to Paul Molnar], *SJT* 52/1 (1999): 132; "Response to Watson and Hunsinger," *SJT* 55/2 (2002): 225-32, at 230.

152. Jenson, *The Triune Identity*, 140-43; *Systematic Theology*, 1:216.

153. Jenson, *The Triune Identity*, 142.

154. Jenson, *Systematic Theology*, 1:157, italics original. Pannenberg, *Systematic Theology*, 1:308-19, had already made a similar point.

155. Jenson, *Systematic Theology*, 1:161.

ties between these various theologies would allow one to minimize their differences. Nevertheless, by placing these theologies alongside the christological discussions of New Testament scholars, I hope I have enabled a more acute observation of the way in which they all share what has been underplayed in recent New Testament, and specifically Pauline, exegesis. Despite their drastic disagreements, these trinitarian theologies, in marked contrast to the debate in Pauline scholarship over how "low" or "high" Paul's christology was, frustrate any attempt to identify one of the trinitarian persons — "God"/"the Father," "Jesus"/"Christ"/"the Son," or "the Spirit" — in a way that does not also implicate the other two.[156] If "God" is to be defined, it is as "the Father," which implies a corresponding "Son"; if "Jesus" is to be identified, it is as "the Son," which implies a corresponding "Father"; if the Spirit's identity is to be explicated, it is as "the Spirit of God"/"the Spirit of Christ," which implies the Spirit's inseparability from God (the Father) and Jesus (the Son). Although *the way in which* this is to be spelled out is understood very differently among contemporary (and historic) trinitarian theologians, the necessity of its being spelled out is a common starting point — which is precisely what has been neglected or rejected among contemporary readers of Paul.

iii. Interpretive Method: Retrieving a Trinitarian Conceptuality for Pauline Exegesis

So far, then, I have attempted to accomplish three tasks. First, I outlined the approach taken in several recent influential treatments of Pauline christology. Focusing on a representative sampling of scholarship, I noted the descriptors "high christology" and "low christology" and discussed some of the exegetical bases for these descriptors, as well as the varied dynamics of the positions represented by these labels. Despite the differences between their approaches, I noted that those who adopt the "low christology" designation as well as those preferring the "high christology" label are

---

156. Cf. the elegantly compressed summary of trinitarian doctrine in Thomas F. Torrance, *The Christian Doctrine of God: One Being, Three Persons* (Edinburgh: T&T Clark, 1996), 157: "no divine person is what he is without relation to the other two, and yet each divine person is other than and distinct from the other two." Similarly, according to David F. Ford and Frances Young, *Meaning and Truth in 2 Corinthians* (London: SPCK, 1987), 257, one should "always identify God through Father, Son and Holy Spirit, and intend this even when only one is mentioned."

both operating with what might be termed a "vertical axis" conceptuality, whereby the all-important question is whether Christ rises to the level of God and reconfigures the definition of monotheism or whether he remains subordinate to God and Paul's inherited Jewish monotheism remains to that degree unmodified.

From there I suggested that these recent discussions of Pauline christology — whether they be "high" or "low" — owe some of their plausibility to broader currents in the discipline of New Testament studies, particularly the loss of confidence, after the rise of critical scholarship, in the strength of trinitarian conceptualities as historically credible accounts of Pauline theology/christology. This loss of confidence, as well as the lifting of christology from its original (e.g., patristic)[157] place within the matrix of trinitarian theology, contributed to the abandonment of trinitarian accounts of Pauline theology and the resultant dominance of debates over Pauline *christology,* conceived now as a separate area of inquiry from the question of Christ's relations within the trinity.

Finally, I described the category of "relations" as it appears in the development of trinitarian theologies. Although these theologies differ dramatically from each other, they coalesce strikingly precisely at their point of disagreement *when compared with the treatments of Pauline christology in recent New Testament scholarship.* Although each conceives of what the trinitarian "relations" are in a different way, their very disagreements underscore a shared commitment to the importance of the category of "relations" in the first place. Despite their mutually exclusive formulations, they all emphasize the mutual involvement of the trinitarian persons in the identities of the other persons: *each person is only identifiable by means of reference to the others.* Thus, the question of whether Jesus/"the Son" occupies a "high" or "low" position relative to "God" is not likely to appear as an urgent one, since "God" is never construed as identifiable apart from "the Son." And, vice versa, "the Son" is never taken to denote an identity explicable apart from his relation to God.

Having summarized what I have attempted so far, now in conclusion, before turning to Paul's texts, it seems important to indicate what role trinitarian theologies of "relations" will play in the subsequent exe-

---

157. Cf. Brian E. Daley, " 'One Thing and Another': The Persons in God and the Person of Christ in Patristic Theology," *Pro Ecclesia* 15 (2006): 17-46, at 42: " 'Trinitarian theology' and 'Christology' are modern terms, not ancient ones, and represent tracts in the theological curriculum of the modern Western university rather than categories of patristic discussion."

gesis. The methodological danger that lurks here is one that may be described as a certain kind of "projection": first, a (rather vague) category of "relations"/"relationality" is sketched, then it is read back into the Pauline texts, at which point the Pauline texts are interpreted as having led to that "relational" category themselves — and thus a vicious hermeneutical circle is constructed.[158] To avoid this pitfall, I will adopt a twofold approach: First, the readings of Paul I will offer in the chapters that follow will be self-consciously *historical* readings, guided by the canons of "critical" modes of exegesis. At no point will a trinitarian conclusion be allowed to "trump" what Paul's texts may be plausibly shown to have communicated within his own context. Second, trinitarian theologies will be employed as hermeneutical *resources* and, thus, mined for conceptualities which may better *enable* a genuinely historical exegesis to articulate what other equally "historical" approaches may have (unwittingly or not) obscured. In other words, if it can be shown that certain critical approaches and conclusions leave crucial texts unsatisfactorily accounted for, or that they construct a version of Paul's theology with significant unresolved tensions and internal difficulties, and if trinitarian categories and conceptualities may offer help in achieving solutions to those tensions and difficulties, then my use of those trinitarian conceptualities may carry its own justification.

What will be avoided in this thesis is the consideration of either "Pauline theology" or "trinitarian theology" as entities fully "given" and thus needing no constructive effort on the part of their interpreters. On the contrary, both Pauline theology and trinitarian theology will be treated in dialectical fashion. Adopting a trinitarian grammar for rereading Paul is not the same as fitting Pauline texts to a Procrustean bed. Instead, as systematic theologians regularly emphasize, "trinitarian theology" is in need of specification to indicate what *sort* of trinitarian theology is in view. Or, put differently, trinitarian theology is in need of critical retrieval and appropriation, since creedal and conciliar dogmas and formulations are

---

158. Cf. Karen Kilby's critique of the way the concept of "perichoresis" is employed in some current forms of "social trinitarianism": "In short, then, I am suggesting we have here something like a three-stage process. First, a concept, perichoresis, is used to name what is not understood, to name whatever it is that makes the three Persons one. Secondly, the concept is filled out rather suggestively with notions borrowed from our own experience of relationships and relatedness. And then, finally, it is presented as an exciting resource Christian theology has to offer the wider world in its reflections upon relationships and relatedness" ("Perichoresis and Projection: Problems with Social Doctrines of the Trinity," 442).

not brute "facts" requiring no active reception.[159] Trinitarian theology, rather, always elicits some measure of constructive reflection on the part of its interpreters if its formulations are to appear in a genuinely "renewed" contemporary form and not simply as repeated affirmations whose original import has ceased to be clear.

Likewise with regard to Paul's theology: it does not exist in a static form to which its interpreters are then beholden as passive receivers. Rather, its patterns and dynamics may be newly illumined and realized within new contexts and by means of later conceptualities, which are to some degree "foreign" to the texts themselves.

The movement from trinitarian formulations to their redeployment in contemporary discussions of Pauline theology should thus be a spiraling one in which exegetes and theologians play a creative role as they seek to respond dynamically to the "givenness" and continuing influence of past confessional and textual norms while at the same time incorporating what has been learned in the ongoing work of interpretation since those doctrines and texts were originally formed. The creeds and doctrinal heritage of the church invite reflection and hermeneutical appropriation, just as the Pauline texts themselves do; they shape their interpreters' horizons and, in turn, are shaped by their readers' interpretive efforts.

To say more than that at this stage would be to beg the crucial questions. In the end, the validity and usefulness of discussing Pauline theology and trinitarian theology together may only be shown through exegesis. Lengthy prolegomena justifying the use of trinitarian theology in the task of reading Paul in an authentically historical mode is unlikely to convince skeptics of its merit apart from its demonstrating explanatory power in close textual work. Only if the exegesis I offer in subsequent chapters proves able to establish a more coherent and compelling account of the data and dynamics of the Pauline texts than the ones I have criticized above may it be seen as an improvement on the more standard approaches to Paul's christology and theology currently on offer.

Before turning to that exegesis itself, I want to make one more caveat. Although my argument is largely aimed at the guild of biblical and Pauline interpreters, the conviction underlying the argument — and, it is hoped,

---

159. Cf. Jason Byassee, "Closer than Kissing: Sarah Coakley's Early Work," *Anglican Theological Review* 90/1 (2007): 139-55, at 154: "no 'orthodox' theologian who mindlessly parrots orthodox Trinitarian formulation without exploring the metaphorical and elastic qualities of those terms . . . is actually being faithful to the fathers themselves."

vindicated (in part) *by* the argument — is that theology and exegesis are, or ought to be, mutually dependent. This means that I hope the argument is accessible and of interest to theologians as well as exegetes. If trinitarian theology can assist in the task of interpreting Paul, it is equally the case that interpreting Paul is of benefit to trinitarian theology. Contemporary exegesis is often in danger of dismissing theology out of hand as so much anachronistic accretion distorting the biblical texts. On the other hand, though, much contemporary theology is likewise in danger of dismissing exegesis, opting instead to engage great thinkers of the Christian past or contemporary philosophers of religion or social scientists or any number of other disciplines before it turns (or in lieu of turning) to Scripture. Therefore it is hoped that the following chapters, although written in an idiom foreign to that of much contemporary theology, may nonetheless prove useful to theologians, reminding them of the exegetical roots of their own enterprise.

CHAPTER TWO

God in Relation to Jesus

In the foregoing survey of research, I noted a tendency in discussions of Pauline christology to interpret all christological references against the benchmark of Paul's monotheism, which he is said to have inherited from his pre-Christian Jewish background and left basically intact after his conversion. This interpretive tendency is observable among a range of Pauline exegetes, regardless of whether they construe Paul's christology in a "high" or "low" direction — and in fact, adopting the categories "high" and "low" themselves already insures that this tendency will continue, since the distances "high" and "low" are assessed by measuring, respectively, Jesus' nearness or distance from the one God. The movement of thought thus runs from Paul's theology proper — his understanding of God — to his christology, in that the former conditions or limits the latter. Christology is always *situated within* Paul's theology: "christology [is] an aspect of theology."[1]

In contrast to this trend among Pauline scholars, we observed that trinitarian theologies utilize the concept of "relations" as a way to articulate what might be called the "bi-directionality" (and, as will be explored in Chapter 5, the "tri-directionality") of God-talk: In order to identify Jesus, it is necessary to refer to God, *but also,* in order to identify God, it is necessary to refer to Jesus. *Mutuality,* rather than a unilateral movement

---

1. James D. G. Dunn, "Christology as an Aspect of Theology," in *The Christ and the Spirit;* Volume 1: *Christology* (Grand Rapids: Eerdmans, 1998), 377-87. Elsewhere Dunn writes that "the context of Paul's christology was Paul's continuing monotheism which narrows the possible avenues of interpreting Paul's christology" ("In Quest of Paul's Theology: Retrospect and Prospect," in E. Elizabeth Johnson and David M. Hay [eds.], *Pauline Theology,* Volume IV: *Looking Back, Pressing On* [Atlanta: Scholars Press, 1997], 95-115, at 108).

(in either direction), is the watchword here. Jesus, the Son, is who he is only in relation to the Father, and likewise the Father is who he is only in relation to Jesus the Son.

However, the link between these two perspectives is far from clear. The road from Paul's theology/christology to trinitarian doctrine seems strewn with journey-disrupting rubble. For many Pauline scholars, there is no possibility of uniting the two, since the trinitarian category of "relations," emerging as it did within intricate fourth-century debates, was the product of an idiom foreign to the grammar of Paul's texts. Specifying intra-divine relations may have been an eventual theological necessity, given the development of Christian thought and the challenges posed to it by various detractors, but such a specification should not, simply for that reason, be allowed to determine the shape of Pauline exegesis. Others, however, have suggested that the trinitarian category of "relations" may be just the sort of conceptual resource we need for a fresh approach to Paul's theology.[2] It is the purpose of this chapter to advocate for the latter position.

Toward that end, this chapter will explore a few select Pauline texts which appear to resist assimilation to the dominant paradigms of Pauline christology and to allow those texts, consequently, to pose some questions about ways in which the paradigms themselves might be reconfigured. The argument here will function as the first step in a reconfiguration that will not be complete without the next three chapters. In this chapter, I will discuss a variety of texts, drawn from the undisputed Pauline letters, which demonstrate one half of a double movement — from Jesus to God and from God to Jesus — and I will observe their various resonances with trinitarian theologies along the way. The half under consideration here will be those texts that move from Jesus to God, which is to say, those texts that interpret God's being and action by way of "the Christ-event."

1. Establishing Textual Parameters

The complex textual dynamics I will explore in this chapter are generated by the way in which Paul's God-language[3] interacts and is intertwined

2. Cf., e.g., the suggestions offered in Leander E. Keck, "Toward the Renewal of New Testament Christology," *NTS* 32 (1986): 362-77, although Keck makes use of "relational" categories without recourse to trinitarian theologies.

3. The word θεός occurs 430 times in the undisputed letters and 118 times in the so-called contested letters. Such a figure, of course, leaves out other references to "God," such

with Christ-language.[4] This feature of Paul's letters is well known.[5] Neil Richardson helpfully classifies the range of this material under several headings, noting linguistic patterns: texts in which "God" (θεός) and "Christ" (Χριστός) share the same preposition (e.g., χάρις ὑμῖν καὶ εἰρήνη ἀπὸ θεοῦ πατρὸς ἡμῶν καὶ κυρίου Ἰησοῦ Χριστοῦ, Gal 1:3); texts in which Jesus/Christ is the object of a verb governed by "God" (e.g., ἐξαπέστειλεν ὁ θεὸς τὸν υἱὸν αὐτοῦ, Gal 4:4); texts in which "Christ" in a prepositional phrase accompanies a reference or implied reference to God (e.g., ἡ χάρις τοῦ θεοῦ τῇ δοθείσῃ ὑμῖν ἐν Χριστῷ Ἰησοῦ, 1 Cor 1:4); texts in which "God," usually in a prepositional phrase or in the dative case, follows or expands on a reference to Christ (e.g., Χριστός . . . ὁ δοὺς ἑαυτὸν ὑπὲρ τῶν ἁμαρτιῶν ἡμῶν . . . κατὰ τὸ θέλημα τοῦ θεοῦ καὶ πατρὸς ἡμῶν, Gal 1:4); and what Richardson calls "other" juxtapositions, a miscellaneous category that he uses to collect occurrences that fall outside his other categories.[6]

This chapter will seek to uncover and better explain the *theological import* of the texts that Richardson has highlighted. Two overarching questions will guide this effort: (1) Do the conceptual categories of "high" versus "low" christologies — and, by implication, the wider christological discussions in critical New Testament theologies that make use of these conceptual categories and give them their force — enable a penetrating grasp of this material? (2) Does the conceptual category of "relations" in trinitarian theologies — and the wider matrix of trinitarian reflection within which that category of "relations" finds its rationale — offer hermeneutical assistance in the attempt to explain the dynamics found in these texts?

---

as personal pronouns and the implied subjects of certain passive verbs. In addition, θεός must be located among other titles: for example, κύριος, πατήρ, and various participial constructions (e.g., ὁ δικαιῶν τὸν ἀσεβῆ, Rom 4:5). For concise summaries of the data, see Halvor Moxnes, *Theology in Conflict: Studies in Paul's Understanding of God in Romans* (NovTSup 53; Leiden: Brill, 1980), 15-16; Paul-Gerhard Klumbies, *Die Rede von Gott bei Paulus in ihrem zeitgeschichtlichen Kontext* (Göttingen: Vandenhoeck & Ruprecht, 1992), 11; Gordon D. Fee, *Pauline Christology: An Exegetical-Theological Study* (Peabody, MA: Hendrickson, 2007), 25-27.

4. E.g., κύριος, Ἰησοῦς, Χριστός, υἱός, etc.

5. See Fee, *Pauline Christology,* 25-27; Wilhelm Thüsing, *Per Christum in Deum. Das Verhältnis der Christozentrik zur Theozentrik* (vol. 1; Münster: Aschendorff, 1965).

6. Neil Richardson, *Paul's Language about God* (JSNTSup 99; Sheffield: Sheffield Academic Press, 1994), 256-73.

2. Texts in Which God Is Identified
by Actions Done by/to/in Jesus

One of the notable places to observe Paul's intertwining of God- and Christ-language is in his substantival participial constructions.[7] Especially prominent, judged by its place at rhetorically central moments in several letters, is Paul's designation of God as "the one who raised Jesus from the dead":[8]

... καὶ θεοῦ πατρὸς τοῦ ἐγείραντος αὐτὸν ἐκ νεκρῶν ("God the Father, who raised him from the dead," Gal 1:1)

... ἐπὶ τὸν ἐγείραντα Ἰησοῦν τὸν κύριον ἡμῶν ἐκ νεκρῶν ("the one who raised Jesus our Lord from the dead," Rom 4:24)

... τοῦ ἐγείραντος τὸν Ἰησοῦν ἐκ νεκρῶν ("the one who raised Jesus our Lord from the dead," Rom 8:11a)

... ἐγείρας Χριστὸν ἐκ νεκρῶν ("the one who raised Christ from the dead," Rom 8:11b)

At least three factors warrant the devotion of sustained attention to these constructions. First, these phrases are Paul's modifications of liturgical formulas already in use in Christian worship and, therefore, Paul cites them as evidence for his gospel's continuity with the gospel he "received" (cf. 1 Cor 15:1).[9] As such, they bear a certain *rhetorical* prominence. Even if their pre-Pauline pedigree does not, by itself, serve as an argument for

7. The most sustained treatment of these constructions remains G. Delling, "Partizipiale Gottesprädikationen in den Briefen des Neuen Testaments," *Studia Theologica* 17 (1963): 1-59.

8. Cf. 2 Cor 1:9 (ὁ θεὸς ὁ εγειρῶν τοὺς νεκρούς) and 4:14 (ὁ ἐγείρας τὸν κύριον Ἰησοῦν) as well as the similar forms in the disputed letters: Eph 1:20; Col 2:12 (ἡ ἐνέργεια τοῦ θεοῦ τοῦ ἐγείραντος αὐτὸν ἐκ νεκρῶν). In other places, Paul refers to God's raising of Jesus with a finite verb (see Rom 4:25; 6:4 [cf. v. 9]; 10:9; 1 Cor 6:14; 15:15 [2x]; 1 Thess 1:10).

9. For an extensive treatment of these phrases as an early Christian formula, see Werner Kramer, *Christ, Lord, Son of God* (trans. Brian Hardy; Studies in Biblical Theology 50; London: SCM, 1966 [1963]), 20-26; Klaus Wengst, *Christologische Formeln und Lieder des Urchristentums* (StNT 7; Gütersloh: Mohn, 1972), 21-23, 92-104; Henning Paulsen, *Überlieferung und Auslegung in Römer 8* (WMANT 43; Neukirchen-Vluyn: Neukirchener Verlag, 1974), 51-55.

their theological priority, which must be established by a close exegesis of the predications in their immediate context, their continuity with well-known liturgical forms helps ensure their status in Pauline discourse.

Second, by form, these constructions present themselves as "identity descriptions."[10] The aim of such formulations is not merely to reference some divine action but also to "name" God or specify his unique character by that action.[11] As Werner Kramer remarks, "We can see how vividly God is regarded as the agent in the resurrection from the fact that Paul uses statements of [creedal formulas], re-cast in participial form, as descriptions of God himself."[12] In other words, it is the combination of the participial form with the liturgical "ring" that constitutes these statements as identity descriptions.

Third, these constructions are selected for special attention in part because they appear in contexts that Dunn, Hurtado, and others have used to argue for a two-stage movement from a pre-Pauline "monotheism" which Paul assumes and preserves (largely) intact to an explicitly christological refashioning or determination of that monotheism.[13] Since it is this model that I hope to challenge, these Pauline phrases may provide a fresh hermeneutical entry point into this discussion.

i. The God Who Gives Life to the Dead (Romans 4:24)

My primary reason for beginning here — with Rom 4:24 — rather than, for example, with the more straightforwardly "trinitarian" Rom 8:9-11, is that Romans 4 and its context has served as the baseline for Dunn's and others' claim that Paul's God-talk enjoys a largely unaltered *axiomatic* sta-

10. See Robert W. Jenson, "Identity, Jesus, and Exegesis," in Beverly Roberts Gaventa and Richard B. Hays (eds.), *Seeking the Identity of Jesus: A Pilgrimage* (Grand Rapids: Eerdmans, 2008), 43-59, at 44.

11. I borrow the notion of identifying descriptions as those ways of "picking out" a subject from Bruce D. Marshall, "Trinity," in Gareth Jones (ed.), *The Blackwell Companion to Modern Theology* (Oxford: Blackwell, 2004), 183-203, at 187, 190-93. "To identify God" is "to pick God out from the crowd, as it were" (Bruce D. Marshall, "Christ and the Cultures: The Jewish People and Christian Theology," in Colin E. Gunton [ed.], *The Cambridge Companion to Christian Doctrine* [Cambridge: Cambridge University Press, 1997], 81-100, at 95).

12. Kramer, *Christ, Lord, Son of God*, 22.

13. See, e.g., James D. G. Dunn, *The Theology of Paul the Apostle* (Grand Rapids: Eerdmans, 1998), 378-79; Larry W. Hurtado, *Lord Jesus Christ: Devotion to Jesus in Earliest Christianity* (Grand Rapids: Eerdmans, 2003), 105-6.

tus as an inheritance from his pre-Christian Jewish past *from which* he goes on to construct a distinctively Christian position on justification.[14] Richard B. Hays, for example, after offering a detailed discussion of Paul's use of the Abraham material from Genesis, says this: "Paul has developed this reading of the story [of Abraham] directly through exegesis of Scripture, without any appeal to the language of Christian confession. This reading intends to be and is a Jewish theological interpretation of the significance of Abraham."[15] It will be my purpose in this section to challenge that construal by arguing that what Paul predicates of God in relation to Abraham *does* depend on "the language of Christian confession" — specifically, the language of the Christ-event itself — though it is not for that reason any less Jewish.[16]

The rhetorical climax of Romans 4, vv. 23-25, contains a participial "identity description" embedded in it: God is described as "the one who raised Jesus our Lord from the dead" (ὁ εγείρας Ἰησοῦν ιὸν κύριον ἡμῶν ἐκ νεκρῶν, v. 24). That identity description is anticipated within Paul's argument in two earlier participial constructions found in vv. 5 and 17: God is "the one who justifies the ungodly" (ὁ δικαιῶν τὸν ἀσεβῆ, v. 5) as well as "the one gives life to the dead" (ὁ ζῳοποιῶν τοὺς νεκρούς, v. 17). In order to see what links — if any — these earlier identity descriptions have with v. 24, I will examine each of them in turn.

For Paul, the justification of the ungodly is the present experience of the believers to whom he writes, as 3:21-26 makes clear, and Abraham is drawn in to establish the reality of justification by faith for Paul's hearers: Abraham is "our" forefather (4:1). Thus, after quoting Gen 15:6, Paul makes clear that the "one" in view in 4:4-5 who will be justified is the same "one" Paul's argument has constructed in 1:18–3:20, namely, the "human" under sin (3:9) who receives the gift of justification (3:24). Abraham's faith is cited as the basis on which believers can remain con-

---

14. The argument usually begins by noting the reference to monotheism in 3:27-31, which 4:1-25 is then said to expand on; see Jochen Flebbe, *Solus Deus. Untersuchungen zur Rede von Gott im Brief des Paulus an die Römer* (BZNW 158; Berlin: Walter de Gruyter, 2008), 260; Richard B. Hays, "Abraham as Father of Jews and Gentiles," in *The Conversion of the Imagination: Paul as Interpreter of Israel's Scripture* (Grand Rapids: Eerdmans, 2005), 61-84, at 69-74; cf. Richard B. Hays, *Echoes of Scripture in the Letters of Paul* (New Haven: Yale University Press, 1989), 54-57; Dunn, *The Theology of Paul the Apostle*, 32, 363-64, 366-67.

15. Hays, *Echoes of Scripture*, 57.

16. There is an implicit contrast between a "Christian" and "Jewish" reading in Hays's remark that anachronistically distorts what Paul attempts in Romans 4.

fident of God's justifying activity, and in this way his experience of being justified apart from works is elucidated as scriptural precedent for Paul's addressees' faith.[17]

The circumstances out of which Abraham's faith grew were doubly hopeless: Abraham's body was "already dead" and Sarah's womb was "dead" also (4:19).[18] Yet it is out of these dire conditions that Abraham trusts God, the one who gives life to the dead and calls the things that are not as though they are (v. 17). On the other side of this description of Abraham's believing, forming a somewhat oblique inclusio with vv. 1-5, lies the conclusion to which Paul has been driving since v. 1: "Now the words, 'it was reckoned to him,' were written not for his sake alone, but for ours also. It will be reckoned to us who believe in him who raised Jesus our Lord from the dead" (vv. 23-24). The description of Abraham's faith as aimed toward the God who gives life to the dead thus supports a twofold, unified affirmation: Paul's addressees are those who believe in the God who justifies the ungodly (v. 5) and the God who raised Jesus our Lord from the dead (v. 24).[19]

This much has been frequently noticed in discussions of Romans 4. What has gone relatively unremarked on is the way in which Paul has *chosen* to read the Abraham material he adduces in a particular way. The Genesis story emphasizes the advanced age of Abraham and Sarah and implies that they are well past the point of physical ability to conceive (Gen 17:17), but it does not describe this as a condition of *death* out of which Isaac will be born, as though by resurrection.[20] That metaphor is one Paul

---

17. Cf. Stephen Westerholm, *Perspectives Old and New on Paul: The "Lutheran" Paul and His Critics* (Grand Rapids: Eerdmans, 2004), 280-81. My understanding of the structure of Romans 4 is based on an understanding of the unit's purpose: to present Abraham's faith as of the same law-free character as that which Paul has already described as the occasion of justification for both Jew and Gentile (3:22, 25, 26, 27-31). Abraham's faith is first presented as the occasion of his own justification (4:1-8) and then as prior to his circumcision (vv. 9-15), thus ensuring that his progeny are not only his ethnic offspring but also those who share the same faith (vv. 16-25).

18. The difficulty of describing Abraham's obviously still physically existing body as ἤδη νενεκρωμένον probably indicates that the omission of ἤδη in mss. B, F, G, etc. was a purposeful editorial decision on the part of the scribe; cf. J. R. Daniel Kirk, *Unlocking Romans: Resurrection and the Justification of God* (Grand Rapids: Eerdmans, 2008), 72.

19. Mark A. Seifrid, *Christ, Our Righteousness: Paul's Theology of Justification* (NSBT 9; Leicester: Apollos, 2000), 68, notes the link between 4:5 and 4:17 and concludes that Paul understands justification as a *creatio ex nihilo*, like the granting of life to Abraham and Sarah.

20. But cf. Heb 11:12, 17-19, drawing on Genesis 22.

brings *to* the text of Genesis,[21] which raises the question of where it comes from and why Paul has decided to use it here.[22]

Viewed in the light of this question, we can see that the conclusion of the argument in Rom 4:23-25 determines the shape of the argument's development. The deadness of Jesus and God's subsequent raising of him to new life (vv. 23-25) is what prompts Paul to reread the Abrahamic narrative as one of deadness and resurrection.[23] In other words, God's raising of Jesus from the dead enables Paul to limn God's identity, as the guarantor of offspring for Abraham, as already bearing a christological shape even before the raising of Jesus.[24] Thus, to paraphrase E. P. Sanders's famous description of Pauline theology, the argument of Romans 4 runs from God's solution (i.e., God's raising Jesus from the dead) to the human plight — in this case, the plight of Abraham and Sarah's childlessness. The resurrection of Jesus becomes for Paul the key to discerning God's identity as the giver of life to Abraham, in a kind of chronological confusion[25] — with the result that the present, eschatological event of Jesus' resurrection becomes newly visible as figured in the past event of Sarah's pregnancy.[26]

This line of thought receives confirmation from the identity description in 4:5: God is the one who justifies the ungodly. As is often noted, this description of God is in tension with what the Old Testament affirms God will not do (i.e., justify the ungodly: see Exod 23:7; cf. Prov 17:15; 24:24;

21. Flebbe, *Solus Deus,* 257.

22. Paul's designation of God as "the one who gives life to the dead" (4:17) is not original with him. It was already in use in Jewish texts contemporary with Paul; e.g., *Joseph and Asenath* 8.9; 20.7 and the second of the *Eighteen Benedictions.* C. Burchard, "Joseph and Asenath: A New Translation and Introduction," in *The Old Testament Pseudepigrapha* (vol. 2; ed. James H. Charlesworth; New York: Doubleday, 1985), 177-247, at 234, comments: "Around the beginning of our era 'He who gives life to the dead' had become all but a definition of God in Judaism." But it must still be explained why, theologically, Paul chose to invoke this (relatively fixed) formula here.

23. Francis Watson, *Paul and the Hermeneutics of Faith* (London: T&T Clark, 2004), 217 n. 64.

24. Moxnes, *Theology in Conflict,* 269-82. Cf. Ulrich Wilckens, *Der Brief an die Römer* (3rd ed.; 3 vols.; EKKNT 6; Zurich: Benziger, 1997), 1:279-85; Kirk, *Unlocking Romans,* 72-74.

25. John M. G. Barclay, "Paul's Story: Theology as Testimony," in Bruce W. Longenecker (ed.), *Narrative Dynamics in Paul: A Critical Assessment* (Louisville/London: Westminster John Knox, 2002), 133-56, at 146.

26. John David Dawson, *Christian Figural Reading and the Fashioning of Identity* (Berkeley: University of California, 2002), 136 speaks of "a strange retroactive power in which a present occurrence makes possible the reality of the event which prefigures it."

Isa 5:23; Sir 9:12; CD 1:19), and there have consequently been numerous attempts to plot Paul's apparently radical formulation on a trajectory that begins in pre-Christian Jewish texts.[27] But these efforts fail to reckon with where Paul's formulation appears within the argument of Romans itself, a place that demonstrates its theologically novel character.

Within Romans, the description of God in 4:5 as the one who justifies the *ungodly* harks back to 3:21-26 and anticipates 5:6-10.[28] In 3:23-24, it is those who are identified as having sinned and fallen short of God's glory (v. 23) who are justified (v. 24). From the point of view of many Jewish texts contemporary with Paul, such a formulation would appear dangerously paradoxical in that it involves the correct identification of the sinner as sinner but then undermines the expected outcome of that judgment by declaring the sinner's condemnation to be averted.[29] What accounts for this paradox? Within Romans, the answer is christology. In other words, it is Paul's appeal to the Christ-event (3:24) that allows him to interpret God's justification as the giving of righteousness *to the sinner.* Christ Jesus became the place of atonement (v. 25) to enable *both* the sinner's justification *and* the upholding of the righteousness of God (v. 26). Paul theologizes *from* this christological affirmation to a reinterpretation of justification as the event whereby the "wrong" objects receive the verdict intended for the "righteous."

That the Christ-event is the occasion for Paul to reinterpret justification finds support in 5:6-10, where Christ's death on behalf of the ungodly

---

27. It is instructive to compare Dunn's treatment of Rom 4:5 in his commentary, where he observes that "Paul's language would jar with normal Jewish presuppositions" (James D. G. Dunn, *Romans 1–8* [WBC 38A; Dallas: Word, 1988], 204), and his later treatment of the same text in his *Theology of Paul the Apostle,* where he attempts to remove the novelty of Paul's phrase by noting that "Israel also knew that God's covenant obligation was sustained only by grace" (367 n. 134) and thus God's justification of the ungodly is a "theologoumenon . . . [uncontested] by other (Christian) Jews" (367). The thrust of this later argument is to qualify the sense in which Paul represents a departure from Jewish views, apparently in some tension with Dunn's admission that " '[t]o justify the ungodly' breached a primary canon of covenant law" (367 n. 134). Peter Stuhlmacher, *Der Brief an die Römer* (NTD 6; Göttingen: Vandenhoeck & Ruprecht, 1989), 68, points to Ezek 18:23 as a partial anticipation of Paul's view, as well as the prayers of the wicked for mercy at the judgment (e.g., Psalm 51; Dan 9:18ff.; 4 Ezra 8:35-36; 1QS 11.11ff.).

28. C. E. B. Cranfield, *The Epistle to the Romans* (2 vols.; ICC; Edinburgh: T&T Clark, 1975), 1:232.

29. Jonathan A. Linebaugh, "Debating Diagonal Δικαιοσύνη: The Epistle of Enoch and Paul in Theological Conversation," *Early Christianity* 1 (2010): 107-28.

(v. 6) constitutes a verbal echo of 4:5. The thought of Christ's death being "for" (ὑπέρ) others was already circulating in Christian proclamation before Paul (see 1 Cor 15:1-3), but as many commentators observe, the thought of that death being *for the "ungodly"* (ἀσεβεῖς) is Paul's way of radicalizing the tradition.[30] As in Rom 3:21-26, then, the formulation is not wholly new in terms of its form, but it *is* strangely radical in terms of its content. Just as 3:21-26 employs the language of the Old Testament — that is, the language of righteousness/justification — toward a radical end — that is, its application to a new object (the sinner) — so too 5:6-10 takes the familiar language of Christian confession and deepens its paradoxical character. In both cases, the ground for the reworking of traditional forms appears to lie in the peculiar way Paul reads the nature of the Christ-event.

These brief comments on 3:21-26 and 5:6-10 should help to underscore the surprising sharpness of 4:5 and should, in turn, show how 4:5 is embedded in the christological affirmation of 4:24-25. That it is *the ungodly* who are justified suggests that for Paul justification is an act of resurrection, an act of bringing life out of death, its opposite.[31] Or, stated more straightforwardly, Paul's exposition of Abraham's faith in 4:4-5 suggests that Paul has *constructed* Abraham's faith so that it bears a particular shape — so that it may be seen as, to borrow J. R. Daniel Kirk's words, "belief in the God who is responsible for the Christ event (so 4:23-25). Paul's reinterpretation of the Abraham narrative is . . . based on . . . discovering the grace of God in bringing about justification through the death and resurrection of Jesus (cf. esp. 3:26; 4:25)."[32] The christological endpoint determines the contours of the beginning.

This way of interpreting Romans 4 invites further theological reflection. If I am right that Paul's use of a traditional resurrection formula in 4:17, as well as a startlingly novel God-predication in v. 5, is determined by his conclusion that God raised Jesus from the dead (v. 24), then this forces the question of the relationship between theology and christology to the

---

30. Robert Jewett, *Romans* (Hermeneia; Minneapolis: Fortress, 2007), 358. Dunn, *Romans 1–8*, 255, finds the Pauline innovation to be in "shocking contrast" to the Maccabean martyrological tradition in which martyrs were said to die "for the sake/benefit of" the Torah or the Jewish nation (2 Macc 7:9; 8:21; *4 Macc* 1:8, 10; Josephus, *Ant.* 13.5-6).

31. Ernst Käsemann, *Commentary on Romans* (trans. G. W. Bromiley; London: SCM, 1980), 123; Wilckens, *Römer*, 1:188.

32. Kirk, *Unlocking Romans*, 63. Cf. N. T. Wright, "The Letter to the Romans: Introduction, Commentary, and Reflections," *NIB* 10 (ed. Leander Keck; Nashville: Abingdon, 2002), 393-770, at 492.

forefront of the effort to gauge the theological significance of Romans 4, since it is precisely the relationship between the oneness of God as the God of Abraham and the "newness" of invoking this God by means of formulas involving Jesus that creates the difficulty Dunn, Hays, and others mentioned above were attempting to solve. In other words, Paul's apparently deliberate invocation of the God of Abraham by reference to Christ makes it necessary to try to discern the nature of the correlation between God and Christ.

At this point, several options are available to interpreters who wish to engage this theological issue directly. First, one may attempt to preserve the priority of "traditional"/"Jewish" God-language over christologically-shaped God-language by noting the sequential progression of Romans 4. This is, as we have seen, a well-worn path. Observing the absence of explicit Christ-language until 4:24, and highlighting the allusion to Israel's primary monotheistic text (Deut 6:4) at 3:30, these readings move from the God-predications in 4:5 and 17, as affirmations that either were made explicitly or were approximated within Judaism, to the fully Christian God-predication of v. 24.[33] On this view, v. 24 *flows from* vv. 5 and 17 organically, and this flow is one-way.[34] In addition, interpreters who choose to go this route may note that the acting subject even in v. 24 is God. Thus, even in the climactic moment when the traditional Old Testament God-language of vv. 5 and 17 gives way to explicitly christological language in v. 24, Christ remains the *object,* while *God,* the acting subject, raises *him* from the dead. Taking this interpretive route would be to move *away* from trinitarian, "relational" conceptualities.

The problem with this interpretation is that if Paul were simply following a linear, progressive historical development and refusing to allow his christology to shape his reading of the Old Testament, then one would not expect Rom 4:5 to jar with the Old Testament. But since it does jar, we are driven to explore a second possible way of interpreting the significance of the identifying description of God in Romans 4.

Before we explore that option, however, I want to acknowledge that Paul's strategy of arguing from Gen 15:6 in Romans 4 differs from his treatment of Abraham's faith in Galatians 3. In Galatians, the past scriptural

---

33. Flebbe, *Solus Deus,* 257. Dunn makes this move clearly in his "In Quest of Paul's Theology," 111-12. Cf. his mention of 4:17 in *Theology of Paul the Apostle,* 29, as an instance of a traditional Jewish affirmation of God, without asking why *this particular* traditional affirmation is employed within an interpretation of Abraham's faith.

34. Flebbe, *Solus Deus,* 256.

testimony to God's decisive act of salvation in Christ is made present in a way that telescopes the temporal distance between Abraham and believers in Jesus (Gal 3:16). In Romans 4, however, there are no such straightforward equations. Paul constructs his argument for Abraham's paradigmatic status from the chronological order of the Genesis narrative, in which faith (Gen 15:6) precedes circumcision (Gen 17:10), as well as the promise that Abraham would be the father of many nations (Gen 17:5), saving the correlation of Abraham's faith with Christian faith for the end of his discussion (Rom 4:24-25). It could be argued that this difference between Galatians and Romans represents Paul's effort to respect "the prophetic writer's antecedent knowledge of [the Christ-event] and the apostle's *a posteriori* knowledge of it," so that a sense of chronological unfolding is preserved.[35] In other words, Paul's argument *appears* sequentially *progressive* or linear. But chronological order is not necessarily a reliable index to what is most important theologically.

The essential point is that, in Watson's words, Romans 4 remains "oriented towards the claims of the gospel from the very outset."[36] Theological priority is accorded to the christological identification of God in v. 24, even though that identification comes after vv. 5 and 17 in the sequential order of Romans 4. Paul's obvious reticence to introduce explicit christology into the quotations of Genesis should not be allowed to obscure the fact that the Genesis quotations are adduced and, to some degree, shaped with the argumentative conclusion of 4:24-25 in mind. Moreover, that Paul maintains the distinction between God and Christ — it is Abraham's God who raises Jesus from the dead (v. 24)[37] — does not invalidate or undermine the claim that identifying God of Abraham is now dependent upon that act of resurrection.[38]

<hr>

35. Watson, *Paul and the Hermeneutics of Faith,* 519.

36. Watson, *Paul and the Hermeneutics of Faith,* 519.

37. Here, to invoke trinitarian grammar, we must conclude that Abraham's God is identified with *the Father only* and that the distinction between the "persons" of God (the Father) and Jesus (the Son) is not blurred. Cf. C. Kavin Rowe, "Biblical Pressure and Trinitarian Hermeneutics," *Pro Ecclesia* 11 (2002): 295-312 (302-3).

38. A similar conclusion may be reached about the "monotheistic" affirmation in 3:30a. Regardless of whether the εἴπερ begins a new sentence whose protasis ends at πίστεως and whose elliptical apodosis consequently starts with the καί (as Hays, "Abraham as Father of Jews and Gentiles," 70, argues) or, as the more usual rendering has it, εἴπερ εἷς ὁ θεὸς κτλ. is considered to be the apodosis of the affirmation ναὶ καὶ ἐθνῶν in v. 29b (so most interpreters), it is difficult to maintain, as many commentators do (e.g., N. A. Dahl, "The One God of Jews and Gentiles," in *Studies in Paul* [Minneapolis: Augsburg, 1977], 178-

To sum up: we have seen that Paul used resurrection language ("deadness" and "life" in Rom 4:17) and a theological account of the Christ-event's effects (justification of the ungodly; cf. 5:6-10) in his description of the God in whom Abraham trusted. In other words, Paul specifies who God is, even prior to the resurrection of Jesus, by reference to Jesus. Paul identifies the God of Abraham by means of what he knows of that God through the Christ-event. But if so, then that suggests that Paul not only believes that God was once operative in one way (giving life to Abraham and Sarah) and now, in Jesus, confirms his previous actions (by raising Jesus). My argument is stronger than that: The identity of the God of Abraham — who God was in the past, for Abraham — is bound up with the identity of God as the God of Jesus — who God is as the one who raised Jesus. God *was* for Abraham the God who would raise Jesus. Paul suggests that to lay hold of the identity of the God of Abraham must involve reference to Jesus.

ii. *The Christ-Shaped Divine Telos (Romans 8:11)*

Having observed Paul's christological identification of God in a passage not usually interpreted along those lines, we can now move more rapidly through another participial identifying description of God and note how it chimes with my reading of Rom 4:24. As already mentioned, Rom 8:11 is parallel to 4:17 and 24 in several ways. First, the same participial construction is used twice: a substantival aorist form of ἐγείρειν designating God ("the one who raised . . ."), followed by "Jesus" (τὸν Ἰησοῦν) or "Christ" (Χριστόν) as the object of the participle's action (both are used in 8:11a and b), with the prepositional phrase "from the dead" (ἐκ νεκρῶν) specifying the realm out of which God raised Jesus. Furthermore, this action of God

---

91), that Paul is arguing from a definition of monotheism shared by most Jews and Jewish Christians. The grammar of v. 30a, in which εἷς ὁ θεός is modified by the relative clause ὃς δικαιώσει περιτομὴν ἐκ πίστεως καὶ ἀκροβυστίαν διὰ τῆς πίστεως, suggests that Paul has defined monotheism in a particular way — as entailing God's justifying Gentiles χωρὶς ἔργων (v. 28), a "monotheism" with which even most Jewish Christians would not have agreed (as Gal 2:15-21 indicates). This relative pronoun clause, formally and materially similar to the participial God-predications of Romans 4, suggests, furthermore, that this *redefined* monotheism is deduced from God's justifying activity. In this way, even here in the most clearly monotheistic text found in Paul's argument so far, God's oneness is not a theological axiom but is instead understood by Paul only in light of God's action in Christ (3:28 read as the continuation of vv. 21-26).

serves as the basis for confidence that God will give life to believers' bodies in the future, in a repetition of the same verb associated with Abraham's faith in 4:17 (ζῳοποιήσει).

The small unit of text in which this description of God finds its place (8:9-11) has received renewed attention recently, among systematic theologians[39] as well as New Testament exegetes,[40] as one of the prime places for rethinking the relation between Paul and trinitarian doctrine. My purpose here is to note what it suggests about the relation between Christ and God and to ask whether that harmonizes with what we have already seen in Romans 4.

The text's main actor is indicated in 8:9b — the Spirit of God — and invoked as the ground for the unit's opening assertion that Paul's hearers

---

39. Robert Jenson, *The Triune Identity: God according to the Gospel* (Philadelphia: Fortress, 1982), 44, refers to Romans 8 as the "most remarkable trinitarian passage in the New Testament" and to v. 11 as its "conceptual and argumentative heart." Thomas Weinandy, *The Father's Spirit of Sonship: Reconceiving the Trinity* (Edinburgh: T&T Clark, 1995), 31-38, has made much of this text, as has Sarah Coakley in several essays (e.g., "God as Trinity: An Approach through Prayer," in *We Believe in God: A Report by the Doctrine Commission of the General Synod of the Church of England* [Wilton, Conn.: Morehouse-Barlow, 1987], 104-21; "Why Three? Some Further Reflections on the Origins of the Doctrine of the Trinity," in *The Making and Remaking of Christian Doctrine: Essays in Honor of Maurice Wiles* [ed. Sarah Coakley and David A. Pailin; Oxford: Clarendon Press, 1993], 29-56; "Living into the Mystery of the Holy Trinity: Trinity, Prayer, and Sexuality," *Anglican Theological Review* 80/2 [1998]: 223-32). With reference to Coakley, Jason Byassee, "Closer than Kissing: Sarah Coakley's Early Work," *Anglican Theological Review* 90/1 (2007): 139-55, at 141, notes that "[w]e clearly do not have in Romans 8 the working out of a Trinitarian doctrine with anything like the theological sophistication of the Nicene-Constantinopolitan creed. But we do have a surprisingly elaborate description of the irreducibly triadic character of God." Cf. Eugene F. Rogers, Jr., *After the Spirit: A Constructive Pneumatology from Resources outside the Modern West* (Grand Rapids: Eerdmans, 2005), 75-97.

40. In addition to Francis Watson, "The Triune Divine Identity," *JSNT* 80 (2000): 104, 106-8, and Rowe, "Biblical Pressure and Trinitarian Hermeneutics," 305-6, see Gordon D. Fee, "Christology and Pneumatology in Romans 8:9-11 — and Elsewhere: Some Reflections on Paul as a Trinitarian," in Joel B. Green and Max Turner (eds.), *Jesus of Nazareth: Lord and Christ* (Grand Rapids: Eerdmans, 1994), 312-31; "Paul and the Trinity: The Experience of Christ and the Spirit for Paul's Understanding of God," in Stephen T. Davis, Daniel Kendall, SJ, and Gerald O'Collins, SJ (eds.), *The Trinity: An Interdisciplinary Symposium* (Oxford: Oxford University Press, 1999), 49-72, at 66. Compare also the comment in Richard B. Hays, "The God of Mercy Who Rescues Us from the Present Evil Age," in A. Andrew Das and Frank J. Matera (eds.), *The Forgotten God: Perspectives in Biblical Theology* (Louisville: Westminster John Knox, 2002), 123-43, at 137: "This passage comes as close as anything in Paul to an explicitly trinitarian understanding of God."

are not in the flesh but in the Spirit (v. 9a). Moreover, the Spirit's presence in the community of believers (v. 9a) and possession by the individual believer (v. 9b) guarantee that the one *from whom* that Spirit comes — that is, God — will raise the mortal bodies of believers, just as he raised Christ (vv. 10-11). Consequently, although remaining the focal point (mentioned six times in vv. 9-11), the Spirit is only so in the way a spotlight can remain an object of fascination — its brightness, while impressive and worthy of notice, is meant to direct attention away from itself to its object (in this case, God). The Spirit's role here, as an agent intertwined with the action of another, is to offer assurance of the effectiveness of that other's agency — namely, of the one who raised Christ. That God raised Jesus — and that the Spirit of that same God (v. 9a; and of Christ, v. 9b) now dwells among/ in believers — is the basis of the confidence believers may have in God's ability to raise them as well through the same Spirit. Again, we are dealing here with an "identifying description," a circumlocution whereby God is "picked out" by reference to his action — in this case, as in 4:24, his action of raising Jesus from the dead.

But, as with the conjunction of the divine identity descriptions in 4:5, 17, and 24, the identifying description in 8:11 finds an echo in its immediate context. The relative clause in 8:32, "he who did not spare his own son . . . ," is parallel to v. 11, both in form[41] and in that both probably draw on fixed formulas already in use in Christian confession.[42] These additional identity descriptions serve to situate the identification of God in v. 11. If God is identified by his act of raising Jesus (v. 11), he is equally identified by his "giving up" Jesus as his Son (v. 32) whom he "sent" for that purpose (v. 3). And, similarly to what we saw in ch. 4, Paul retrojects this complex divine action of giving up and raising Jesus back into the identity of God prior to its temporal outworking in the human life of Jesus. It is not simply

---

41. Moxnes, *Theology in Conflict,* 25: "The one form that is most easily interchangeable with the participial predication is the relative clause." The relative clause of 8:32 is also parallel to the adjectival participial construction in v. 3, ὁ θεὸς τὸν ἑαυτοῦ υἱὸν πέμψας κτλ. Note, e.g., the possessive pronouns in both texts (ἰδίου, v. 32; ἑαυτοῦ, v. 3) as well as the similarity of the thoughts of "giving up" and "sending."

42. Cf. Otto Michel, *Der Brief an die Römer* (Göttingen: Vandenhoeck & Ruprecht, 1955), 184, who also points out the link between God's "giving up" (παραδιδόναι) in 8:32 and in 4:25. On this, compare also E. Schweizer, "υἱός, υἱοθεσία, κτλ," *TDNT* 8:334-99, who notes the link between 8:3 and 32; and Nils A. Dahl, "The Atonement: An Adequate Reward for the Akedah?," in Donald H. Juel (ed.), *Jesus the Christ: The Historical Origins of Christological Doctrine* (Minneapolis: Fortress, 1991), 137-51, at 139.

that God *has been* identified in one way (as, e.g., the creator [1:25] or the God who made promises to Abraham [9:7]) and is now identified as the one who sent his son (8:3) and raised him from the dead (v. 11). Instead, this latter, christological divine action determines Paul's understanding of God's purpose as it was prior *to* the Christ-event (v. 29).[43] The foreknowledge (προγινώσκειν) and predestination (προορίζειν) of the believers to whom Paul writes is, at least in this context, probably best understood as the witness to Gentile inclusion that Paul hears in Israel's Scriptures. And Paul reads that scriptural witness as indicating God's determination that believers would be conformed to the image of his Son and that that Son might attain preeminence as the pattern of believers' adoption (8.29b). In this way, God's foreknowing and predestining of believers before the "sending" of his Son were already oriented toward a christological telos. God foreordained Paul's Gentile hearers with a view to those believers being conformed to God's Son Jesus. And that means that there is no space left for identifying God apart from the Christ-event.

What is disallowed here, as in Romans 4, is a two-stage identification of God, whereby Paul might conceive of certain pre-Christian designations of God (e.g. the one who "predestined" [8:29] or "called" [v. 30] Israel and the Gentiles) as bearing validity in their own right *until* the sending of the Son at a particular point, *after* which time God may then, *newly,* be identified in some other way (i.e., by reference to Jesus). If God's foreordination of the Gentiles, already discernible in Scripture, is oriented toward establishing the Son as "firstborn among many brothers" (8.29b), then no such stages may be delineated. God is, from the time before the sending of the Son, the God whose identity is bound up with the Son. God's christological aim in God's foreknowledge enables Paul to discern a Christ-oriented identity of God prior to the Christ-event. God does not become what God was not, for Paul does not know a time when God was not already the God who would send his Son so that believers might be conformed to his image.

iii. *"The Primal Mark of God's Identity" (Galatians 1:1)*

The opening of Galatians (1:1) uses the same divine identifying description as Rom 4:24 and 8:11. Here, however, God is the one who raised Jesus

---

43. Watson, "The Triune Divine Identity," 105-6, 113, 116-17.

from the dead as "God the Father," a title heralding a theme — father-hood — whose melody will reverberate beyond the letter's introduction (in addition to 1:3, 4, see 4:2, 6). By juxtaposing God's act of raising Jesus with the title "Father," Paul anticipates his development of an organic link between the sonship of Jesus and the sonship of the Galatians themselves (3:26; 4:4-7), the precise nature of which is disputed and therefore must be clarified by Paul by way of an appeal to Abraham (3:7, 15-18; 4:22-31).[44]

This is our first clue that what is at stake in the reference to God raising Jesus in 1:1 is not simply the pinpointing of one divine action in distinction from another (e.g., raising the dead as opposed to making promises or issuing commands) but instead the specification of the unique divine nature vis-à-vis another, competing specification of it put forward by Paul's opponents.

Moreover, Paul's identifying God here as "the one who raised him from the dead" is bound up with similar themes in Romans: in Rom 4:24, as we saw above, God's act of raising Jesus illumines God's act of giving life to Abraham (4:17), just as here in Gal 1:1 that same act, with its accompanying name "Father," is part of an argument that Paul's hearers are to look to Abraham as their father and share in his faith (3:7) in a particular way (i.e., apart from circumcision). In Rom 8:11, God's act of raising Jesus results in the guarantee that the Spirit will give life, since it is by the Spirit of adoption (v. 15) that the sons of God (v. 14) cry out, as they do in Gal 4:6, "Abba, Father" (Rom 8:15). Most important for our purposes is how Paul here, as in Rom 4:17, draws a link between God as the one who raised Jesus from the dead (Gal 1:1) and God as the one who calls (Gal 1:6). In Rom 4:17, God's act of "giving life" (ζωοποιεῖν) is explained as his "calling the things that are not as though they were" (καλεῖν τὰ μὴ ὄντα ὡς ὄντα). Here in Galatians, God, as "the one who raised Jesus Christ from the dead" (1:1), is followed immediately by another participial identification of God as "the one who called you in grace" (v. 6).[45] This, in turn, suggests that

---

44. H. D. Betz, *Galatians* (Hermeneia; Philadelphia: Fortress, 1979), 39 n. 27, explains the initial repeated emphasis on God as πατήρ (1:1, 3, 4) by way of the prominence of the (polemical) theme of adoption in the letter as a whole. Cf. Ben Witherington III and Laura M. Ice, *The Shadow of the Almighty: Father, Son, and Spirit in Biblical Perspective* (Grand Rapids: Eerdmans, 2002), 34: "The story that undergirds the references to the Fatherhood of God in Paul's letters is the story of Jesus, and the Father's relationship to him, not the story of Israel as a nation and God's relationship to Israel."

45. Normal Pauline usage suggests that θεός is implied as the agent designated in the participial phrase ὁ καλῶν ὑμᾶς (Gal 1:6); see Gal 5:8, 13; Rom 4:17; 8:30; 9:12, 24; 11:29;

an effort to grasp the theological import of v. 1 must attend closely to vv. 6 and 15 and the conceptual links between them.

Within the argument of Galatians, for Paul to specify God with this description — "the one who called you in grace" (1:6) — is to begin to articulate what will occupy him for the duration of the letter, namely, what we might call the Galatians' "narrative identity"[46] — their personal history involving the memory of their initial faith (ἀκοὴ πίστεως, 3:2) and their concomitant circumcision-free reception of the Spirit (3:2-3, 5) — and why that past experience, if interpreted correctly, should lead them to reject the alternative gospel (cf. 1:6b) of Paul's opponents. To see how Paul incorporates the identifying description of 1:6 within this broader rhetorical purpose, we turn first to the closely similar divine identifying description in 1:15.

On the heels of 1:6, Paul identifies God as "the one who set me apart from my mother's womb and called me through his grace" (ὁ ἀφορίσας με ἐκ κοιλίας μητρός μου καὶ καλέσας διὰ τῆς χάριτος αὐτοῦ, v. 15).[47] The repetition of the verb "to call" (καλεῖν) allows Paul to connect his own experience with the Galatians'; highlighting his "calling" gives him the opportunity to interpret their "calling." Contrary to the different story his opponents tell, Paul attempts his own construal of the Galatians' identity and consequently urges a particular course of action on their part (i.e., their hoped-for refusal to accept circumcision) by way of an appeal to *his* conversion experience. As Paul narrates it, God's calling and Paul's subsequent conversion interrupted a story in which Paul was making progress in Judaism and in the buttressing of his ancestral traditions (vv. 13-14).[48] But if God's calling cut against the grain of this progressive narrative, and if the bestowal of God's grace (v. 15) occurred before Paul was born and

---

1 Cor 1:9, 26; 7:15, 17, 18-24; Phil 3:14; 1 Thess 2:12; 4:7; 5:24; 2 Thess 1:11; 2:14; cf. 2 Tim 1:9 (J. Louis Martyn, *Galatians: A New Translation with Introduction and Commentary* [AB 33A; New York: Doubleday, 1997], 108-9).

46. I borrow the term from Paul Ricoeur, "Interpretative Narrative," in Regina M. Schwartz (ed.), *The Book and the Text: The Bible and Literary Theory* (Cambridge, MA: Basil Blackwell, 1990), 237-57, at 241.

47. Paul's use of καλεῖν here is likely determined by the use of the same verb in Isa 49:1, since Paul's being set aside ἐκ κοιλίας μητρός μου is best understood as an echo of LXX prophetic call narratives (Jer 1:4-5; Isa 49:1-6; cf. Roy E. Ciampa, *The Presence and Function of Scripture in Galatians 1 and 2* [WUNT 2/102; Tübingen: Mohr Siebeck, 1998], 78-79, 111-17).

48. Note the shift in subject: Paul is the agent of the verbs in 1:13-14, but (δέ) God sharply intrudes on this narrative from outside (1:15-16).

therefore happened only by divine agency and without regard for Paul's cultural and moral attainments,[49] then the Galatians must consider the implications of such a radical prioritization of divine agency and grace in their case as well. John Barclay expresses this fundamental link between vv. 6 and 15 especially clearly:

> It was not because [Paul] was a good Jew (though he was) that he was called by divine gift; nor did his calling have regard to the fact that he had set himself violently against God's church. What he experienced in the revelation of Christ was the impact of a grace that called him before he was born, unconditioned by his ethnicity, tradition or advance in Judaism (1:11-17). In the same way, sinful and idolatrous Gentiles have been called by grace, without regard to their ethnicity, their moral behaviour or their intellectual achievements (Gal 1:6; 4:8-9).[50]

The identification of God as the one whose calling operates irrespective of human cultural identities and traditions becomes, on this reading, integral to the letter's basic purpose of persuading the Galatians to reject Paul's opponents' gospel of circumcision. Because God acted thus with Paul, the Galatians may be sure that he has acted similarly with them.

But Paul does not leave his configuration of the divine identity there. As we saw in the case of Rom 4:24 and 8:11, here in Galatians, too, Paul appears to locate his description of the divine identity not only in the present context — downwind of the Christ-event, as it were — but also in the past, anticipating the Christ-event and therefore, even prior to its historical eruption, as determined by it. In Galatians, God is who he is in relation to Christ even before the historically particular sending of Christ.

To be sure, there are indications in Galatians that Paul is well aware that the God who calls Gentiles irrespective of their circumcision is, in some sense, doing so *newly*. The "sending" of the Son, for example, is punctiliar (4:4a), which entails a historically dateable rescue of Gentiles (1:4) and an eschatological depiction of the Spirit's outpouring (3:14; 4:6). Yet, at the same time, Paul resists the conclusion that the Christ-event — inseparable from its *telos* in Paul's law-free mission of Gentile inclusion — was not always and already the intention of God prior to that

---

49. Barclay, "Paul's Story," 138-39.

50. John M. G. Barclay, "Paul, the Gift and the Battle over Gentile Circumcision: Revisiting the Logic of Galatians," *Australian Biblical Review* 58 (2010): 36-56, at 50.

event's historical occurrence. This may be seen clearly, for example, in Paul's christological interpretation of Gen 13:15 in 3:16: "Now the promises were made to Abraham and to his offspring; it does not say, 'And to offsprings,' as of many; but it says, 'And to your offspring,' that is, to one person, who is Christ." By drawing attention to the wording of the original Genesis text itself, Paul presents his interpretation not as a later imposition of a newly disclosed understanding layered onto the Genesis text but instead as the discovery of the meaning Gen 13:15 bore all along. He finds a christologically-grounded determination to include uncircumcised Gentiles within the scope of God's promises to Abraham in the original form of that promise itself. In other words, it is not simply that Gen 13:15 may be read as bearing that meaning now, in light of what God has done in Christ and in view of Gentile Spirit-experience (3:1-5). Rather, the "seed" of Gen 13:15 *already* referred to Christ in its first utterance.[51] If God made promises to Abraham, they were not fulfilled in Christ in an unexpected way; rather, the original formulation of the promise in Genesis intended Christ as its object. Here, as J. Louis Martyn has aptly put it, what Paul emphasizes is the "nonethnic character of God's promise *both at its inception and in its fulfillment.*"[52] Christ as the singular seed who incorporates uncircumcised Gentiles into his salvific achievement, according to Paul, should not be seen as the present, surprising climax of the promises, though he is that climax; he is also the originally determined object of those promises.

All of this indicates something of the wider web of divine identifying descriptions within which Gal 1:1 finds its place. Having observed a few of the threads of that web, we are now better able to make sense of the theological force of 1:1. That Paul's identification of God by way of his act of raising Jesus occurs alongside Paul's rhetorically loaded description of God's "calling" (1:6, 15) suggests that the first identification — God as "the one who raised [Jesus] from the dead" — is not simply a theologoumenon on which Paul assumes his opponents agree with him. Rather, it is a polemically-loaded assertion of the core of his own gospel. As Martyn puts it,

> God's identity is here given by his having raised Jesus from the dead. Especially in writing to the Galatians, Paul will make clear that, like

51. Cf. N. T. Wright, "The Seed and the Mediator: Galatians 3.15-20," in *The Climax of the Covenant: Christ and the Law in Pauline Theology* (London: T&T Clark, 1991), 157-74, at 166: "[Paul] is arguing that God *always intended,* from the time of the promise to Abraham, that his people should be a single family" (emphasis added).

52. Martyn, *Galatians,* 352, emphasis added.

the Teachers, he knows there is only one God (see 3:20; 1 Cor 8:4-6). Equally important, however: this one God has now identified himself by his act in Jesus Christ, making that act, indeed, the primal mark of his identity.[53]

In other words, Paul's identification of God by his act of raising Jesus is a preparation for Paul's later, more explicit polemics against his opponents, so that the scriptural argument that dominates chs. 2 and 3 becomes not only a battle for the right interpretation of Abraham's faith and circumcision but, more deeply, a struggle for a right identification of God himself. Again, as Martyn puts it in another place,

> [I]t is against [the Teachers'] view that Paul waged battle precisely in order to bear witness to the true identity of the God of Abraham by speaking of him as the Father of Jesus Christ. With his deed in the crucified Christ, that is to say, this God is announcing who he is, and thus showing that, however wrongly he may have been perceived in the past, he always was the one who rectifies the ungodly.[54]

Certainly Paul and his opponents did not disagree on whether God had raised Jesus from the dead (1:1). Yet their disagreement about the entailments of this act (e.g., at 2:15-16; 3:10-14) constitutes, by the time Paul arrives at the letter's heart, a disagreement about the fundamental character of the one God himself.[55] In other words, we may say that Paul constructs the disagreement between himself and his opponents in such a way that it may be seen to involve not merely the grasping of a new act of divine self-identification (i.e., the resurrection) but rather — more deeply — a grasping of what that act implies about who God has always been. If Paul's opponents added God's act of raising Jesus to God's previous biography as the one who commanded Abraham's circumcision, Paul will press

53. Martyn, *Galatians,* 85. "The Teachers" is Martyn's preferred term for Paul's opponents in Galatia, the Jewish-Christian missionaries.

54. J. Louis Martyn, "John and Paul on the Subject of Gospel and Scripture," in *Theological Issues in the Letters of Paul* (Nashville: Abingdon, 1997), 209-30, at 226.

55. Moxnes, *Theology in Conflict,* 214, correctly notes that a shared formulaic or liturgical starting point between Paul and his opponents does not mean that its material content or implications were agreed upon: "[T]he statement that 'God is one' [3:20] was part of a common set of beliefs for Paul and his opponents. However, in Paul's theology it is understood in light of the antithesis between promise and law."

beyond this formulation and argue for a stronger claim. For Paul, God's act of raising Jesus and its inextricable link with God's calling of Paul and of the Galatians while they were still uncircumcised suggests that God is not only *identifiable* by that act but that, even more dramatically, God's *identity* — what makes God the God that he is — is revealed in that act. That God's act of raising Jesus was an agreed-upon theologoumenon between Paul and his opponents should not obscure the fact that, for Paul, God's act of raising and its concomitant act of calling Paul and the Gentiles highlights the way God has always been and always determined himself to be from the time he made promises to Abraham.

3. Rereading Pauline God-Language in Light of Trinitarian Theologies

It is now time to step back and draw some theological conclusions on the basis of the exegesis offered above. At the beginning of this chapter, I suggested that two broad questions would guide our evaluation of the Pauline texts we have considered: (1) Do the conceptual categories of "high" versus "low" christologies (and the christological discussions within NT scholarship that give these conceptual categories their force) enable a rich penetration of these texts, so that the contours and subtleties of the Pauline texts are better grasped with these categories than without them?; and (2) Does the conceptual category of "relations" in trinitarian theologies (and, by implication, the trinitarian theologies themselves within which that category of "relations" is explicated) open a fresh hermeneutical angle from which to view the dynamics discovered in these texts? Drawing on the exegesis of the previous section of this chapter, I will now treat each of these questions in turn.

i. The Preservation of "Monotheism"?

Recall Dunn's comment, quoted in Chapter 1 above, that early Christianity witnessed a transition from "a debate oriented to the question of monotheism to one oriented to the question of the internal relationships within the Godhead."[56] The former may be observed in the texts of the New Testa-

---

56. James D. G. Dunn and Maurice Wiles, "M. Wiles on *Christology in the Making* and

ment while the latter does not fully emerge until the "Arian" debates of the fourth century. On Dunn's reading, Paul was able to preserve monotheism by making christology a sort of subset of theology by interpreting it against a prior doctrine of God's oneness as the boundary *beyond which* christology must not transgress. Nor are such statements limited to Dunn. Hurtado, advocating a self-consciously "higher" view of christology than Dunn's, nevertheless comments in the same basic vein: "Paul (with other Christian Jews of his time) saw [the] stunning prominence that they gave to Christ as fitting within a faithful commitment to one God. . . . Paul's christology did not involve any conscious abandonment of the monotheistic stance that he inherited from the Jewish tradition."[57] Such ways of accounting for the innovative character of Paul's theology/christology depend on an assumption that monotheism remains the larger explanatory category that encloses and thereby determines the character of christology.

But in each of the God-predications we discussed (Rom 4:24; 8:11; Gal 1:1), it became apparent that not only was God identifiable, after the Christ-event, by means of his raising Jesus from the dead but that, in a more radical move, Paul makes that act of resurrection determine what he says of God when he describes God's purposes and activity *prior* to the Christ-event. Such a move seems to disallow the separation of a supposedly more fundamental God-talk (designated by the term "monotheism") that may then be said to condition and constrain Paul's christology as something separable from it, since Paul himself rereads the God-language he is said to have "inherited" from a christologically-determined vantage point.

In the case of Rom 4, we observed that the God-predications of 4:5 and 4:17 — the former addressing God's present self-identification (albeit on the basis of his past relation to Abraham) and the latter specifying his past self-identification vis-à-vis Abraham — were best seen as arising from the explicitly christological predication of 4:24. Paul discerns the character and actions of the God of Abraham only through the lens of his act of giving up (4:25) and raising (4:24) Jesus. At the very least, this represents the granting of a kind of epistemological priority to the God-predication of 4:24 — the God of Abraham *is known* by means of the Christ-event — and arguably by the time Paul arrives at ch. 8, that epistemological priority

---

Responses by the Author," in Dunn, *The Christ and the Spirit;* Volume 1: *Christology* (Grand Rapids: Eerdmans, 1998), 257-69, at 264.

57. Larry W. Hurtado, "Paul's Christology," in James D. G. Dunn (ed.), *The Cambridge Companion to St. Paul* (Cambridge: Cambridge University Press, 2003), 185-98, at 187.

has become what we might term a *teleological* priority — the God of Israel *was already* oriented toward the Christ-event from before that event's enactment in history. Paul's apparent retrojection of God's saving action of giving up his son (Rom 8:32) and raising him from the dead (8:11) back into his eternal purpose of predestination (8:29) exerts pressure on interpreters to reach for some such formulation.

Paul's link in Galatians between God's raising Jesus (1.1), "calling" Paul himself (1:15), and calling the Galatians (1:6) without regard to his or their respective circumcision and uncircumcision makes similar demands on interpreters. If God's raising Jesus and calling the Galatians are organically connected, and, furthermore, if this law-free calling is explained by way of God's promise to Abraham of a singular seed — Christ (3:16) — then the significance of God's relation to Jesus for rightly identifying God is pushed back into the time before God sent his Son. The Christ-event has priority when it comes to specifying who the God of Abraham is. God was not first the God of Abraham and then, later, the God who raised Jesus and called the Galatians. He was, *as* the God of Abraham, the one who promised Christ to Abraham, whom he sent and raised from the dead. What is at stake in the Galatian controversy is the fundamental identity of God itself.

Already — prior to the Christ-event — the theology of Paul is christocentric (or christo-telic).[58] In each of the above textual instances, we have observed this radicalizing dynamic at work. God's act of raising Jesus from the dead becomes the occasion for picking God out from the crowd, as it were, but also discloses a christological shape to God's character and actions before the historically determinate Christ-event. If there is a theologically-determined shape to Pauline christology, the texts we have examined necessitate some complementary speech about a fundamental christologically-determined shape to Pauline theology proper. Or, put more sharply, there is no "monotheism" without christology.

ii. Trinitarian Theologies as Hermeneutical Aids

Several times already in the above exegesis I have used terminology suggesting that the substantival participial constructions under consideration

---

58. Cf. Richardson, *Paul's Language about God,* 307: "If it is true that Paul uses God-language in order to interpret and 'define' Christ, it is also true that language about Christ in turn redefines the identity of God."

are "identifying descriptions" that serve to specify the subject in question. To quote Watson, "If we ask Paul which god he is speaking of, his answer is, 'the one who raised Jesus our Lord from the dead' (Rom. 4:24, cf. 8:11), or, 'the one who justifies the ungodly' (Rom. 4:5, cf. 4:24, cf. 8:11)."[59] The God of whom Paul speaks is *this* God — the one who raised Jesus from the dead. In spite of its necessary limitation to only a few select texts, our discussion has appeared to confirm this. For Paul to "pick out" the God in whom his addressees are to believe in the present involves Paul's describing particular actions of that God.

But I hope it has by now become clear that my argument has moved beyond this claim and offered what amounts to a theological interpretation of the significance of the identifying descriptions of Rom 4:5, 17, 24; 8:11, 32; Gal 1:1, 6, 15. I have suggested, in Watson's words, that "[t]he deity and identity of God are bound up with those particular divine actions [of raising Jesus, justifying the ungodly, and 'calling' by grace]."[60] Or, in other words, I have approached the claim that Paul means for God's raising of Jesus not only to become the occasion of *identifying* God but also to enable a grasp of *God's identity* — what makes God the unique "person" he is vis-à-vis Jesus Christ. In order to clarify what this shift entails, we could cite any number of classic formulations, but I take this recent one by Bruce Marshall to be an especially lucid representative:

> The persons of the Trinity . . . can only be identified together. Thus in order to pick out the Father as a particular person — to grasp his unsubstitutable personal uniqueness — we have to be able to pick out the Son and the Spirit as particular persons; the same goes, *mutatis mutandis,* for identifying the Son and the Spirit as well. The reason for this is that the persons of the Trinity have their personal uniqueness only in their relations to and interactions with one another. . . . We become acquainted with the relations and interactions of the divine persons, and so are able actually to identify them, through the way in which the Father sends the Son and the Spirit into the world. . . . Not just the Son and the Spirit, but also the Father, can be identified by us only through this sequence of actions and events.[61]

59. Watson, "The Triune Divine Identity," 104.
60. Watson, "The Triune Divine Identity," 104.
61. Marshall, "Christ and the Cultures," 96. Marshall goes on to note that this way of speaking raises the question of "supersessionism" acutely — i.e., whether the Christian identification of God has replaced or demoted the Old Testament or Jewish one — since if

What is at issue here is not exactly what others have described as the inclusion of Jesus within the identity of God, in such a way that "monotheism" is opened up or expanded so that it might enclose Jesus' actions and identity. Rather, to employ trinitarian categories, at stake in this context is the way the unique personal identity of God is disclosed and grasped by means of his relation to Jesus. The *person* "God" — traditionally referred to as "the Father" in trinitarian discourse — is who he is by virtue of this relation with Jesus ("the Son," in traditional terms); by his act of giving up and raising Jesus (and the soteriological effects of that act) God defines himself as a distinct person, in such a way that the relation is internal to the self-definition.[62]

It is true, as far as it goes, that Paul's theology and christology as we have discussed them here in relation to Romans 4, 8, and Galatians 1 does not offer *direct* assistance in the effort to construct a doctrine of the

---

the "one God" is not rightly identified without reference to Jesus and the Spirit, then the status of continuing Jewish worship of the God of Israel is rendered ambiguous at best and problematic at worst (95-98). Christopher Seitz, in his review of Richard Bauckham, *God Crucified: Monotheism and Christology in the New Testament* (Grand Rapids: Eerdmans, 1998), pushes the question back into the realm of the continuing authority of the Old Testament for Christian trinitarian theology: "Does the God of the Old Testament, . . . scripture's true subject matter, become something different in Christian thought as a consequence of the crucifixion of Jesus?" (Review of Richard Bauckham, *God Crucified,* in *IJST* 2/1 [2000]: 112-16, at 116). Space does not permit a full discussion of this problem, but the distinction Marshall makes between *identify* and *identity* may go some way toward suggesting a solution. God may be *identified* without reference to Jesus, but in order to grasp his full *identity* — his personal uniqueness in the continuity of the salvation narrative — reference to the Christ-event is required.

62. Here classic trinitarianism has wished to distinguish between, on the one hand, God's temporal act of raising Jesus as the act whereby the person of the Father individuates himself from the Son and, on the other hand, the eternal *constitution* of the Father as Father through his begetting of the Son apart from any work *ad extra*. In other words, the unique act of the Father — raising Jesus — allows one to "pick out" the Father from the Son, but for traditional trinitarian theology, it does not *constitute* the Father as Father. See, e.g, Aquinas's discussion in *Summa theologiae* 1.32.3c. For a radically different construal, in which the Father's temporal acts of raising Jesus and entering into saving fellowship with humanity are constitutive for the eternal trinitarian persons, see, e.g., Jenson's *Triune Identity* cited above, as well as the recent rereading of Barth's doctrine of election in Bruce L. McCormack, "Grace and Being: The Role of God's Gracious Election in Karl Barth's Theological Ontology," in John Webster (ed.), *The Cambridge Companion to Karl Barth* (Cambridge: Cambridge University Press, 2000), 92-110; "Seek God Where He May Be Found: A Response to Edwin Chr. van Driel," *SJT* 60/1 (2007): 62-79; "Election and the Trinity: Theses in Response to George Hunsinger," *SJT* 63/2 (2010): 203-24.

"immanent trinity," or the "eternal" relations of Father, Son, and Spirit, considered apart from God's *ad extra* works of creation and redemption.[63] The "intra-trinitarian divine relations" *in that sense* are beyond the scope of Paul's interest, since his God-talk and Christ-language occur in soteriological contexts. But the central trinitarian claim on which I am drawing — that the identities of the persons of the trinity are determined by means of their relations with and to each other — holds true. If we are to ask about what makes God the God who justifies the ungodly, the answer is that God is the God of Jesus Christ. If we are to ask about what individuates God as the God who gave life in the deadness of Sarah's womb, the answer is that God is the God who raised Jesus from the dead. If we are to inquire into what makes God the God who predestines and foreknows a people and adopts them in fulfillment of promises made to Abraham, the answer is that God is the God whose *telos* has always involved God's son, Jesus Christ. "God," in other words, is known by Paul always as the God of Jesus Christ.

In the next chapter, we will come at the same issues from a different starting point. How do the texts in which Paul identifies *Jesus* in relation to God cast light on the thesis I have argued here?

---

63. Gordon D. Fee, *God's Empowering Presence: The Holy Spirit in the Letters of Paul* (Peabody, MA: Hendrickson, 1994), 841, speaks of Paul's "soteriological Trinitarianism" and avers that Paul's trinitarian presuppositions and formulations "never wrestle with [their own] ontological implications" (842), a sentiment which his later work *(Pauline Christology)* suggests that he would extend to Paul's christological formulations.

CHAPTER THREE

Jesus in Relation to God: Philippians 2:6-11

For Paul to "pick God out of the crowd," for him to identify God, involves his talking about God's act in Jesus and, in turn, about the light shed on God by that act. Correspondingly, for Paul to specify who Jesus is involves his following Jesus' life and death back to their origins in God's purpose and action. In more technical language, the relation that obtains between God and Jesus is constitutive for the identities of *both* God *and* Jesus. The identities of God and Jesus are *mutually determined.*

Arguing for such a position in the present climate of scholarship, however, requires some reckoning with a different, more prevalent way of describing the contours of Pauline christology. According to the more standard account, Paul specifies the identity of *Jesus* with reference to God but does not go on to make an accompanying specification of the identity of *God* by reference to Jesus.[1] The building blocks for this more standard construal are by now, I hope, clear: Paul's "monotheism" serves to limit and constrain his christology; Pauline christology may, consequently, be fruitfully discussed as either "high" or "low" depending on the degree to which monotheism is taken for granted or else "redefined"; and God's iden-

1. As I have been emphasizing in the foregoing chapters, this claim is not undermined by pointing out that New Testament scholars are able to make assertions such as the following: "[I]n the NT just as Jesus' status is expressed consistently with reference to the actions of 'God' ('the Father'), so in turn the identity of 'God' is expressed typically in connection with Jesus" (Larry W. Hurtado, *God in New Testament Theology* [Library of Biblical Theology; Nashville: Abingdon, 2010], 37). The central issue is whether the relations between God and Jesus are understood to be fully mutual in such a way that "God" is not seen as a delimiting boundary for christology but, in the crucial sense we explored in Chapter 2, *defined by* his relation to Jesus.

tity is the relatively known or stable quantity that determines or governs what may be said of Jesus without a reciprocal movement back to God.

Each of these building blocks for what I have termed "the standard account" is up for renewed consideration, and I sought in the previous chapter to qualify drastically or reconfigure almost all of them. My argument is for *bi-directionality*[2] rather than unilateralism in Pauline christology and theology. I am attempting exegesis of select Pauline passages in order to demonstrate that what Kathryn Tanner has called the "full mutuality of co-implication" holds true for Paul's theology:[3] who God is is determined by his relation to Jesus, and who Jesus is is determined by his relation to God. The aim of the last chapter was to demonstrate that Paul identifies *God* by reference to *Jesus*. Now, it is time to turn our attention to the complementary claim that Paul identifies *Jesus* by reference to *God*.

It may appear, on the one hand, as if all that can be said on this topic has already been said. Leander Keck's 1986 article "Toward the Renewal of New Testament Christology" famously suggested that Pauline christology had neglected the *relational* matrix of christological texts by focusing too much on christological titles (e.g., κύριος) and not enough on the implicit and sometimes explicit ties to God and humanity by which Jesus' identity is specified.[4] But, arguably, Keck's call has been heeded in the time since he published his article. Partially in response to Keck, Neil Richardson has helpfully spoken of the "grammatical subordination" of Christ-language to God-language, noting the ordered relation of subject and object in these two strands of Pauline discourse.[5] Not only in the use of titles such as "Son of God" (υἱὸς θεοῦ) which obviously indicate the relation between God as source and Jesus as dependent, but also in soteriological and ecclesiological contexts (in which Christ-language occurs most frequently) Jesus is invariably the agent or emissary *from* God, and God is the initiator or goal

---

2. Chapter 5 will expand this claim by examining Pauline pneumatology; thus, *tri-directionality* will in the end be a better descriptor.

3. Kathryn Tanner, *Christ the Key* (Current Issues in Theology; Cambridge: Cambridge University Press, 2010), 152.

4. Leander E. Keck, "Toward the Renewal of New Testament Christology," *NTS* 32 (1986): 362-77, at 363, 373.

5. Neil Richardson, *Paul's Language about God* (JSNTSup 99; Sheffield: Sheffield Academic Press, 1994), 245. Cf. Ferdinand Hahn, *Theologie des Neuen Testaments,* vol. II: *Die Einheit des Neuen Testaments* (Tübingen: Mohr Siebeck, 2005), 299: "Die Zu- und Unterordnung Jesu gegenüber Gott ist jedenfalls ein Leitmotiv in allen christologischen Texten," including — perhaps especially — those by Paul.

of Jesus' life and actions. Jesus is "sent" from God (Rom 8:3; Gal 4:4), but never vice-versa, nor is he "self-sent"; Jesus is the one "given up" by God (Rom 4:25; 8:32; 1 Cor 11:23) and raised from death by God (Rom 4:24, 25; 6:4, 9; 8:11; 10:9; 1 Cor 6:14; 15:15; Gal 1:1; 1 Thess 1:10; cf. Eph 1:20; Col 2:12).[6] Jesus, as the agent of God, is the one in whom or through whom God acts; as Werner Kramer notes, God is almost always the subject in contexts where Paul employs the "in Jesus Christ" (ἐν Ἰησοῦ Χριστῷ), "in Christ" (ἐν Χριστῷ), or "through Christ" (διὰ Χριστοῦ) prepositional phrases (e.g., Rom 3:24; 6:23; 8:2, 39; 15:17; 1 Cor 1:4; 15:19, 22, 31; 2 Cor 2:14; 3:14; Gal 2:17; Phil 1:26).[7]

Even in texts dominated by christology to the virtual eclipse of theology proper, one can find the identity and action of Jesus grounded in the identity and action of God. Thus, for example, in the "Christ-hymn" of Phil 2:6-11, Christ is, as it were, *enclosed* by references to God: the initial indication of Christ's status takes "God" as its orientating coordinate (Jesus is "in the form of God," v. 6), and from v. 9 to 11 the subject of all the verbs in the independent clauses is "God" — God exalts (v. 9a) and graciously bestows a name on Jesus (v. 9b) — all of which redounds to the glory of God (εἰς δόξαν θεοῦ πατρός, v. 11).

These divine actions are inscribed, so to speak, into the identity of Jesus. The actions of God denoted by the verbs of sending, giving up, raising, and exalting Jesus indicate that the identity of Jesus is to be understood as inseparable from the purpose and action of God in and through him. Thus, it is not surprising that Paul casts Jesus' history, involving as it does the action of God, in the form of an identity description:[8] in Rom 4:25, Jesus

---

6. Richardson, *Paul's Language about God,* 244: "[T]here can be no doubt about the *theocentric* character of almost all Paul's references to the resurrection." Cf. Werner Kramer, *Christ, Lord, Son of God* (trans. Brian Hardy; Studies in Biblical Theology 50; London: SCM, 1966 [1963]), 20-26.

7. Kramer, *Christ, Lord, Son of God,* 143. Note Dunn's description of "the more objective usage [of the ἐν Χριστῷ formula], referring particularly to [God's] redemptive act which has happened 'in Christ' or depends on what Christ is yet to do"; and, with reference to the διὰ Χριστοῦ formula, "[Christ is] a living intermediary through whom God acted" (James D. G. Dunn, *The Theology of Paul the Apostle* [Grand Rapids: Eerdmans, 1998], 397, 406). For a fuller discussion of the overlap and distinctiveness of these two prepositional expressions, see Wilhelm Thüsing, *Per Christum in Deum. Das Verhältnis der Christozentrik zur Theozentrik,* vol. 1 (Münster: Aschendorff, 1965), 233-37, and A. J. M. Wedderburn, "Some Observations on Paul's Use of the Phrases 'in Christ' and 'with Christ,'" *JSNT* 25 (1985): 83-97.

8. See Chapter 2 above and the literature on substantival participial God-predications cited there. These relative clauses are formally equivalent to participial identifying descrip-

is *the one who* was handed over and raised from the dead (ὃς παρεδόθη ... καὶ ἠγέρθη); likewise in 8:34, Jesus is *the one who* died, was raised (by God), who is at the right hand of God and intercedes for believers (Χριστὸς ['Ιησοῦς] ὁ ἀποθανών, μᾶλλον δὲ ἐγερθείς, ὅς καί ἐστιν ἐν δεξιᾷ τοῦ θεοῦ, ὃς καὶ ἐντυγχάνει ὑπὲρ ἡμῶν) — presumably, in parallel with the Spirit's intercession in v. 27, κατὰ θεόν.[9] These actions, simultaneously Jesus' own and at God's initiative, are the constitutive features of Jesus' identity.

The question I need to face is whether this obvious asymmetrical relationship between God and Jesus — in which God is Father, sender, giver, and raiser, and Jesus is Son, sent, given, and raised — requires me to qualify or even abandon the position I proposed in Chapter 2: that there is a fully *mutual* relationship of bi-directionality in which God's identity is determined by reference to Jesus, and Jesus' identity is determined by reference to God, in such a way that christology is not simply an "aspect" of a God-talk whose essential contours were shaped independently of that christology. In order to face this question squarely, I will devote the rest of this chapter to examining one of the three most prominent texts that advocates of both "low" and "high" christologies use to make their case for the "subordination" of Christ to God in Pauline theology: Phil 2:5-11.[10] I will read the text first through the lenses of what I have been describing as "unilateral" understandings of the relationship between God and Christ, understandings that distance themselves from trinitarian conceptualities of mutually constituting "relations" and adopt, instead, the judgments and terms of "high" and "low" christology. As part of this endeavor, I will be asking whether the concept of "subordination" — used by almost all parties — enables the kind of specificity and fineness of observation that is needed to do justice to these texts.[11] Finally, I will be suggesting — again — that the trinitarian conceptuality of "relations" may be fruitful here as a hermeneutical resource. This conceptuality, brought *to* Paul's texts from

tions (cf. Halvor Moxnes, *Theology in Conflict: Studies in Paul's Understanding of God in Romans* [NovTSup 53; Leiden: Brill, 1980], 25).

9. The link between 8:27 and 8:34 is noted in Robert Jewett, *Romans* (Hermeneia; Minneapolis: Fortress, 2007), 542.

10. The other two most prominent "subordinationist" texts — 1 Cor 8:6 and 15:20-28 — I will discuss in Chapter 4.

11. That Richardson, e.g., can speak of the "grammatical subordination" of Christ-language to God-language while distancing himself from other forms of "subordination" (such as "ontic") should suggest that some more discriminating categories and terminology are needed to explicate these texts.

its location amid later theological readings *of* Paul's texts, may provide a hitherto unexplored way of handling *both* Paul's asymmetrical ordering of God and Christ *and also* the "full mutuality of [their] co-implication."[12]

In brief, my argument will be this: God and Jesus are determined in their unique identities — who they are as distinct "persons" vis-à-vis one another — by a set of asymmetrical relations whereby God sends and exalts Jesus and Jesus obeys and returns glory to God. And at the same time, these asymmetrical relations do not compromise the fundamental "oneness" or "unity" that obtains between God and Jesus. Concepts such as "subordination" attempt to capture the asymmetrical distinction between God and Jesus but fail to reckon with the way that distinction does not infringe or diminish their unity. Likewise, rubrics such as "high" or "low" christology also attempt to do justice to the distinction between God and Jesus, but, as with "subordination," they fail to integrate all the theological and christological elements of Phil 2:6-11 in a way that respects the twofold, interlocking, complementary character of Paul's discourse there.

1. Competition between Philippians 2:6-11a and 2:11b?

So I turn first to Phil 2:6-11. Already, prior to the more explicit 1 Cor 15:28,[13] one finds in the final phrase of Phil 2:11 (εἰς δόξαν θεοῦ πατρός) an instance of what interpreters regularly refer to as the "subordination" of Christ to God. Larry J. Kreitzer states the case for such an interpretive judgment with admirable clarity:

> The crucial point is that however exalted Christ is, even to the point of being raised to the highest place and being endowed with the very name of God himself, this is followed by a resounding proclamation that God the Father is the one who is worthy to receive the glory. We could say that the hymn ends on a note of subordination, with the Son stepping aside to allow God the Father to take his place as the focus of worship. The hymn thus proclaims that the wonders of what Christ has done in his obedience are more than matched by the wonders that

---

12. Tanner, *Christ the Key*, 152.

13. It should be remembered that for many interpreters, these two texts are linked via "Adam christology," which is explicit in 1 Cor 15 and implicit (so it is argued) in Philippians 2; see James D. G. Dunn, *Christology in the Making: A New Testament Inquiry into the Origins of the Doctrine of the Incarnation* (2nd ed.; London: SCM, 1989), 107-21.

God has done in his grace, and deliberately culminates in a line which makes that abundantly clear. At the end of the day everything has been accomplished "to the glory of God the Father."[14]

Although Paul has spoken of Jesus' exaltation (ὁ θεὸς αὐτὸν ὑπερύψωσεν, v. 9a) and reception of the divine name (ἐχαρίσατο αὐτῷ τὸ ὄνομα τὸ ὑπὲρ πᾶν ὄνομα, v. 9b) and the intended acclamation of that name in worship (ἵνα ἐν τῷ ὀνόματι Ἰησοῦ πᾶν γόνυ κάμψῃ . . . καὶ πᾶσα γλῶσσα ἐξομολογήσηται, vv. 10, 11), the last line of the hymn should be understood to *qualify* Jesus' exalted status and underscore its place in relation to the greater status and glory of God.

One finds repeatedly in the literature on this passage a concern to stress that God's position of most supreme glory is not "threatened"[15] or "rivaled"[16] or "displaced"[17] by Jesus' exaltation. Käsemann is concerned lest it be thought that God's divinity *(Gottheit)* is "endangered" *(angetastet)* by Jesus' being given the divine name, and he suggests that Paul added the final phrase to the hymn to express the same qualification he gives in 1 Cor 15:28.[18] Similarly, according to Dunn, "the acclamation of Jesus Christ as Lord involved no heavenly coup or takeover, no replacement of God by Christ. On the contrary, it was *God* who would be glorified in the confession of *Jesus*. . . . The universal lordship of Jesus Christ has been determined and effected by God, but the supreme glory is God's."[19] And in the same vein, James McGrath summarizes the force of 2:11 as implying that God "shares his own exalted status with Jesus in a way that does not jeopardize

---

14. Larry J. Kreitzer, "'When He at Last Is First!' Philippians 2:9-11 and the Exaltation of the Lord," in Ralph P. Martin and Brian J. Dodd (eds.), *Where Christology Began: Essays on Philippians 2* (Louisville: Westminster/John Knox, 1998), 111-27, at 121. Ralph P. Martin, *Carmen Christi: Philippians ii.5-11 in Recent Interpretation and in the Setting of Early Christian Worship* (rev. ed.; Grand Rapids: Eerdmans, 1983 [1967]), 274, observes that some think "Paul adds the phrase in order to safeguard the unity of the Godhead — for him as a Jew, a precious inheritance with which he never parted, for all his concern to assert the universality of the Gospel and the divinity of Christ."

15. David B. Capes, *Old Testament Yahweh Texts in Paul's Christology* (WUNT 2/47; Tübingen: Mohr Siebeck, 1992), 160.

16. Peter T. O'Brien, *The Epistle to the Philippians* (NIGTC; Grand Rapids: Eerdmans, 1991), 251.

17. Kramer, *Christ, Lord, Son of God,* 83.

18. Ernst Käsemann, "Kritische Analyse von Phil. 2,5-11," *Zeitschrift für Theologie und Kirche* 47 (1950): 313-60, at 349, 353.

19. Dunn, *Theology of Paul the Apostle,* 251-52. Italics original.

God's ultimate supremacy."[20] What these readings hold in common is an understanding that Paul's final reference to "the glory of God the Father" is meant to forestall any notion that Jesus' lordship *competes* with God's sovereignty. Effectively, then, this final doxological flourish functions as a kind of rear-guard action to preserve what appears under siege from the foregoing affirmations.

i. Hurtado's Interpretation of Philippians 2:6-11

In order to see how this perspective — shared by a large range of interpreters — plays itself out in the course of exegesis of this passage, I will look in some detail at one example of an extended treatment of these verses that adopts this perspective. Larry Hurtado's essay, "A 'Case Study' in Early Christian Devotion to Jesus: Philippians 2:6-11,"[21] represents a useful example in that Hurtado clearly shares the concern I have noted above in other interpreters' treatments while also engaging in a thorough and lucid discussion of each strophe of the hymn. Near his conclusion, he writes:

> [W]hile asserting an astonishing "binitarian" view, in which Jesus is linked with God and with divine purposes in an unprecedented way, the passage also reflects a concern to emphasize that Jesus' career and his subsequent exaltation as well do not really represent a threat to the one God of biblical tradition. Jesus' exaltation, in fact, has its basis and its ultimate meaning in the glory of the one God.[22]

Tracing the moves Hurtado makes that allow him to arrive at this conclusion will position us to offer our own reading of Phil 2:5-11, one that will suggest a different way forward through some of the questions Hurtado identifies.

Before examining the hymn in detail, Hurtado notes the social setting of Phil 2:5-11 as (most likely) a hymn sung in early Christian worship. That Jesus should be acclaimed in corporate gatherings by means of an ode/

---

20. James F. McGrath, *The Only True God: Early Christian Monotheism in Its Jewish Context* (Urbana and Chicago: University of Illinois Press, 2009), 51.

21. In Larry W. Hurtado, *How on Earth Did Jesus Become a God? Historical Questions about Earliest Devotion to Jesus* (Grand Rapids: Eerdmans, 2005), 83-107.

22. Hurtado, "A 'Case Study' in Early Christian Devotion to Jesus: Philippians 2:6-11," in *How on Earth Did Jesus Become a God?* 83-107, here 106.

song is one among several phenomena that indicate Jesus' inclusion in "devotional patterns" otherwise limited to God alone.[23] Also as prolegomena to detailed exegesis, Hurtado rejects the need to posit any conceptual scheme lying behind the hymn, choosing to follow inductively the indications of the textual data themselves.[24]

Exegetically, Hurtado begins discussion of Phil 2:5-11 with vv. 9-11. The "therefore" (διό) which opens v. 9 demonstrates that vv. 9-11 provide the divine intention and result of vv. 6-8: "The humiliation and exaltation of Jesus, thus, are treated here as one connected set of actions, with one final outcome and purpose."[25] Rather than begin with the thorny exegetical problems that beset vv. 6-8, Hurtado's approach thus allows the climax of the hymn — vv. 9-11 — to shape and determine what we may conclude with regard to the hymn's first half.

Hurtado begins his exposition by observing that the wording of 2:10-11 is drawn from Isa 45:23 LXX. But whereas the Isaianic text in its LXX context depicts a universal acclamation of *God's* sovereignty, Paul reads that acclamation as directed toward *Jesus* as "Lord" (κύριος). Yet, this does not, for Hurtado, mean that Paul has simply made a substitution, so that where the LXX refers to God, Paul can now find a reference to Jesus, as though Jesus had replaced God without remainder. Paul's move is considerably more subtle than that. The text of Isa 45:23 contains both a first person pronoun ("to me") and a third person referent ("God"): "every knee shall bow to me and every tongue confess to God" (ἐμοὶ κάμψει πᾶν γόνυ καὶ ἐξομολογήσεται πᾶσα γλῶσσα τῷ θεῷ). A natural reading of this alternation in its original context would be to take both the pronominal and the nominal references as referring to the same figure, that is, God. Likewise with the alternation found two verses later, in Isa 45:25, the shift between "Lord" (κύριος) and "God" (θεός) could be most straightforwardly treated, in its LXX context, as a stylistic variation meant in both instances to indicate the same being, "God": "from the Lord shall be justified and in God shall be glorified all the seed of the sons of Israel" (ἀπὸ κυρίου

23. Hurtado, "A 'Case Study' in Early Christian Devotion to Jesus: Philippians 2:6-11," 86-87.

24. Hurtado, "A 'Case Study' in Early Christian Devotion to Jesus: Philippians 2:6-11," 88-89.

25. Hurtado, "A 'Case Study' in Early Christian Devotion to Jesus: Philippians 2:6-11," 90. Hurtado appears to sidestep the debate as to whether the ἵνα governing the clauses of vv. 10-11 indicates a divine purpose or a result, on which cf. Gordon D. Fee, *Paul's Letter to the Philippians* (NICNT; Grand Rapids: Eerdmans, 1995), 223 n. 27.

δικαιωθήσονται καὶ ἐν τῷ θεῷ ἐνδοξασθήσονται πᾶν τὸ σπέρμα τῶν υἱῶν Ἰσραήλ). But because Jesus was already acclaimed as κύριος (2:11) in early Christian circles as part and parcel of early Christian charismatic experience, Hurtado thinks Paul would certainly have found a reference to Jesus in the κύριος mentioned in Isa 45:25. From there, it would have been a short step to locating *two* figures in Isa 45:23-25, one designated as κύριος and referring to himself with a first person pronoun (ἐμοὶ, v. 23) and the other called θεός and referred to in that third person manner.[26] So, in this way, Jesus is, as it were, *inserted* into a classic text of Jewish monotheism, but at the same time his identity as a distinct agent from the one God is preserved. Jesus shares the divine name and receives the acclamation that Isa 45:23-25 depicts as belonging to God alone. But he does so not *as* the one God but rather as one who is somehow within the ambit of the one God's sovereignty and as that God's unique representative.

Having outlined his understanding of Phil 2:9-11, then, Hurtado turns next to vv. 6-8 and the highly disputed matters of its interpretation. The conclusions reached with regard to the former provide the basis for the examination of the latter. Several of Hurtado's interpretive moves are worth noting. After distinguishing between two primary interpretations of vv. 6-8, one designated with the term "Adam christology" in which Jesus' humanity is in view from v. 6 onward and one designated by the shorthand "pre-existence" in which Jesus' divinity is in view at first (v. 6) followed by his humanity (v. 7-8), Hurtado opts for the latter, "pre-existent" view. The approach of "Adam christology" founders on the fact that there are no clear allusive links between the Philippians text and the LXX Genesis text, despite the once popular suggestion that Paul's "in the form of God" (ἐν μορφῇ θεοῦ) is parallel to κατ' εἰκόνα in Gen 1:26 LXX.[27] This fact, together with the aorist verb "he emptied himself" (ἐκένωσεν) and its participial parallel "becoming" (γενόμενος), suggests the transition from one state to another state characterized by the human traits delineated in v. 7 (μορφὴ δούλου . . . ἐν ὁμοιώματι ἀνθρώπων . . . σχήματι . . . ὡς ἄνθρωπος): "it seems . . . likely that vv. 6-7 refer to Jesus as being in some way 'divine' in status or mode, and then becoming a human being."[28] Or, expressed more fully:

26. Hurtado, "A 'Case Study' in Early Christian Devotion to Jesus: Philippians 2:6-11," 91-93.

27. Hurtado, "A 'Case Study' in Early Christian Devotion to Jesus: Philippians 2:6-11," 98-99. Cf. David Steenburg, "The Case against the Synonymity of Morphê and Eikôn," *JSNT* 34 (1988): 77-86.

28. Hurtado, "A 'Case Study' in Early Christian Devotion to Jesus: Philippians 2:6-

In Philippians 2:6 Jesus "being in the form of God" is clearly intended as in some way a contrast/comparison with his then "taking the form of a slave" in v. 7. If the latter represents his status and mode as a historical, earthly, human figure, then "being in the form of God" is surely best taken to represent a different and prior status or mode of being much higher than being human, which he chose not to exploit for his own advantage.[29]

The important point to underscore about this reading is that it is formed retrospectively from the vantage point of the eschatological scenario pictured in vv. 9-11. Hurtado argues that already in pre-Christian Jewish tradition "there was a freedom, a tendency perhaps, to link particular characters of exceptional importance to the heavenly and pretemporal state."[30] Thus, if God exalted Jesus in the manner that vv. 9-11 describes, then the significance of that exaltation would need to be thought retrospectively into the realm of protology as well. In the case of Phil 2:6-7, read from the vantage point of vv. 9-11 with the latter's elevation of Jesus to the status of the supreme representative of God's ultimate sovereignty, "it would perhaps have been a logical move to think that he must also be ascribed a prior, heavenly status or existence, however that was understood."[31] In other words, since Jesus is the eschatologically exalted one, called upon by the divine name "Lord" (κύριος, vv. 10-11), then he must have been "in the form of God" and "equal with God" (v. 6) from the time before the humiliation described in v. 7.

At this point, Hurtado concludes, in the passage already quoted above, that Jesus' exalted status does not endanger God's greater glory:

> I suggest that the ode may reflect the desire to emphasize that the earthly events of Jesus' life are to be seen as the career of the uniquely obedient one, that the outcome of that career was God's unique exal-

---

11," 101. Cf. G. B. Caird, *New Testament Theology* (ed. L. D. Hurst; Oxford: Clarendon Press, 1994), 300 n. 31.

29. Hurtado, "A 'Case Study' in Early Christian Devotion to Jesus: Philippians 2:6-11," 102.

30. Larry W. Hurtado, "Pre-existence," in G. F. Hawthorne, R. P. Martin, and D. G. Reid (eds.), *Dictionary of Paul and His Letters* (Downers Grove, IL: InterVarsity Press, 1993), 743-46, at 744.

31. Hurtado, "A 'Case Study' in Early Christian Devotion to Jesus: Philippians 2:6-11," 102.

tation and vindication of him, and that all this in turn both manifests and serves the glory of God. That is, while asserting an astonishing "binitarian" view, in which Jesus is linked with God and with divine purposes in an unprecedented way, the passage also reflects a concern to emphasize that Jesus' career and his subsequent exaltation as well do not really represent a threat to the one God of biblical tradition. Jesus' exaltation, in fact, has its basis and its ultimate meaning in the glory of the one God.[32]

Having sketched the outline of Hurtado's reading of Phil 2:6-11, I now want to offer a critique and propose a different reading in conversation with Hurtado's. What Hurtado leaves undiscussed in his treatment is the way in which his construal depends upon, first, distinguishing between those elements of vv. 6-11 that seem to suggest a close association between God and Jesus and the elements that appear to distance God from Jesus. But more than that, second, his reading hinges on juxtaposing these elements in a kind of competitive relationship, whereby one set is read as qualifying or limiting the other. Thus, his interpretation begins by highlighting the closeness between God and Jesus: Jesus is acclaimed with language lifted directly from the monotheistic Isa 45:23-25 (Phil 2:10-11) and is said to be "in the form of God" and "equal with God" (2:6). On the other hand, there are elements of Phil 2:6-11 that Hurtado reads as placing a condition on that closeness: it is God who exalts Jesus, not the other way around, nor does Jesus exalt himself (v. 9); and Jesus' acclamation as "Lord" is "to the glory of God the Father," rather than to his own ultimate honor (v. 11). Hurtado constructs his reading from the interplay of these two sets of observations, attempting to do justice to both. However, at no point does he explicitly reflect on whether articulating such a distinction between the text's elements in the manner he does is the only or best way to describe the text's dynamics. For example, Hurtado does not ask if the elements that suggest closeness between God and Jesus may operate on a different plane, as it were, from the elements that suggest distance and hence whether they ought to be construed as in any way competing with one another. Might the suggestions of *closeness* between God and Jesus and the suggestions of *distance* coalesce in such a way that they are not meant to be *antithetically* complementary to one another, as Hurtado's treatment

32. Hurtado, "A 'Case Study' in Early Christian Devotion to Jesus: Philippians 2:6-11," 106.

implies, but function in an *overlapping* complementarity? Having observed the presence of *both* sets of elements in Phil 2:6-11 (i.e., closeness and distance), is it necessary to see those sets in conflict with each other, so that more of one means a limitation on the other?

I want to answer these questions with the help of trinitarian conceptualities of "relations." My reading of Phil 2:6-11, carried out below with Hurtado's reading visible in the background, will proceed in three stages. First, I will offer my own (necessarily circumscribed) exegesis of Phil 2:6-11, focusing on the elements of the text that indicate a closeness or identification between God and Jesus as well as the elements that indicate "subordination" or distinction between God and Jesus. Second, I will lay out the trinitarian conceptualities that will, as before, serve as exegetical prompts and heuristic aids. The questions these conceptualities generate and their suggested lines of inquiry will, third, lead me to sketch an alternative to Hurtado's reading, concluding with a response to the question of whether Phil 2:6-11 undermines the bi-directional, mutually definitive relations between God and Jesus which my previous chapter suggested is characteristic of Paul's theology and christology.

2. Elements of "Oneness" and "Subordination" between God and Jesus in Philippians 2:6-11

As will become apparent, Phil 2:6-11 resists attempts to keep its various elements hermetically sealed off from one another or to pit its various elements against one another in a kind of zero-sum game. Admittedly, any effort — including the one I will present below — to separate the aspects of the text that indicate some kind of "unity," "oneness," or "equality" between Jesus and God from those other elements that indicate "distinction," "order," or "subordination" between Jesus and God appears strained and artificial from the standpoint of the text's own formal presentation. Even a simple phrase such as "Jesus is presented as equal to God" carries the seeds of its own complication. This construction requires distinguishing two figures able to be picked out by different designations — *Jesus* and *God.* Yet the syntactical link between the figures — "is presented as equal to" — places them not only in an opposed relation but also simultaneously specifies their essential unity. All of this is to acknowledge that what follows is determined in large measure by my need to break Phil 2:6-11 down into various components for the purpose of examining those components more closely. For the purpose of probing a two-poled affirmation like "Jesus is equal to God," I will consider each of these double aspects of Phil 2:6-11 in sequence rather than in an overlapping fashion — though along the way I will observe the intermingling of these paired patterns of speech within the hymn. And the theological significance of that intermingling, its precise shape and import, will be the sustained focus of this chapter's final section.

i. The "Identification" of Jesus with God

The first step in my exegesis, then, will be to observe those elements of Phil 2:6-11 that seem to suggest unity or "oneness" between Jesus and God. Opening the passage in v. 6 is the designation of Jesus as "in the form of God" (ἐν μορφῇ θεοῦ). Here "God" refers to the same "God" named in v. 9 — that is, the "God" who is identifiably distinct from Jesus.[33] Yet Jesus is said to be in the form of that God. Regardless of whether one takes μορφή to denote the visible characteristics of God's heavenly existence[34] or the shape or expression that corresponds to an underlying divine "being,"[35] the point is the same: Jesus' μορφή is the same as God's μορφή, since Jesus is said to be "in" (ἐν) that μορφή.[36] As Fee puts it, Jesus "was characterized by what was essential to being God."[37]

But this interpretation of μορφή depends not simply on establishing the lexical range of that word but on understanding the function of the verb "to be" (ὑπάρχειν) in 2:6 in relation to the finite verb and participles that follow it in v. 7. The participial phrase ἐν μορφῇ θεοῦ ὑπάρχων docs not stand in direct relationship to ἡγεῖσθαι but rather to the sentence's main verb, κενοῦν, as signaled by the οὐχ/ἀλλά construction. Thus: "being in the form of God . . . he emptied himself." The

---

33. Cf. Augustine, *The Trinity* (trans. Edmund Hill; Hyde Park, NY: New City Press, 1991), 73 (= *De Trinitate* 1.12): "here [the apostle uses] 'God' as a proper name for the Father."

34. So Markus Bockmuehl, "'The Form of God' (Phil. 2:6): Variations on a Theme of Jewish Mysticism," *JTS* 48/1 (1997): 1-23.

35. Cf. J. H. Moulton and G. Milligan, *The Vocabulary of the Greek New Testament* (Peabody, MA: Hendrickson, 1995 [1930]), 417: μορφή refers to "a form which truly and fully expresses the being which underlies it."

36. The understanding that μορφὴ θεοῦ denotes the visible splendor that Jesus later exchanged for the visible appearance of μορφὴ δούλου (2:7) probably best explains the use of ἐν, "as though the form of God was a sphere in which he existed or a garment in which he was clothed" (O'Brien, *Philippians*, 206).

37. Gordon F. Fee, *Pauline Christology*, (Peabody, MA: Hendrickson, 2007), 379.

force of κενοῦν is, in turn, spelled out by μορφὴν δούλου λαβών and ἐν ὁμοιώματι ἀνθρώπων γενόμενος. The emptying is explained as "taking the form of a slave" and sharing "the likeness of human beings." This means that ὑπάρχειν takes its time reference from the aorist finite verb κενοῦν, standing in temporal contrast with it ("being in the form of God [in the past] . . . he emptied himself") and with the participles whose role is to fill in the content of what it means for Jesus to have "emptied himself."[38] On this reading, then, for Jesus to be ἐν μορφῇ θεοῦ expresses what was temporally prior to the movement described with the first two participles of v. 7. That the "becoming" of v. 7 is in contrast to the "being" of v. 6 suggests that what is in view is not simply the movement from one state of human existence to another but rather Jesus' movement *into* the human sphere not previously experienced.[39] The upshot is that Jesus — or more precisely the one who *would become* Jesus[40] — existed prior to his state of self-emptying and obedience and is thereby understood on the "God" side of the contrast here between "God" (θεός) and the merely "human" (ἄνθρωπος).

---

38. So Fee, *Philippians*, 203.

39. So I. Howard Marshall, "Incarnational Christology in the New Testament," in H. H. Rowdon (ed.), *Christ the Lord: Studies in Christology Presented to Donald Guthrie* (Leicester: InterVarsity Press), 1-16, at 6. That it is *Jesus'* movement is open to at least two misunderstandings. On the one hand, it could be argued that, since the personal name of the man Jesus is employed, Paul cannot have in mind the divine "Son" who, as in John 1:1-8 (there, of course, as ὁ λόγος), exists prior to becoming human (cf. Phil 2:7). Rather, Paul must have in mind a change of status that occurs within the temporal boundaries of the human life of Jesus. But this challenge can be met by observing that the name "Jesus" functions here in the way that "President" does in the sentence, "President Obama attended elementary school in Jakarta." Obama was not president at the time he was in grade school, but we may use his present title without confusion when referring to his life before he became president. So, the fact that Paul refers to "Christ Jesus" as "being in the form of God" (2:6) does not, by itself, require that "being in the form of God" refer only to some reality predicable of his life *qua* human. The second potential misunderstanding that arises at this point is that the man Jesus may be thought to pre-exist his life of self-emptying in an abstracted, non-personal way. But that the subject of the actions of 2:6-8 is "Christ Jesus" prevents an abstracted interpretation of the state of Jesus' existence prior to the actions of 2:7. It is the *person* of Jesus who is determinative for any "preexistence" that is posited. See Simon J. Gathercole, "Pre-Existence, and the Freedom of the Son in Creation and Redemption: An Exposition in Dialogue with Robert Jenson," *IJST* 7/1 (2005): 38-51, at 42: "the person of Jesus Christ defines the 'that' and the 'how' of pre-existence."

40. N. T. Wright, "Jesus Christ is Lord: Philippians 2.5-11," in *The Climax of the Covenant: Christ and the Law in Pauline Theology* (London: T&T Clark, 1991), 56-98, at 96-97.

In addition to discussing the meaning of "in the form of God" together with the participle ὑπάρχων and the finite verb it modifies (κενοῦν, v. 7), it is important to note the connection between that clause and τὸ εἶναι ἴσα θεῷ at the end of v. 6. Although the article τό is not anaphoric and so τὸ εἶναι ἴσα θεῷ is not simply synonymously parallel with ἐν μορφῇ θεοῦ ὑπάρχων,[41] nonetheless there is a resonance between the phrases that makes them mutually illuminating, especially when both are read as the counterpart to the actions described in v. 7.[42] Grammatically, τὸ εἶναι ἴσα θεῷ receives the emphasis in the second half of v. 6 by its placement in the final position after οὐχ ἁρπαγμὸν ἡγήσατο. The definite article indicates its role as the sentence's subject, which leaves ἁρπαγμόν as the predicate noun with an implied "to be" linking the two. If we take Roy Hoover and N. T. Wright's work on ἁρπαγμός to represent the most likely meaning of the word,[43] the clause could be rendered literally, if somewhat woodenly, in English as "Not as something to take advantage of did [Christ Jesus] consider the being equal with God."[44]

What this reading implies is that equality with God is not the uncertain *aim* of the action denoted by the noun ἁρπαγμός ("taking advantage"), as though it were out of reach, but is rather the already-held *presupposition* for the "not taking advantage."[45] Further, τὸ εἶναι ἴσα θεῷ is not something that Jesus gives up in 2:7; it is, instead, something he chooses to express in a particular way — not as something to be retained for his own advantage but rather as the basis for self-abnegation, generosity, and service. As N. T. Wright has put it, "The pre-existent son regarded equality with God not as excusing him from the task of (redemptive) suffering and death, but actually as uniquely qualifying him for that vocation."[46] Jesus' sharing the form of God and being equal with God is *expressed in* his self-emptying — his taking the form of a servant and being found in the likeness of humans.[47]

41. Denny Burk, "On the Articular Infinitive in Philippians 2:6: A Grammatical Note with Christological Implications," *Tyndale Bulletin* 55/2 (2004): 253-74.

42. So Bockmuehl, "'The Form of God'," 6. Karl Barth, *The Epistle to the Philippians* (Louisville: Westminister/John Knox, 2002 [1962]), 61, suggests that the meaning of ἐν μορφῇ θεοῦ ὑπάρχων is best determined from τὸ εἶναι ἴσα θεῷ.

43. R. W. Hoover, "The *Harpagmos* Enigma: A Philological Solution," *HTR* 64 (1971): 95-119; Wright, "Jesus Christ is Lord: Philippians 2.5-11."

44. Cf. Fee's whole discussion of the phrase in *Pauline Christology*, 379-81.

45. Wright, "Jesus Christ is Lord: Philippians 2.5-11," 82: "The idiom here used clearly assumes that the object in question — in this case equality with God — is already possessed."

46. Wright, "Jesus Christ is Lord: Philippians 2.5-11," 83-84.

47. It could be argued that Jesus does give up μορφὴ θεοῦ — the visible divine splen-

Seeing such self-emptying, the hearers/readers of the Christ-hymn see what it looks like to be God.

But this still leaves unanswered the question of what the phrase denotes. If its function in relation to ἁρπαγμός is now pinpointed, to what does it refer? Bauckham notes the infrequency with which this question is even posed,[48] as well as the inadequacy of attempts to water down the meaning of the phrase to something denoting similarity.[49] The question Bauckham proposes as an interpretive key here is a good one: In the context of Phil 2:6-11 as a whole, with its allusive invocation of a key monotheistic passage from the LXX (Isa 45:21-23), could τὸ εἶναι ἴσα θεῷ fail to be heard as bearing a strongly monotheistic resonance?[50] To speak of the quality or state of being ἴσος θεῷ in this particular context, in other words, would seem to require an understanding of that quality or state against the backdrop of the theology embodied in Isa 45:21-23. Jesus, in other words, is being deliberately placed *within* the boundaries of what separated God from all other reality in one LXX text.

This understanding of 2:6 leads inexorably into a consideration of the other elements of 2:6-11 that suggest the closest possible association or oneness between God and Jesus. The first of these elements is God's action of "highly exalting" Jesus (v. 9), which is best taken as an allusion to Isa 52:13 LXX (ὁ παῖς [δοῦλος][51] μου καὶ ὑψωθήσεται) which is, in turn, linked to the evocation of Isa 53:12 LXX in vv. 7 and 9.[52] The result

dor — trading it for a different visible form, μορφὴ δούλου, even while he does *not* give up being ἴσος θεῷ but chooses to express that "equality" *as* self-emptying.

48. Bauckham, "Paul's Christology of Divine Identity," in *Jesus and the God of Israel: God Crucified and Other Studies on the New Testament's Christology of Divine Identity* (Grand Rapids: Eerdmans, 2008), 182-232, at 207.

49. Dunn, *Christology,* 116, speaks of "the degree of equality with God which [Adam] already enjoyed," but as Bauckham, "Paul's Christology of Divine Identity," 207 n. 61 observes, in the evidence Dunn cites for this reading from the LXX, ἴσος appears in similes — a different kind of usage from τὸ εἶναι ἴσα θεῷ. Cf. BDF §434.1.

50. Bauckham, "Paul's Christology of Divine Identity," 208, cf. 207.

51. Aquila and Symmachus have δοῦλος here in place of παῖς (J. Ziegler, *Isaias* [Septuaginta 14, 2nd ed.; Göttingen: Vandenhoeck & Ruprecht, 1967]).

52. The verbal/structural links noted by Bauckham and Lucien Cerfaux are as follows: παρεδόθη . . . ἡ ψυχὴ αὐτοῦ (Isa 53:12) — ἑαυτὸν ἐκένωσεν (Phil 2:7); εἰς θάνατον (Isa 53:12) — μέχρι θανάτου (Phil 2:8); διὰ τοῦτο (Isa 53:12) — διὸ (Phil 2:9); ὑψωθήσεται (Isa 52:13) — ὑπερύψωσεν (Phil 2:9); cf. L. Cerfaux, "Hymne au Christ — Serviteur de Dieu (Phil., II, 6-11 = Is., LII, 13–LIII, 12)," in *Receuil Lucien Cerfaux: Études d"Exégèse et d'Histoire Religieuse* (vol. 2, BETL 6-7; Gembloux: Duculot, 1954), 425-37. But see also Francis Watson, "Mistranslation and the Death of Christ: Isaiah 53 LXX and Its Pauline

is a complex fusion of Isaiah 52 and 53, which treat the suffering servant's self-humiliation, *together with* Isaiah 45 and its picture of the revelation of God's unique sovereignty, definitively acclaimed in the eschatological acts of bowing knees and confessing tongues (Phil 2:10-11a). In other words, Paul reads the self-emptying of Jesus *alongside* the affirmation of God's unique reign in such a way that Jesus' exaltation, as an interpretation of Isa 52:13, is at the same time the moment of the acknowledgement of God's rule, as an interpretation of Isa 45:23. If it is asked when and how God will be acknowledged as God in accordance with Isa 45:23, Paul's answer appears to be: at and by the exaltation of Jesus, in and as a consequence of his obedience, which led to death.[53]

The second element of "oneness" or "identification" in 2:9-11 is the bestowal on Jesus of "the name that is above every name" (τὸ ὄνομα τὸ ὑπὲρ πᾶν ὄνομα). This is most likely not an additional honor beyond that specified by ὑπερυψοῦν in the first half of v. 9 but rather the explication of what that exaltation entails: for Jesus to be exalted *is* to be the beneficiary of the divine name.

The "name" in question must be, as Bauckham maintains, the reverential substitute for the divine name YHWH — that is, κύριος. The appendage τὸ ὑπὲρ πᾶν ὄνομα is the primary piece of evidence for this, since it appears highly unlikely that it could have been applied to any other name but the address by which God's deity was specified.[54] As many interpreters have noted, this represents a startling transference of κύριος from one subject to another: Jesus is now addressed by the identifier that

---

Reception," in Stanley E. Porter and Mark J. Boda (eds.), *Translating the New Testament: Text, Translation, Theology* (Grand Rapids: Eerdmans, 2009), 215-50, esp. 246-48, who argues that "possible connections between the Philippian Christ-hymn and Isaiah 53 are more persuasive if we suppose an influence from whatever prior translations or revisions underlie the later work attributed to Aquila, Symmachus, and Theodotion" (246) and proceeds to highlight a greater range of parallels than those found in Bauckham's treatment: e.g., πεπλήγοτα ὑπὸ [τοῦ] θεοῦ καὶ τεταπεινώμενον (Isa 53:4, Aquila, Symmachus, and Theodotion for the final word) — ἐταπείνωσεν ἑαυτὸν (Phil 2:8); προσήχθη καὶ αὐτὸς ὑπήκουσεν καὶ οὐκ ἤνοιξεν τὸ στόμα αὐτου (Isa 53:8, possibly Symmachus) — γενόμενος ὑπήκοος (Phil 2:8).

53. David S. Yeago, "The New Testament and the Nicene Dogma: A Contribution to the Recovery of Theological Exegesis," *Pro Ecclesia* 3/2 (1994): 152-64, at 155.

54. Richard J. Bauckham, "The Worship of Jesus in Philippians 2:9-11," in Ralph P. Martin and Brian J. Dodd (eds.), *Where Christology Began: Essays on Philippians 2* (Louisville: Westminster/John Knox, 1998), 128-39, at 131: "it is inconceivable that any Jewish writer could use this phrase for a name other than God's own unique name."

in its original context was YHWH's.[55] The question becomes, then, what it might mean for Jesus to share not simply a divine title but to be given the divine *name*. What does this transference say about the "oneness" between Jesus and God?

Once a position on the theological import of κύριος as the name of YHWH has been adopted, the range of possible answers to this question narrows considerably. It seems impossible to say that Jesus merely shares the same *functions* as YHWH in the LXX and that it is appropriate for him to be acclaimed as κύριος for that reason. If that were the case, then κύριος would have to be an indicator of *role* rather than *identity*. But that is not borne out by wider Pauline usage of κύριος. Regardless of how one decides the complicated issue of whether the LXX consistently substituted κύριος for יהוה, it appears that Paul himself did so when quoting the Old Testament.[56] Grasping this point disrupts any effort to read κύριος *merely* as a title. Insofar as it retains its lexical meaning, it may *connote* "sovereignty" or "rulership" when used of God.[57] But when it functions as the circumlocution by which the divine name YHWH is indicated, κύριος is not simply the designation of an office or function (i.e., one of lordship or sovereignty) and thereby transferable to different subjects. Rather, in that distinctive usage, it is inseparable from the divine identity and being. Rowe expresses this point with particular clarity:

> [O]ther titles are appellations connected with who YHWH is, but κύριος is the unique identity of the God of Israel. Further, there is no cleft between YHWH and his name. The divine subject is totally identified with and present in his name — κύριος *is* YHWH.[58]

If that is the case, then Jesus is not simply the sharer of YHWH's *functions* but *is YHWH*. Other interpreters have entertained the possibility that Jesus bears the divine name *representatively*, as a divinely commissioned agent in the way that, for example, the angel Yahoel does in the *Apocalypse*

---

55. E.g., L. Joseph Kreitzer, *Jesus and God in Paul's Eschatology* (JSNTSup 19; Sheffield: JSOT, 1987), 114, 116; Capes, *Old Testament Yahweh Texts in Paul's Christology*, 159; Fee, *Pauline Christology*, 396.

56. C. Kavin Rowe, "Romans 10:13: What Is the Name of the Lord?," *Horizons in Biblical Theology* 22/2 (2000): 135-73, at 157 n. 66.

57. Bauckham, "The Worship of Jesus in Philippians 2:9-11," 131.

58. C. Kavin Rowe, "Luke and the Trinity: An Essay in Ecclesial Biblical Theology," *SJT* 56/1 (2003): 1-26, at 20-21.

of Abraham.[59] But this overlooks the context of Isa 45:21-23, which is decisive for the meaning of κύριος in Phil 2:10. That deutero-Isaianic context precludes God's sharing his lordship with another.[60] In addition, maintaining that Jesus simply takes on the divine name as an emissary of the one God neglects to reckon with the full implications of the worship of Jesus in Phil 2:10, which stands in contrast to Yahoel's joining Abraham in worshiping God instead of receiving worship himself (*Apoc. Abr.* 17.2, 7). If Jesus is performing a role similar to Yahoel's, one would expect him to refuse the bended knees of others and join them in bending his own knees to God alone.

Finally, one might attempt to maintain, with Joseph Fitzmyer, that Jesus' reception of the name κύριος "suggest[s] a *Gleichsetzung* of Jesus with Yahweh, a setting of him on a par with Yahweh, but not an *Identifizierung* — because he is not" God the Father.[61] But this option fails for the same reasons as the first two. It obscures the fact that the "name" in view is, as Christopher Seitz has so provocatively put it, "God's very self, and by giving it to Jesus, maximal identity [between the 'name' and Jesus] is affirmed."[62] If Jesus does not simply gain a title or an office but instead receives the divine name, then a distinction between some kind of functional equality and personal identity does not appear supple and subtle enough to do justice to the dynamics of Philippians 2.

Jesus is not, then, brought into a close relationship with YHWH. He is not simply given some of YHWH's prerogatives. He is, rather, shown to belong within what makes YHWH unique; he is shown to be the rightful

59. McGrath, *The Only True God,* 49, suggests that Yahoel's role in the *Apocalypse of Abraham* parallels Jesus' role in Phil 2:10-11.

60. Wright, "Jesus Christ is Lord: Philippians 2.5-11," 93-94.

61. Joseph A. Fitzmyer, SJ, "New Testament *Kyrios* and *Maranatha* and Their Aramaic Background," in *To Advance the Gospel: New Testament Studies* (New York: Crossroad, 1981), 218-35, at 223. Fitzmyer's other essay, "The Semitic Background of the New Testament *Kyrios*-Title," in *A Wandering Aramean: Collected Aramaic Essays* (Chico, Calif.: Scholars Press, 1979), 115-42, explicitly places this understanding in contrast to the affirmations of "the Councils of Nicaea [and] Chalcedon" (130). In that essay, Fitzmyer maintains that "the gradual awareness of [Jesus] as θεός, as someone on a par with Yahweh, and yet not [*abba*] himself, eventually led to the development of the Christian doctrine of the Trinity" (131). As I will discuss more fully below, this approach depends upon the correct observation of a distinction between θεός and Ἰησοῦς in Phil 2:6-11 (the context of Fitzmyer's comments is an interpretation of that passage) but also the *incorrect* presupposition that that distinction necessitates a qualification of the *identity* between Ἰησοῦς and the κύριος of Isaiah 45.

62. Christopher R. Seitz, "Handing Over the Name: Christian Reflection on the Divine Name YHWH," in *Figured Out: Typology and Providence in Christian Scripture* (Louisville: Westminster/John Knox, 2001), 131-44, at 143.

bearer of the divine name. The overlapping use of κύριος for both God and Jesus exerts a "unitive pressure"[63] whereby the unique name of God in the LXX — κύριος — becomes an assertion of oneness between the "persons" of Father and Son in Phil 2:6-11.[64] Or, to put in Rowe's more lapidary formulation, "to ask after the identity of the κύριος [in Phil 2:6-11] is to answer θεός and 'Iησοῦς."[65] The application of κύριος to Jesus, while not synonymous with the earlier affirmations that he is "in the form of God" (v. 6a) and "equal with God" (v. 6b), is of a piece with them in terms of theological function. Jesus' reception of the name κύριος in vv. 10-11 is the consequence of his self-humbling and obedience outlined in vv. 6-8, for which ἐν μορφῇ θεοῦ ὑπάρχων and being ἴσα θεῷ (v. 6) are the enabling presuppositions.[66] The relationship between all these elements must be of the closest possible organic kind. As Yeago puts it, with blunt forcefulness, if Isa 45:21-24 is not to be undermined, then the "relationship between YHWH and Jesus . . . must *always have been* intrinsic to YHWH's identity."[67] In other words, the consequence of Jesus' obedience all the way to death can be the bestowal of the divine name (2:10) only if Jesus' has already been identified with God (2:6).

In these multiple ways, then, Phil 2:6-11 affirms a unity or oneness between God and Jesus. But does that mean Hurtado is right to see the other elements of vv. 6-11 as existing in some tension with that unity or oneness? In the next section, I examine the notes of distinction and separation between God and Jesus before going on in the following section to ask whether Hurtado's explanation of how these two elements of the text

63. C. Kavin Rowe, "Biblical Pressure and Trinitarian Hermeneutics," *Pro Ecclesia* 11 (2002): 295-312, at 303.

64. Cf. Robert Jenson's intriguing comment that the resonance between the Father and Son created by their sharing of the κύριος title "is *itself* the doctrine" of their unity or "oneness" (*Systematic Theology* [2 vols.; Oxford: Oxford University Press, 1997], 1:92, italics original).

65. C. Kavin Rowe, *Early Narrative Christology: The Lord in the Gospel of Luke* (Grand Rapids: Baker Academic, 2009), 200.

66. Barth, *The Epistle to the Philippians*, 66, astutely observes that the hymn does not come full circle, as it were, and speak of the simple *resumption* of the form of God: "No, he who became Man and was crucified, whose abasement and humiliation is not by any means washed out or canceled — it is *he* who is exalted, it is to *him* the great name is given, it is of *him*, as the Equal of God that he never ceased to be, but as the Equal of God who abased and humbled himself, that all that follows is said. . . . [P]recisely he who was abased and humbled even to the obedience of death on the cross is also the Exalted Lord" (order slightly altered).

67. Yeago, "The New Testament and the Nicene Dogma," 157. Cf. Wright, "Jesus Christ is Lord: Philippians 2.5-11," 94-95.

fit together is an adequate way of keeping the entirety of vv. 6-11 in play and not relegating some of its affirmations to the periphery.

ii. The "Subordination" of Jesus to God

Susan Grove Eastman notes that the dynamism and complexity of the entirety of the Christ-hymn is owing to its "travers[ing of] the spectrum between difference and equivalence" — the difference and equivalence between God and Jesus.[68] Having examined closely the elements of Phil 2:6-11 that stress the equivalence, I turn now to those elements that indicate the "difference" between Jesus and God. It is obvious that, while Jesus is identified with the κύριος of Isaiah 45 (as discussed above), he is also *distinguished* from the God who exalts him and gives him the name κύριος in vv. 9-11. As Barth puts it, boldly: "What is beyond question is that the κύριος Ἰησοῦς Χριστὸς is separate from and subordinate to θεὸς πατήρ."[69] This is evident not only in the grammar of vv. 6-11, as Jesus yields his role as acting subject in vv. 6-8 to God in vv. 9-11, but also in his acclamation in vv. 10-11a redounding "to the glory of God the Father" (v. 11b).

Lingering with this final affirmation of 2:11b, we may ask whether the designation of God as "Father" implies the correlate "Son." Although some interpreters set the various senses in which God is "Father" against one another in the effort to pinpoint Paul's meaning here in v. 11b, the term "Father" in Paul's wider corpus is only applicable to believers (e.g., πατὴρ ἡμῶν, Phil 1:2; 4:20) because God is first the Father of Jesus.[70] If Paul's wider usage determines his meaning here, then "God the Father" in 2:11b serves to place God face to face with the one who has been exalted — Jesus — distinguishing God from Jesus in language that simultaneously binds them both together.[71] As R. W. L. Moberly puts it:

68. Susan Grove Eastman, "Philippians 2:6-11: Incarnation as Mimetic Participation," *Journal for the Study of Paul and His Letters* 1/1 (2010): 1-22, at 6. Eastman's point is made specifically with regard to the dialectic between Jesus' being ἐν μορφῇ θεοῦ and being found σχήματι . . . ὡς ἄνθρωπος, but her point has wider application to the entirety of the passage.

69. Karl Barth, *Church Dogmatics* I/1 (Edinburgh: T&T Clark, 1936), 385.

70. This is the Pauline pattern: Believers' sonship is derivative from *Jesus'*, as Rom 8:14-17, 29 and Gal 4:4-7 make clear. If God is Father of believers, it is because adoption enables believers to share in Jesus' sonship and, in turn, Abraham's (Gal 3:7, 29).

71. C. A. Wanamaker, "Philippians 2.6-11: Son of God or Adam Christology," *NTS* 33 (1987): 179-93, at 184-85, makes this point especially clearly.

[I]n Philippians 2:9-11, the exaltation of Jesus, the bestowal of a supreme name upon him, and the confession of Jesus as Lord is directed to a perhaps surprising goal — to the glory of God the Father. It is striking because it could so easily have been otherwise. The sentence beginning in verse 9 could have ended with the confession "that Jesus Christ is Lord"; or, if extended, then extended solely "to the glory of God." Yet in fact all that is bestowed on Jesus is "to the glory of God the Father" (*eis doxan theou patros,* anarthrous). Although, the passage has not mentioned the sonship of Jesus, it relates the significance of Jesus as Lord to the worship of God as God is known in relation to Jesus, that is as Father.[72]

Jesus' exaltation by God and acclamation as "Lord" redounds to the glory of the God whose identity is specified *precisely in terms of that God's relationship to Jesus.* In other words, "[Jesus] has been raised by God to an exalted position where his identity and God's identity are inextricably intertwined."[73] Jesus is exalted by God as the one whose acclamation gives glory to God the Father, and in this way Jesus' identity as "Lord" is bound up with God's and is not explicable apart from God's. But God, in turn, is glorified as the one who is Jesus' *Father,* whose unique sovereignty is acclaimed and acknowledged precisely in his act of exalting Jesus, and in this way *God's* identity is bound up with *Jesus',* and Paul does not describe it as separable from Jesus' identity. There is an *ordering* or an *asymmetry* between God and Jesus, but one that is mutually definitive for both. To borrow a comment from Augustine, "He is not the Father if he does not have a Son; and he is not the Son if he does not have a Father" — thus the closeness and bi-directionality — "[b]ut still, the Son is God from the Father [Jesus is ἐν μορφῇ θεοῦ]; and indeed, the Father is God, but not

---

72. R. W. L. Moberly, *The Bible, Theology, and Faith: A Study of Abraham and Jesus* (Cambridge Studies in Christian Doctrine; Cambridge: Cambridge University Press, 2000), 221.

73. Moberly, *The Bible, Theology, and Faith,* 222. The same point is made in N. T. Wright, "Adam, Israel and the Messiah," in *The Climax of the Covenant: Christ and the Law in Pauline Theology* (London: T&T Clark, 1991), 18-40, at 30, with specific reference to the υἱός/θεός-language in 1 Cor 15:28, and in Seitz, "Handing Over the Name: Christian Reflection on the Divine Name YHWH," 143, who writes, "The condescension of Jesus has its counterpart in the giving over of the name. God surrenders his name and himself to his Son and his name, *that at the name of Jesus* every knee shall bow. The identification is two-way, of Jesus with YHWH and of YHWH with Jesus."

from the Son [God is not ἐν μορφῇ ʼΙησοῦ]" — and thus the distinction and asymmetry.[74]

Thus, to summarize, we have seen an admittedly somewhat artificial parsing out of two sets of affirmations, both of which are found in Phil 2:6-11. The first set of affirmations discloses the unity or oneness between God and Jesus, while the second set of affirmations distinguishes God and Jesus from one another. What remains to be done in this chapter is to offer a synthetic reading of precisely these — allegedly competing — dynamics in 2:6-11. I will proceed from here by way of dialogue with Hurtado's reading (and by implication with others who share its basic approach), aided hermeneutically by some trinitarian conceptual resources. The next section will place the trinitarian resources on the table, in preparation for the synthetic conclusion to follow in this chapter's final section.

3. "Redoublement" and Relationality in Trinitarian Theologies

The questions leading into our discussion of trinitarian conceptualities here are as follows: Do historic and contemporary accounts of "persons" and "relations" in trinitarian doctrine speak of the "persons" as constituted by their mutual relations? If they do speak in such a way, do they allow for asymmetry in those relations? And if so, what then becomes of the allegedly central trinitarian claim, that the "persons" in the Godhead are all "equal" or "one"? Does the affirmation of oneness among the persons diminish trinitarian theology's emphasis on distinction between the persons? And do the notes of distinction reach their limit with the notes of oneness, so that there is a kind of competitive relationship between these various elements?

Across the range of trinitarian theologies, both "Eastern" and "Western," theologians have regularly spoken of the need for repetition or reduplication — *redoublement*, as Ghislain Lafont has termed it[75] — in descrip-

---

74. Augustine, *Tractates on John 28-54* (trans. John W. Rettig; Washington, DC: Catholic University of America Press, 1993), Tract. 29.5.1, p. 17 (John 7:14-18), as quoted in Tanner, *Christ the Key*, 192.

75. Ghislain Lafont, *Peut-on Connaître Dieu en Jésus-Christ?* (Paris: Cerf, 1969), at 130, 160, 234. See also Gilles Emery, OP, "Essentialism or Personalism in the Treatise on God in Saint Thomas Aquinas?," *The Thomist* 64 (2000): 521-64, and Matthew Levering, *Scripture and Metaphysics: Aquinas and the Renewal of Trinitarian Theology* (Challenges in Contemporary Theology; Oxford: Blackwell, 2004), 214-16.

tions of what is one (or what is "common") and what is three (or what is "proper" to a specific divine person) in God. Lewis Ayres summarizes the Augustinian version of this feature of trinitarian discourse in this way: "If we are to do any justice to the mystery revealed in scriptural language . . . , we must describe the same ground twice over, using the language of irreducible persons and the language of a unity of essence and will."[76] The language of "persons" and the language of "essence" thus serve different functions in the construction of trinitarian doctrine. " 'Substance' and 'relation' are two aspects of, or perspectives on, God's triune being, as are 'nature' and 'person.' "[77] Or, as Gregory of Nazianzus puts it succinctly: "The Three are One from the perspective of their divinity, and the One is Three from the perspective of the properties."[78]

Each one of the divine persons may be spoken of with both sets of language. As Augustine says, "[E]very being that is called something by way of relationship is also something besides the relationship."[79] The relationship (e.g., "fatherhood") names what is distinctive, or "proper," to the particular person in view (in this case the Father), while Augustine's phrase "besides the relationship" names what is shared, or "common," between the persons in view (i.e., the Father is "God").

Statements making this point are scattered throughout the tradition of Eastern and Western trinitarian reflection. One more instance, this one from Basil of Caesarea, will be enough to illustrate its importance for my purposes:

The divinity is common, but the paternity and the filiation are properties (ἰδιώματα); and combining the two elements, the common (κοινόν) and the proper (ἴδιον), brings about in us the comprehension of the truth. Thus, when we want to speak of an *unbegotten light*, we think of the Father, and when we want to speak of a *begotten light*, we

76. Lewis Ayres, *Augustine and the Trinity* (Cambridge: Cambridge University Press, 2010), 260.

77. Kevin J. Vanhoozer, *Remythologizing Theology: Divine Action, Passion, and Authorship* (Cambridge Studies in Christian Doctrine; Cambridge: Cambridge University Press, 2010), 145.

78. Gregory of Nazianzus, *Orations* 31.9, as quoted in Gilles Emery, OP, *The Trinitarian Theology of St Thomas Aquinas* (trans. Francesca Aran Murphy; Oxford: Oxford University Press, 2007), 45.

79. Augustine, *The Trinity* (trans. Edmund Hill; Hyde Park, NY: New City Press, 1991), 219 (= *De Trinitate* 7.1.2: "omnis essentia quae relativa dicitur est enim etiam aliquid excepto relativo").

conceive the notion of the Son. As light and light, there is no opposition between them, but as begotten and unbegotten, one considers them under the aspect of their opposition (ἀντίθεσις). The properties (ἰδιωμάτα) effectively have the character of showing the alterity within the identity of substance (οὐσία). The properties are distinguished from one another by opposing themselves, . . . but they do not divide the unity of substance.[80]

In the example Basil offers, the Father is marked out as Father by being "begetter," while the Son is picked out as Son by being "begotten." The Father's identity as the unique hypostasis he is — his identity *qua* Father — is only specifiable in terms of his relation to the Son, and this relation *distinguishes* him from the Son, marking him out as the Father and not the Son. But, to borrow Kevin Vanhoozer's words, "The relations that distinguish . . . the Father from the Son and the Spirit are constitutive of the Father's distinct personal identity rather than the Father's personhood *simpliciter*."[81] So, in addition to being described as the unique person that he is, the Father may also be spoken of as identical to the divine essence — the same essence with which the Son is identical. The Father may be described in terms of what he holds in *common* with the Son, in addition to being described by what distinguishes them.

This redoubled way of speaking of the divine persons arose in response to "Arian" introduction — and subsequent repudiation — of it, as an examination of Book 5 of Augustine's *De Trinitate* indicates.[82] An Arian approach distinguishes between what is said substantially or with reference to being *(ad se)* and what is said relationally or relatively or with reference to another *(ad aliquid)*.[83] After granting that Father and Son are

---

80. Basil, *Against Eunomius* 2.28, as cited in Emery, *The Trinitarian Theology of St Thomas Aquinas,* 45. Compare Steven D. Boyer, "Articulating Order: Trinitarian Discourse in an Egalitarian Age," *Pro Ecclesia* 18/3 (2009): 255-72, at 260: "The Son eternally comes from and is eternally dependent upon the Father, yet in a manner that in no way entails the Son's being less than or inferior to the Father. To connect dependence to inferiority is in fact to accept an axiom of Neoplatonism that the fourth-century Fathers who knew Neoplatonism best went out of their way to reject. . . . And by rejecting this tenet of Platonism, the Fathers paved the way for a full-blooded Trinitarian tradition that speaks over and over not of equality *or* order, but of equality *and* order."

81. Vanhoozer, *Remythologizing Theology,* 144.

82. Augustine, *The Trinity,* 190-94 (= *De Trinitate* 5.3-8).

83. Luigi Gioia, *The Theological Epistemology of Augustine's* De Trinitate (Oxford: Oxford University Press, 2008), 150.

relative terms *(ad aliquid)* that imply one another and so denote a certain sort of unity, the key Arian move is to argue that the Father's being unbegotten *(ingenitus)* is predicated of the Father substantially *(ad se),* whereas the Son's being begotten *(genitus)* is predicated of the Son substantially *(ad se).* If that is the case, then one is forced to conclude that the Son's substance differs from the Father's, and therefore Father and Son may not be said to be consubstantial.

Augustine's response to this tack is twofold. First, he agrees with the Arians that no "accidents" (i.e., properties inessential to a being's nature) can be predicated of God. But second, he denies that what is predicated of God relationally — being Father and Son — may be thought to be predicated "in terms of modification [*accidens*], because what is signified by calling them Father and Son belongs to them eternally and unchangeably." Hence Augustine concludes, "Therefore, although being Father is different from being Son, there is no difference of substance, because they are not called these things according to substance [*secundum substantiam*] but according to relationship [*secundum relatiuum*]; and yet this relationship is not a modification, because it is not changeable."[84] With this deft move, Augustine eliminates the possibility that the relations predicated of the persons of the Godhead — paternity and filiation, in this case, which is to say, being Father and Son — allow one to distinguish between the essence of the Father and the essence of the Son. And in this way Augustine develops a method of keeping separate and yet holding together the divine *unity* with the *relationality* that obtains among the persons.[85]

The primary point of interest for my reading of Phil 2:6-11 is the way in which these two perspectives on each of the triune persons exist in a non-competitive relationship. Although they overlap in that both sets of language are used to describe the same person, they operate on distinct levels: the language of what is "proper" to each person does not indicate anything about the "essence" that that person shares with the other persons. Likewise, the language of what is "common" to each person does not contribute to itemizing what distinguishes each person from the others. To predicate a shared oneness among the persons does not, in other words, give any further insight into their relations between one another; and vice versa, to speak of three persons and their individual properties does not

---

84. Augustine, *The Trinity,* 192, translation slightly altered (= *De Trinitate* 5.6).

85. The entire discussion in Gioia, *The Theological Epistemology of Augustine's* De Trinitate, 150-52, is well worth consulting.

involve speaking about what those persons hold in common. *Redoublement* in trinitarian discourse, then, means that the language of "persons" and the language of "essence" serve different linguistic or theological functions with respect to their shared object of inquiry.[86] So — again, to take an example — that the Father is "begetter" and the Son is "begotten" in the relations predicated of the immanent trinity, and that the Father "sends" the Son and the Son is "sent" in the relations predicated of the economic trinity, does not mean that the Father and Son differ in essence from one another. Nor does the specification of these relations imply that they are the *same* in essence (although, of course, in the tradition, the persons *do* share the same essence). Rather, specifying their shared essence and naming their distinct postures or directions vis-à-vis one another are tasks of equal priority in trinitarian discourse. Although the twofoldness of the discourse does not imply two different objects of inquiry,[87] those double perspectives also do not, as it were, infringe on one another's area of responsibility: they both attempt to speak of the same reality, but their idioms are distinct.[88] There is a harmonious fit between the interlocking modes of discourse but not a direct correlation.[89]

86. By this, I intend to make a provisionally *constructive* claim solely for the purpose of exegesis of Phil 2:6-11. If I were to attempt a *descriptive* claim with respect to the historical development of Nicene trinitarian theology, then I would need to further qualify the above, since precisely how the language of persons and essence cohered was the subject of much debate among pro-Nicene theologians. For a sample of some of this debate, see Andrew Radde-Gallwitz, *Basil of Caesarea, Gregory of Nyssa, and the Transformation of Divine Simplicity* (Oxford Early Christian Studies; Oxford: Oxford University Press, 2009), 212-18, and the literature cited there, and compare Ayres's comment on Lafont's work: "I suggest that there are in fact many forms of 'redoublement' to be found in Trinitarian tradition, and that the tensions we see in the mature Augustine offer important and distinct examples from the Thomistic patterns to which those who have recently sought to appropriate Lafont have (rightly) pointed" (*Augustine and the Trinity*, 260).

87. Augustine, *The Trinity*, 230 (= *De Trinitate* 7.3.11): "[I]t is not . . . that we talk about the trinity as being three persons or substances, one being and one God, as though they were three things consisting of one material, even if whatever that material might be were wholly used up in these three; for there is nothing else, of course, of this being besides this triad. And yet we do not talk about three persons out of the same being, as though what being is were one thing and what person is another."

88. Vanhoozer, *Remythologizing Theology*, 146: "[T]he oneness (of substance) and the threeness (of persons) are equally ultimate." On this, compare Levering, *Scripture and Metaphysics*, 215: "neither [what is common nor what is proper to the divine persons] is reducible to the other."

89. This way of expressing the relationship between the linguistic registers of what

The question then becomes whether that harmony may serve as a useful hermeneutical resource for rethinking the problem of the alleged tensions found within Phil 2:6-11.

4. Mutuality and Relations in Philippians 2:6-11: A Proposal for a Non-Competitive Relationship between 2:6-11a and 2:11b

In what way do these trinitarian resources have a bearing on exegesis of Paul? None of the terms and conceptualities from the above discussion map *directly* onto Paul's vocabulary in Phil 2:6-11. In itself, this should pose no problem, since my goal is not to "find" trinitarian theology "in" Paul

is "common" among the divine persons and what is "proper" to each person leaves out — intentionally — recent developments in "social trinitarianism." In most forms of social trinitarianism, the point I am making would be obscured in that the description of the divine "essence" — or what is "one" in the divine life — is directly correlated to the unique personal properties of the "three." This is because, again in most versions of social trinitarianism, the essence is conceived as the *communion* that obtains between the three in their relations to and with one another and is thus dependent on an account of the personal relations for its account of the divine essence. Rowan Williams, *"Sapientia* and the Trinity: Reflections on the *De Trinitate,"* in B. Bruning (ed.), *Collectanea Augustiana* (vol. 1; Leuven: Leuven University Press, 1990), 317-32, at 325, for example, although not in other respects a proponent of a strongly "social" doctrine of the trinity, approaches the suggestion (by way of a reading of Augustine) that the divine essence is *constituted by* the *caritas* between the *hypostaseis*. As Bruce D. Marshall, "Trinity," in Gareth Jones (ed.), *The Blackwell Companion to Modern Theology* (Oxford: Blackwell, 2004), 183-203, at 189 notes, similar moves are observable among a range of modern interpreters: "The unity of the three [is] conceived primarily as intimate interpersonal 'communion,' rather than supposing that what makes the three one God is chiefly their common possession of (numerically) the same essence." Cf. John D. Zizioulas, *Being as Communion: Studies in Personhood and the Church* (Crestwood, NY: St. Vladimir's Seminary Press, 1985), 40. This form of social trinitarianism is not directly germane to the reading of Paul I will propose below and thus I will not engage it directly, and in any case, as Marshall's essay goes on to note, it may in fact represent a misreading of much of the trinitarian tradition, not only Augustine and the other "Western" strands but also the Cappadocians (and, indeed, more recent figures such as, e.g., Dumitru Staniloeae). Having made this qualification, however, I also wish to stress that *redoublement* may not only be observed in the traditional account of the "relations of origin" but also in more recent "historicizing" proposals that the trinitarian persons are determined in their identities from their "relations of [eschatological] fulfillment" (e.g., Jenson, *Systematic Theology,* 1:157; cf. Wolfhart Pannenberg, *Systematic Theology* [vol. 1; trans. G. W. Bromiley; Grand Rapids: Eerdmans, 1991], 308-19). Robert Jenson, for example, speaks of the constitution of the irreducible agents of Father, Son, and Spirit in the resurrection of the man Jesus without diminishing his emphasis (quoted above) on the "kyriotic unity" between Father and Son.

so much as to use the conceptual resources of trinitarian doctrine as hermeneutical aids for reading Paul afresh. I also want to stress that closely similar theologies may be expressed in a variety of dialects or vocabularies, and to say that Paul does not speak of "redoublement" and the "divine essence" and the "three persons" of the trinity, besides stating the obvious, does little to address the deeper and more interesting question of whether those trinitarian resources may actualize certain trajectories from Paul's letters that he would have expressed in a different idiom.[90] Is there, then, a version of "redoublement" in Phil 2:6-11, and, if so, how might it affect interpretation of that text if it were highlighted?

i. The Complementarity between Philippians 2:6-11a and 2:11b

The crucial question is whether the elements of the text that draw a sharp contrast between God and Jesus must be read in counterpoint to the exaltation of Jesus and his reception of the divine name. Recall Hurtado's assertion that 2:11b "reflects a concern to emphasize that Jesus' career and his subsequent exaltation . . . do not really represent a threat to the one God of biblical tradition. Jesus' exaltation, in fact, has its basis and its ultimate meaning in the glory of the one God."[91] This sets up the relationship between 2:6, 9-11a and 2:11b as one of potential conflict or competition that must be resolved by limiting one or the other of these two poles. If God and Jesus are equal, that must not be stressed so as to limit their distinctness, and, vice versa, if they are distinct, that must not be allowed to threaten their oneness. In the rest of this chapter, I hope to show how my exegesis has opened the possibility of reading the text without this competitive relationship.

My reading above insisted on Jesus' *identification* with the κύριος of Isaiah 45. Identification in the sense I gave it is not something that may exist in varying degrees. One is either identified with the κύριος — the divine name which stands for the divine *self* or being — or not. If the matter were simply one of sharing functions or approximating a sort of "ontic" equality, then speaking of Jesus' being exalted *highly* but not in the *highest* sense

90. Cf. Yeago, "The New Testament and the Nicene Dogma," on how the same theological "judgments" may be rendered in different "concepts."

91. Hurtado, "A 'Case Study' in Early Christian Devotion to Jesus: Philippians 2:6-11," 106.

possible would be, perhaps, an adequate interpretation of vv. 9-11a. But if the issue is the sharing of the name by which God's deity is named, then no such degree-oriented construal is possible. Jesus is not placed on the same level with YHWH in terms of *association* but is depicted as a participant in the unique designation and activity by which God is distinguished from all other reality.[92] "Monotheism," as Kathryn Tanner incisively expresses it, "means . . . that divinity is not a class term; divinity is not a kind of thing whose defining characteristics might be displayed by many things to greater or lesser degree."[93] That this counts as a good exegesis of vv. 9-11a is confirmed by the reading of v. 6 offered above, in which I argued that μορφὴ θεοῦ and ἴσος θεῷ do not denote similitude but rather Jesus' participation in "what was essential to being God."[94] Vv. 9-11a dovetail, in other words, with v. 6.

If that is the case, then certain interpretations of 2:11b are immediately ruled out. That Jesus' exaltation and acclamation are "to the glory of God the Father" must not be read as placing a limit on some ever-increasing "equality" whose advance must be interrupted lest it endanger God's greater glory. There is no such increase or advance in view; Jesus already shares the kind of identification with deity that cannot be quantified in terms of less or more. Therefore, we must look for another reading of the function of v. 11b.

On the one hand, the distinction between κύριος Ἰησοῦς Χριστός and θεὸς πατήρ must not be brushed aside. Bauckham flirts with such marginalization when he writes, glossing 2:11b, "Since [Jesus bears the name that names the unique divine identity] as the Son of his Father, sharing, not rivaling or usurping, his Father's sovereignty, worship of Jesus is also worship of the Father, but it is nonetheless really worship of Jesus."[95] This is accurate as far as it goes, but at his concluding assertion that Jesus is *"really"* the one who is worshiped, one wonders whether Bauckham feels the need to downplay the finality of the note on which vv. 6-11 conclude. Such an attempted minimization of v. 11b should be resisted. There really is an *ordered* relationship of *asymmetry* between these two agents in the narrative unfolding of vv. 6-11 — Jesus is placed in the

92. This point emerges with great clarity and force in Bauckham's exegesis in, e.g., *God Crucified: Monotheism and Christology in the New Testament* (Grand Rapids: Eerdmans, 1998), 51-53, 56-61.

93. Tanner, *Christ the Key*, 156.

94. Fee, *Pauline Christology*, 379.

95. Bauckham, "Paul's Christology of Divine Identity," 203.

role of reflector opposite God's role as spotlighted. God and Jesus really are *distinguished* here.

But, on the other hand, too many interpretations allow that final note to drown out the clear implications of v. 6 and vv. 10-11a. This is — and here I return to Hurtado's reading — to construe a note of "subordination" as a competitor with the notes of "oneness." The only way to construct such an interpretation of v. 11b is if an assumption has already been made, namely, that the nature of Jesus' identification with the divine κύριος is of such a kind that it might be even possible for it to "threaten" the oneness of God. But this is precisely the assumption that ought not to be made. In other words, Hurtado's interpretation has failed to grasp the point that Jesus is not being posited as more or less, to a greater or lesser degree, "on a par with God" but is instead being included in the divine identity. One may sympathize with Hurtado's rejection of attempts to blur the distinctions between God and Jesus,[96] but one may not view Jesus' distinction from God as the exalted κύριος as evincing any sort of "threat" to God's identity as "God the Father."

To state the same point positively, we could say, in language that echoes the trinitarian linguistic strategy of "redoublement," that Jesus' identification with God (2:6, 9-11a) and his glorification of God (v. 11b) operate correlatively or complementarily.[97] The statements that Jesus is in the form of God, is equal to God, and receives the divine name serve the theological function of indicating Jesus' oneness or identity with God, while the indication that the confession of Jesus as Lord is "to the glory of God the Father" serves to show that Jesus remains not only distinct from God the Father but distinct *in a particularly ordered way,* namely, as the

96. Rowe's *Early Narrative Christology* is again immensely helpful in providing fresh nomenclature for precisely this point. He suggests there that the unity between God and Christ is not a *Vermischung* — God and Jesus are never *vermischt* — but rather, the kind of relationship God and Jesus share is based on a *Verbindung:* There is a *Verbindungsidentität* of unity and differentiation (201).

97. Here, forming a kind of inclusio with the earlier collection of statements to the effect that Jesus' exaltation does not "endanger" or "threaten" God's glory as God, one could mention those statements which attempt to state the matter less in competitive terms and more in complementary ones; see, e.g., Robin Scroggs, *Christology in Paul and John* (Philadelphia: Fortress, 1988), 79 (discussing the Fourth Gospel but with implications for Pauline theology); Morna Hooker, "Philippians 2.6-11," in *From Adam to Christ: Essays on Paul* (Cambridge: Cambridge University Press, 1990), 88-100, at 97 ("Jesus is at once one with the Father, yet dependent upon him"); Capes, *Old Testament Yahweh Texts in Paul's Christology,* 182 ("Jesus is God and yet he is distinct from and subordinate to God").

Father's "Son" who *receives* from God (v. 9) because he has been obedient *to* God (v. 8). Rather than transgressing the other's territory and so causing disharmony, or rather than both operating in a zero-sum economy, these two aspects of Phil 2:6-11 are irreducible to one another, equally ultimate, and non-overlapping in their respective claims and implications.

ii. The Mutuality of Relational Identities

What does this conclusion mean for the position I have been arguing for since Chapter 2? Does Phil 2:6-11 constitute counterevidence for the claim that "God is who God is only in relation to Jesus, and conversely Jesus is who he is only in relation to God"?[98] Is Phil 2:6-11 the nail in the coffin for the view that "it is incredible that [Paul] thought of 'God apart from Christ,' just as it is that he thought of 'Christ apart from God'"?[99] As I noted above in the introduction to this chapter, many interpreters have indeed considered texts such as Phil 2:6-11 as decisive evidence *against* such a thesis. Since Jesus is so clearly shown to be in a subordinate relationship with God the Father (v. 11b), it cannot be that God's identity is determined just as much by his relationship to Jesus as Jesus' identity is determined by his relationship to God.

The exegesis and theological reflection I have offered above would suggest a two-pronged response to this objection. In the first place, we should note that the evident asymmetry of the relationship between God and Christ does not preclude their mutual dependence on one another for the particular identities they possess. Interestingly, in Hurtado's most recent work, there is a clearer acknowledgment of this point than one finds in his reading of Phil 2:6-11 discussed above. With reference to v. 11b, "the glory of 'God' and the triumph of 'God's' purposes," he notes, "are so closely linked with Jesus as to make Jesus essential to them. That is, arguably, 'God' is thereby redefined in a significant degree with reference to Jesus."[100] Jesus is exalted by God and gives glory to God the Father, so that his identity as "Lord" is intertwined with God's and not specifiable apart from God's. But God, likewise, is glorified as Jesus' *Father,* and his

98. Francis Watson, "The Triune Divine Identity: Reflections on Pauline God-language, in Disagreement with J. D. G. Dunn," *JSNT* 80 (2000): 99-124, at 111.

99. E. P. Sanders, *Paul, the Law, and the Jewish People* (Philadelphia: Fortress, 1983), 194.

100. Hurtado, *God in New Testament Theology,* 69.

identity is specified precisely in his act of exalting Jesus, so that who he is as "God the Father" requires the one naming it to specify Jesus' identity as well. It is these actions in the dramatic sequence of Phil 2:6-11 that serve to individuate *both* God and Jesus, so that even though God remains the sender and Jesus remains the exalted one (asymmetry), those very actions of sending, being sent, exalting, and being exalted are all required in order to preserve the identities of God and Jesus as disclosed here in the text.

The second response to the objection above is that certain elements of Phil 2:6-11 resist being coerced into the role the objection scripts for them. Recall what the objection says: since Jesus is exalted by God (rather than self-installed as "Lord") and since his acclamation redounds not to his own glory but to *God's*, it is therefore appropriate to maintain the theological priority of God-talk — variously parsed as "monotheism," "God's greater glory," God's sovereignty not being "endangered" — and the "subordination" of Christ as a subset or "aspect" of that more fundamental God-discourse. Because Jesus is subordinate to God, therefore God remains fundamental and Jesus is secondary (however high — and indeed unprecedented — his exaltation may be). If the identities of God and Jesus were fully "one" or "equal," then there could be no such subordination of Jesus to God. That is how the objection goes.

But to make this interpretation stick, one has to conclude that a theology of unity between God and Jesus is incompatible with their asymmetrical relations. In response to this dubious conclusion, one can make two observations. First, in vv. 6 and 9-11a, Jesus has already been fully identified with the κύριος of Isaiah 45, so there is no question of the "one God" of the LXX somehow remaining "pre-christological" and only then, later, at the moment of Jesus' humbling and exaltation, achieving a different identity in relation to Jesus than the one he bore already. Rather, the God who is κύριος is now *disclosed* as having always been differentiated: the κύριος is both "God" (i.e., "God the Father," cf. 2:11b) and Jesus,[101] and the κύριος *has been* both "God" and "the one who would become Jesus" from before

---

101. As Rowe, "Biblical Pressure and Trinitarian Hermeneutics," 303, puts it, in contrast to a list of Protestant and Catholic exegetes for whom the God of the OT is the Father *only,* "YHWH is not the Father alone." Cf. Bruce D. Marshall, *Trinity and Truth* (Cambridge Studies in Christian Doctrine; Cambridge: Cambridge University Press, 2000), 37, 36: "Christian theology from early in its history has oscillated between saying that the God of Israel is the Father and that the God of Israel is the Trinity," since if the God of Israel "is simply identical with the Father, then the Son and Spirit are not YHWH and not the God of Israel."

Jesus' appearance "in the likeness of humans."[102] And second, the asymmetrical relations that obtain between "God" and "Jesus" in Phil 2:6-11 neither diminish nor enhance the identification of both God and Jesus as κύριος. As I noted at the conclusion of the last chapter, the specifically differentiated agent designated here as "God" — traditionally referred to as "the Father" in trinitarian discourse — is who he is by virtue of this relation with Jesus ("the Son," in traditional terms). By his act of exalting Jesus and giving him the name κύριος, God defines himself as a distinct agent over against Jesus. But this differentiation and self-definition does not contribute anything toward heightening on the one hand, or qualifying on the other, Jesus and "God the Father's" identification at the level of "oneness" or "equality" (ἴσος) or "form" (μορφή). Better, I have argued, to speak of complementary affirmations that nevertheless operate on two planes. In terms of his identification with the κύριος of the LXX, Jesus is *not* differentiated from God (with whom he shares the same form and to whom he is "equal"). In terms of his relation to the *person* or *agent* θεὸς πατήρ, Jesus *is* differentiated from God and ordered in such a way that could be labeled "subordinate." Both of these affirmations are required by the theological grammar of Phil 2:6-11, and, taken together, far from undermining the thesis I have been advancing so far, serve to deepen it.

---

102. Jesus' appearance enabled one to grasp God's identity *as Father,* but because Jesus (or, to be precise, *"the person who became* Jesus Christ" [Wright, "Jesus Christ is Lord: Philippians 2.5-11," 97]) has always existed ἴσος θεῷ, God is not *constituted* as Father by Jesus' temporal acts of self-humbling and exaltation. God has always been Father of the one who would be found in the likeness of humans, but Jesus' temporal life enables one to identify God as such. On this point, see even the more "historicizing" proposal of Wolfhart Pannenberg, *Systematic Theology* (vol. 1; trans. Geoffrey W. Bromiley; Grand Rapids: Eerdmans, 1991), 264, 300.

CHAPTER FOUR

Jesus in Relation to God:
1 Corinthians 8:6 and 15:24-28

In the previous chapter we confronted an objection to my overarching thesis. I have argued that, for Paul, to speak of God and Jesus Christ is to speak of two identities constituted by their mutual relations. God is not who God is apart from his relation to Jesus, and likewise Jesus is not who he is apart from his relation to God. Or to say the same thing positively, specifying the identity of God — who God is — requires reference to the saving act achieved in Jesus Christ; and specifying the identity of Jesus — who Jesus is — requires reference to God as Jesus' originating "sender" and vindicator in the act of raising him from the dead.

But the objection is that, whatever "mutuality" may be said to obtain in God and Jesus' relations to and with one another, there remains a sense in which Jesus is *subordinate* to God, so that God retains a priority over Jesus: God is who God is *first* without Jesus and only *then* further enacts his identity in and through Jesus, whereas Jesus himself enjoys no such priority apart from God. The previous chapter attempted to address this objection by filling out the notion of an *asymmetrical mutuality* between God and Jesus and by distinguishing that relational mutuality from the *oneness* or *unity* they share. In the roles they each assume in the drama of salvation, God and Jesus are differentiated insofar as God is the one who exalts Jesus and bestows on him the divine name (Phil 2:9-11). And yet that differentiation does not prevent Jesus from determining God's particular identity as Father (2:11). God determines Jesus' identity as the exalted one (ὁ θεὸς αὐτὸν ὑπερύψωσεν) and the bearer of the name κύριος, but in a movement of reciprocity, God is thereby determined in his identity as the one who exalts Jesus and is glorified inseparably with Jesus as the one who is "Father" vis-à-vis Jesus as "Son." So the relationship remains asymmet-

111

rical but not for that reason any less *mutual*. And, at the same time, while God and Jesus are differentiated from one another in this way, they enjoy a basic oneness or unity via the κύριος name that remains God's (as the appeal to Isaiah 45 makes clear) even as it is shared with Jesus.

In this chapter I want to sharpen that answer by attending closely to two texts that are usually grouped together with Phil 2:6-11 as making closely similar assertions: 1 Cor 8:6 and 15:20-28.[1] I will discuss each of them in turn.

1. 1 Corinthians 8:6 as "Redoubled" Discourse

A number of features establish the connection between 1 Cor 8:6 and Phil 2:6-11. First, 1 Cor 8:6 distinguishes Jesus Christ as κύριος from the one to whom Jesus relates as θεὸς ὁ πατήρ, as Phil 2:11 does with the same terms. Second, 1 Cor 8:6 preserves an apparently hierarchical relation between these two, with "God the Father" being the one "from whom" (ἐξ οὗ) all things (τὰ πάντα) are said to derive and the "one Lord Jesus Christ" being the one "through whom" (δι' οὗ) they exist, just as Phil 2:9-11 makes God the acting subject who exalts Jesus *to be* "Lord," and the acclamation of Jesus as such redounds to God's glory. And third, 1 Cor 8:6 relies on a classic text of Jewish monotheism (Deut 6:4 LXX) as the medium with which to make its constructive claims, in the same manner that Phil 2:9-11 depends on Isa 45:23 LXX.[2] Taken together, these features have led many

---

1. See, e.g., the discussions in Paul A. Rainbow, "Jewish Monotheism as the Matrix for New Testament Christology: A Review Article," *NovT* 33 (1991): 78-91; Richard Bauckham, *God Crucified: Monotheism and Christology in the New Testament* (Grand Rapids: Eerdmans, 1998), 35-40, 51-53, 56-61; Richard Bauckham, "Paul's Christology of Divine Identity," in *Jesus and the God of Israel: God Crucified and Other Studies on the New Testament's Christology of Divine Identity* (Grand Rapids: Eerdmans, 2008), 182-232, at 197-218; James F. McGrath, *The Only True God: Early Christian Monotheism in Its Jewish Context* (Urbana and Chicago: University of Illinois Press, 2009), 38-54.

2. The dependence of 1 Cor 8:6 on Deut 6:4 has been most fully discussed in Erik Waaler, *The Shema and The First Commandment in First Corinthians: An Intertextual Approach to Paul's Re-reading of Deuteronomy* (WUNT 2/253; Tübingen: Mohr Siebeck, 2008), with which the earlier studies of Hofius may be compared: Otfried Hofius, " 'Einer ist Gott — Einer ist Herr': Erwägungen zu Struktur und Aussage des Bekenntnisses 1 Kor 8,6," in *Paulusstudien II.* (WUNT 143; Tübingen: Mohr Siebeck, 2002), 167-80; "Christus als Schöpfungsmittler und Erlösungsmittler: Das Bekenntnis 1 Kor 8,6 im Kontext der paulinischen Theologie," in *Paulusstudien II.*, 181-92.

interpreters to construe 1 Cor 8:6 along the same lines as they do Phil 2:6-11: the identities of Jesus and God are not mutually constitutive; rather, Jesus exists as God's instrument *through whom* God made all things, and his status as "Lord" is one traceable back to God's prior and superior status, which rules out any bilateral effort to speak of God's identity as God being constituted by and in his relation to Jesus.[3]

My response to this construal is, likewise, parallel with the exegesis of Phil 2:6-11 offered above. As I attempted to do there, I will begin here by separating the elements of 1 Cor 8:6 into two categories: those which highlight oneness between God and Jesus and those which necessitate distinction.

The key structural terms of 1 Cor 8:6 — εἷς, θεός, and κύριος — are all present in the LXX of Deut 6:4 which reads: Ἄκουε, Ἰσραηλ· κύριος ὁ θεὸς ἡμῶν κύριος εἷς ἐστιν.[4] What sets Paul's interpretation apart, however, is its apportioning these terms, all of which denote the same agent in their LXX context, to two different agents — God, designated as ὁ πατήρ, and Ἰησοῦς Χριστός. This interpretive move has been described by some as the "addition"[5] of Jesus as κύριος to the affirmation of "one God," so that a unilateral movement from Jesus back to God is preserved: "God" is the one God of Israel, *and* now also, alongside him, there is Jesus as the exalted agent through whom he acts. This reading can point to the use of καί connecting the two main clauses of 1 Cor 8:6, as well as the non-overlapping roles assumed by God and Jesus that are indicated by the differing prepositions governing their actions (ἐκ and διά respectively). But what this reading does not account for satisfactorily is that the designation given to Jesus — κύριος — is taken from Deut 6:4 itself, not imported into it. As Bauckham writes, "Paul is not adding to the one God of the *Shemaʿ* a

---

3. E.g., Jochen Flebbe, *Solus Deus: Untersuchungen zur Rede von Gott im Brief des Paulus an die Römer* (BZNW 158; Berlin: Walter de Gruyter, 2008), 270, who speaks of "einer klaren, programmatischen Überordnung von Gott über Christus" illustrated in 1 Cor 8:6 and 15:28; cf. Larry W. Hurtado, *One God, One Lord: Early Christian Devotion and Ancient Jewish Monotheism,* 2d. ed. (Edinburgh: T&T Clark, 1998), 98; Adelbert Denaux, "Theology and Christology in 1 Cor 8,4-6: A Contextual-Redactional Reading," in R. Bieringer (ed.), *The Corinthian Correspondence* (BETL; Leuven: Leuven University Press, 1996), 593-606, at 602.

4. These lexical links warrant specific reference to Deut 6:4 as opposed to the more generic claim that Paul's language here is "Jewish" in its affirmation of εἷς θεός to which Paul then adds reference to Jesus as κύριος (so Hans Conzelmann, *1 Corinthians* [trans. James W. Leitch; Hermeneia; Philadelphia: Fortress, 1975], 144).

5. McGrath, *The Only True God,* 40.

'Lord' the *Shema'* does not mention. He is identifying Jesus as the 'Lord' whom the *Shema'* affirms to be one."[6] In other words, Paul is making an interpretive gloss.[7] To pick out the God to whom Deut 6:4 is referring, he says in effect, requires one to mention both "God the Father" and "Jesus Christ"; where Deut 6:4 affirms, "The Lord our God is one," we are to understand "the Lord our God" as inclusive of both "God the Father" and the "Lord Jesus Christ."[8]

Two observations confirm this interpretation. The first is that in addition to Deut 6:4, Paul draws on another monotheistic formula and splits it apart it in a similar way, assigning half of it to "God the Father" and half to the "Lord Jesus Christ." Prior to its Pauline modification, the formula likely would have resembled Rom 11:36a: ἐξ αὐτοῦ καὶ δι᾽ αὐτοῦ καὶ εἰς αὐτὸν τὰ πάντα.[9] In its original form, the object of all the prepositions would have been the same figure, namely, God. But in Paul's adaptation of it, two of the prepositions — ἐκ and εἰς — continue to take "God," now specified as ὁ πατήρ, for their object, while the third of the prepositions — διά — now

6. Bauckham, *God Crucified,* 38, together with his whole discussion of this point (35-40); cf. N. T. Wright, "Monotheism, Christology and Ethics: 1 Corinthians 8," in *The Climax of the Covenant: Christ and the Law in Pauline Theology* (London: T&T Clark, 1991), 120-36, at 128-30; and Hofius, "'Einer ist Gott — Einer ist Herr'," 179: "Das zweigliedrige Bekenntnis sagt mithin *nicht:* Es gibt den *einen* und *einzigen* Gott, von dem das Sch[e]ma' spricht; und neben und unter ihm gibt es noch eine Art δεύτερος θεός, nämlich den κύριος Ἰησοῦς Χριστός. Vielmehr gilt: Der 'Vater' Jesu Christi und der 'Sohn' dieses Vaters *sind* der εἷς θεός, neben dem es keinen anderen Gott gibt" (italics original).

7. Hofius, "'Einer ist Gott — Einer ist Herr'," 180. Cf. David Lincicum, *Paul and the Early Jewish Encounter with Deuteronomy* (WUNT 2/284; Tübingen: Mohr Siebeck, 2010), 142: "This interpretation or refinement is not, according to Paul, the invention of a *novum,* but rather a deepened grasp of the *res* to which the text itself testifies."

8. Traugott Holtz, "Theo-logie und Christologie bei Paulus," in E. Reinmuth and C. Wolff (eds.), *Geschichte und Theologie des Urchristentums: Gesammelte Aufsätze* (WUNT 57; Tübingen: Mohr Siebeck, 1991), 189-204, at 191. This phenomenon has been described by Rowe as "kyriotic overlap" and "kyriotic identity" (C. Kavin Rowe, "Luke and the Trinity: An Essay in Ecclesial Biblical Theology," *SJT* 56/1 [2003]: 1-26, at 19, 22, 25): the κύριος-title/name becomes the medium for Paul's articulating the unity between God and Jesus.

9. Conzelmann, *1 Corinthians,* 144 n. 44 notes the similarity with Rom 11:36, as do Wilhelm Thüsing, *Per Christum in Deum* (Münster: Aschendorff, 1965), 229; Anthony C. Thiselton, *The First Epistle to the Corinthians* (NIGTC; Grand Rapids: Eerdmans, 2000), 636-38. Bauckham, *God Crucified,* 39, observes the parallel with Rom 11:36 and argues for its Jewish background (cf. Josephus, *B.J.* 5.218; Philo, *Cher.* 127). See Gregory E. Sterling, "Prepositional Metaphysics in Jewish Wisdom Speculation and Early Christian Liturgical Texts," *The Studia Philonica Annual* 9 (1997): 219-38, at 235-36 for a nuanced discussion of how Stoic and Middle Platonic conceptualities are here intermingled and modified.

takes the "one Lord Jesus Christ" for its object. In the same way that Paul apportioned the affirmations of Deut 6:4 to both God and Jesus, he now does the same with the affirmations of a similarly well-known monotheistic formula, with the result that God and Jesus are bound together not only by sharing the divine name (κύριος) but by sharing the role as originator as well as concluder of all things. What previously served to demarcate God's uniqueness — that all of creation is from, through, and for him[10] — now functions in 1 Cor 8:6 to emphasize the uniqueness of God *and* Jesus together in contradistinction from the "many gods" and "many lords" of vv. 4 and 5.

This leads to the second confirmation of the present interpretation. The adversative ἀλλά that begins 8:6 places the affirmation that there is εἷς θεός and εἷς κύριος in opposition to the θεοὶ πολλοί and the κύριοι πολλοί of v. 5. Whatever the Corinthians might be inclined to regard (or whatever they may have heard others regard) as divine, in reality there is only *one* true God and one true Lord. This reference to "one" God and "one" Lord is, however, an expansion of the affirmation already made in v. 4: οὐδεὶς θεὸς εἰ μὴ εἷς. There the contrast is not, as in vv. 5-6, simply between gods and lords whose deity may be an object of doubt and the only true God, but is, more sweepingly, a contrast between an idol which is "nothing" (οὐδὲν εἴδωλον) and the God besides whom there is no other. Therefore when Paul comes to fill out the content of that εἷς in v. 6 and includes Jesus within its ambit,[11] the implication is that Jesus is thereby being placed on the side of divinity in a contrast involving what it means to be God over against a vacuous idol or a so-called "god" or "lord." As Erik Waaler puts the matter, "The strongest argument for unity between the Father and the Lord Jesus is found in Paul's use of the 'no God but one' [v. 4] phrase in close association with the 'one Lord' phrase."[12]

None of this, however, should be taken as warrant for blurring the

---

10. It is unnecessary to set creation/protology against soteriology here as, e.g., Neil Richardson, *Paul's Language about God* (Sheffield: Sheffield Academic Press, 1994), 297-98, misleadingly argues. See P. H. Langkammer, "Literarische und theologische Einzelstücke in 1 Kor VIII:6," *NTS* 17 (1970-71): 193-97, at 197; Gordon D. Fee, *Pauline Christology: An Exegetical-Theological Study* (Peabody, MA: Hendrickson, 2007), 91 n. 16.

11. Carl Judson Davis, *The Name and Way of the Lord: Old Testament Themes, New Testament Christology* (JSNTSup 129; Sheffield: Sheffield Academic Press, 1996), 147: "The argument shifts, without support or explanation, from the 'one' in v. 4 to 'one God and one Lord' of v. 6."

12. Waaler, *The* Shema *and The First Commandment in First Corinthians,* 435.

distinction Paul maintains between God and Jesus. The "one Lord Jesus Christ" is not absorbed into the divine identity in such a way that he ceases to remain recognizably distinct from God. Paul's usage elsewhere suggests that he would probably not apply κύριος to God the Father here, even though in its Deut 6:4 context — Paul's source text for this affirmation — it is simply one pole of a twofold designation for one who is both κύριος and ὁ θεός (that is, God in Deut 6:4 is "the Lord our God"). Rather, in keeping with Philippians 2 (and elsewhere), *Jesus* is now the bearer of the κύριος name, and Jesus is the mediating agent (δι' οὖ) of a creation that finds its initiation in God. Jesus, in other words, is not *interchangeable* with God either in role or identity: he is the Lord, the one involved in the divine work of creation and salvation as its instrument, while God is his[13] Father, the one who gives creation its impetus (ἐξ οὖ) and who serves as its (and salvation's) *telos* (εἰς αὐτόν). In line with the temporal sequence of 1 Cor 15:24-28 (on which see further below), the thought here may be that the Lord Jesus is the historical implementer of God's eschatological sovereignty over all things; on this interpretation, Jesus may be best taken not simply as a timeless instrumental agent of creation and salvation but, more specifically, the mediator *in time* of God's pre-scripted fatherly rule. Alongside his fundamental unity with God, therefore, an irreducible *distinction* between Jesus and God remains.

Faced with this problematic tension, interpreters regularly opt for one of two incompatible resolutions. On the one hand, some commentators attempt to downplay the unity or reinterpret it in a "weaker" direction so as to mitigate Jesus' identification with "God the Father." James McGrath, as we have already mentioned, goes this route, claiming, "Paul uses [the Deuteronomic] language of 'one God' and adds to it a reference to 'one Lord.'"[14] Rejecting Dunn's metaphor of the *Shema* being "split," McGrath continues:

> To clarify further that by appending something additional to the Shema one need not "split" it nor be understood to be incorporating the additional person or thing mentioned into the divine identity, we may note an example of similar language from the Hebrew Bible:

13. As with πατήρ in Phil 2:11 and despite the lack of a corresponding υἱός here in 1 Cor 8:6 as there, I take "God the Father" to find its primary counterpart in Jesus rather than in creation; so Langkammer, "Literarische und theologische Einzelstücke in 1 Kor VIII:6," 194; Hofius, "'Einer ist Gott — Einer ist Herr'," 179.

14. McGrath, *The Only True God*, 41.

2 Samuel 7:22-24. There we find a contrast made between Yahweh and other gods in a manner not wholly unlike 1 Corinthians 8:6. In it, the affirmation that God is one ("There is no God but you") is coupled with the affirmation that there is likewise "one nation that God went out to redeem as a people for himself." I doubt whether anyone has ever suggested that in this passage the people of Israel are being included within the Shema.[15]

This interpretation neglects the fact that "one Lord" is not something brought *to* Deut 6:4, as an additional "one" alongside the "one" God. Rather, κύριος is the divine name in apposition to ὁ θεός in Deut 6:4 itself. The "one nation" of 2 Sam 7:23 presented as a parallel to the εἷς κύριος of 1 Cor 8:6 is, in the end, a red herring; κύριος is the name of the "one God," a name that picks out the same being as θεός does in Deut 6:4, and that name is now applied to Ἰησοῦς Χριστός. Jesus is thereby *identified* with God as the co-bearer of the divine name.[16]

On the other hand, however, a different set of interpreters could be read as downplaying or deemphasizing the notes of distinction that feature so prominently in this passage. Some comments from Bauckham furnish a good example:

> The purpose of what is said about Jesus Christ in 1 Corinthians 8:6 is not primarily to designate him the "mediator" (a not strictly appropriate term in this context, but frequently used) of God's creative work or of God's salvific work, but rather to include Jesus in the unique identity of the one God. Jesus is included in God's absolutely unique relationship to all things as their Creator. The purpose of the whole verse, in its context, is strictly monotheistic. Its point is to distinguish

15. McGrath, *The Only True God,* 42.

16. Richardson, *Paul's Language about God,* 300, comments, "Clearly, no simple identification of Christ with God is being made," and Wolfgang Schrage, *Die Erste Briefe an die Korinther (1 Kor. 6,12–11,16)* (EKKNT VII/2; Solothurn and Düsseldorf: Benziger; Neukirchen-Vluyn: Neukirchener, 1995), 243, makes a similar statement: "Die enge Zuordnung bedeutet keine Identität." Much depends on how one defines "simple" and "identification"/"Identität" in these claims, as we have already explored above with respect to Phil 2:6-11. If Richardson and Schrage mean that there is no blurring of the distinction between God and Jesus, then my exegesis confirms their conclusions. But if they mean that there is no *identification* or *unification* at the level of the shared name and joint participation in the work of creation/salvation, then my exegesis indicates the need for subtler, more sophisticated categories that might enable finer distinctions than the ones they are using.

the God to whom Christians owe exclusive allegiance from the many gods and many lords served by pagans. Just as in all Second Temple Jewish monotheistic assertions of this kind, what is said about God is said as a means of *identifying God as unique*. What is said about Jesus Christ only serves this purpose if it *includes Jesus in the unique identity of God*. Paul apportions the words of the Shemaʿ between Jesus and God in order to include Jesus in the unique identity of the one God YHWH confessed in the Shemaʿ. Similarly, he apportions between Jesus and God the threefold description of God's unique identifying relationship as Creator to all things, in order to include Jesus in the unique identity of the one Creator.[17]

At one level, these comments are attentive to the larger context of the Corinthian situation (8:4-5), and they emphasize conclusions we have already reached in our exegesis. But when Bauckham sets up an antithetical relationship between the elements of unity and differentiation in 8:6 — what the text says is *not* meant to distinguish Jesus from God by making him the mediator *but* to include him in the divine identity — clarity has been purchased by sacrificing the *duality* of the text's elements. The desire to pinpoint one overarching "purpose" of 1 Cor 8:6, while it makes sense of the rhetorical force of the text in relation to vv. 4 and 5, is nonetheless overly precise. It minimizes the modifications Paul has made to Deut 6:4, primarily the designation of God as ὁ πατήρ with its corresponding implication that Jesus is his υἱός but also in the apportioning the mediatorial δι' οὗ and δι' αὐτοῦ to him and reserving the generative and ultimate roles for God (ἐξ οὗ and εἰς αὐτόν).[18] Bauckham simply asserts that calling Jesus a "mediator" is "not strictly [an] appropriate term in this context," but he fails to explain why. Were we to adopt not only Bauckham's positive reading of the import of Paul's use of the Shema here but also Bauckham's disavowals of any notions of distinction and sequence, then we would be left with few resources to escape the charge of "modalism" — God is

17. Bauckham, "Paul's Christology of Divine Identity," 216-17.

18. Hans-Christian Kammler, "Die Prädikation Jesu Christi als 'Gott' und die paulinische Christologie: Erwägungen zur Exegese von Röm 9,5b," *ZNW* 95/3-4 (2003): 164-80, at 174-75 states concisely the point of unity-in-distinction underscored by the prepositions: "Die unterschiedlichen präpositionalen Wendungen — ἐξ οὗ and εἰς αὐτὸν beim Vater, δι' οὗ and δι' αὐτοῦ beim Sohn — heben dementsprechend nicht auf eine *ontologische* Differenz zwischen Vater und Sohn ab, sondern sie markieren — im Sinne einer *inner-göttlichen* Unterscheidung — die *Unumkehrbarkeit* der 'Beziehung von Vater und Sohn'" (italics original).

simply an undifferentiated whole who sometimes appears as "Father," sometimes as "Jesus."

It might seem, then, that we are faced with two options. We can either affirm unity between God and Jesus in such a strong, exclusive way that we are no longer able to make sense of their distinction. Otherwise, we can affirm their distinction to such a degree that we are unable to do justice to the robust affirmations of their unity or even "identity." But the trinitarian conceptuality of *redoublement* we have discussed above provides a hermeneutical vantage point from which to reject the choice between these two interpretive options as a false one. As we have seen, classic (both "Eastern" and "Western") trinitarian formulations regularly emphasized the need to speak of God "twice over,"[19] describing the three "persons" or *hypostases* as irreducibly distinct and at the same time describing the three as one in essence or will or power. Neither of these "redoubled" modes of description was taken to be more basic than the other; neither was logically prior and so viewed as delimiting the other. Rather, both operated in concert, as descriptions of the same reality from two vantage points. Thus, in the present discussion of 1 Cor 8:6, this trinitarian conceptuality may serve a twofold function: on the one hand, it enables us to reject the attempt to allow the distinction between "God the Father" (v. 6a) and "Jesus Christ" as κύριος (v. 6c) to mitigate or qualify the identification between God and Jesus at the level of their joint sharing of what is predicated of the one God in Deut 6:4. Only if one is already committed to a particular construal of how *differentiation* between God and Jesus rules out their both being "named" by the predicates contained in Deut 6:4 will one feel compelled to play the *identification* of God and Jesus with one another off against their obvious *distinction* from one another. In the absence of that particular construal of the implications of differentiation, one can affirm distinction and not thereby underplay identification. On the other hand, and conversely, the trinitarian conceptuality of "redoublement" may equally enable one to reject the notion that *identification* between God and Jesus in terms of Jesus' "inclusion" in the affirmations of Deut 6:4 necessarily means downplaying his clearly mediatorial role as κύριος "through whom" all things came to be in distinction from God as (his) "Father." On the contrary, one can take the distinction of Jesus from God and the mediatorial instrumentality of Jesus with full seriousness without thereby qualifying in any way the identification of Jesus with God by means of the *Shema*. To specify Jesus

---

19. Lewis Ayres, *Augustine and the Trinity* (Cambridge: Cambridge University Press, 2010), 260.

Christ as κύριος and as the agent of God the Father's creative initiative (ἐξ οὗ) does not lessen or remove his full sharing of the divine identity acclaimed in Deut 6:4. Rather, in a non-competitive and mutually complementary way, affirming God the Father and Jesus together *as* the "one God" of Deut 6:4 and affirming their irreducible distinction from one another as unique agents or "persons" is to do justice to both of those elements as present in 1 Cor 8:6.[20]

2. 1 Corinthians 15:20-28 and Mutual, Asymmetrical "Subjection"

One final text appears to stand in significant tension with my argument, namely, that God's identity is constituted by his relation to Jesus, and, vice versa, Jesus' identity is constituted by his relation to God. In 1 Cor 15:20-28, Paul presents "Christ" as submitting himself (αὐτὸς ὁ υἱὸς ὑποταγήσεται) to God, "the one who put all things in subjection to him" (ὁ ὑποτάσσων αὐτῷ τὰ πάντα). This submission, according to C. A. Wanamaker, "demonstrates quite clearly that Paul did not believe in Christ's absolute equality with God."[21] Richard B. Hays makes the same point against the backdrop of later Christian reflection:

20. Several older commentators make this point in a way I have been unable to find repeated in more recent studies. E.g., F. Godet, *Commentary on St. Paul's First Epistle to the Corinthians*, 2 vols. (trans. A. Cusin; Edinburgh: T&T Clark, 1886-87), 1:418; 2:370: "the personal distinction between God and Christ is strongly emphasized, though the community of nature between both appears from this very distinction"; "in the notion of Son there are united the two relations of subordination and homogeneity. The living monotheism of Paul, John, and the other apostles was not less rigorous than ours, and yet it found no contradiction between these two affirmations. . . . Subordination was therefore, according to [Paul], in harmony with the essential relation of the Son to the Father, in His *Divine* and *human* existence." Compare also Barth's categorical conclusion — "What is beyond question is that the κύριος Ἰησοῦς Χριστὸς is separate from and subordinate to θεὸς πατήρ" — with his equally strong affirmation of the *homoousios* doctrine: for him 1 Cor 8:6 means "that the Son of God, too, has a share in the work which is ascribed in the first article of the creed to God the Father, the work of creation. Thus understood, it is an indirect but all the more expressive confirmation of the ὁμοούσιος and therewith of all the preceding phrases. If the Son has a share in what was called the special work of the Father, if He works with the Father in the work of creation, then this means, at least in the sense of Athanasius and the theology which finally triumphed in the 4th century, that He is of one essence with Him. In order that all things might be made by Him, in order that He might be the Mediator of creation, He Himself had to be God by nature" (Karl Barth, *Church Dogmatics* I/1 [Edinburgh: T&T Clark, 1936], 385, 442).

21. C. A. Wanamaker, "Philippians 2.6-11: Son of God or Adam Christology," *NTS* 33 (1987): 187-88.

It is impossible to avoid the impression that Paul is operating with what would later come to be called a subordinationist christology. The doctrine of the Trinity was not yet formulated in Paul's day, and his reasoning is based solely on the scriptural texts themselves, read in light of his Jewish monotheistic convictions and his simultaneous conviction that Jesus is proclaimed as "Lord" by virtue of his resurrection.[22]

Negatively, then, Jesus is not equal to God here. Positively, the argument appears to be that Paul begins from "Jewish monotheistic convictions" and must integrate Jesus' acclamation as κύριος with those convictions in some way. In order to achieve such integration, Paul positions Christ in a "subordinate" place beneath the one God of Israel. Or, to return to Wanamaker's reading, "This text clearly refers to Christ's Lordship which is then limited by his participation in a sonship relation with God who is spoken of as Father in vs. 24."[23] Dunn explains the logic of this interpretation a bit more fully when he speaks of "God shar[ing] his kingly rule with Christ who in the end 'hands over the kingdom of *God* to the Father' (15.24)."[24]

> Whereas the lordship of Christ is unqualified in relation to other "lords many" (1 Cor. 8.5-6), his lordship in relation to God as Creator is qualified. This presumably helps explain why Paul's fullest statement of Christ's lordship (1 Cor. 15.24-28) climaxes in the Lord subjecting himself to the one God of all (v. 28).[25]

The upshot of this line of interpretation is that Christ is a kind of divine representative or agent, "a divine plenipotentiary holding absolute sway for a limited period."[26] After the close of that period, God becomes "all things to all people" (15:28; cf. Eph 1:23; Col 3:11) — "God in His sover-

---

22. Richard B. Hays, *First Corinthians* (Interpretation; Louisville: Westminster/John Knox, 1997), 266. Hays has indicated to me in personal conversation that he would not say things the same way now. For Raymond Brown, *An Introduction to New Testament Christology* (New York: Paulist Press, 1994), 194, n. 289, the only passage in the NT that causes significant difficulty for a fully trinitarian theology is 1 Cor 15:24. "This text needs more study in the light of Nicene christology," he concludes laconically.

23. Wanamaker, "Philippians 2.6-11," 192 n. 30.

24. J. D. G. Dunn, *Theology of Paul the Apostle,* 249 n. 74.

25. Dunn, *Theology of Paul the Apostle* (Grand Rapids: Eerdmans, 1998), 248-49.

26. David M. Hay, *Glory at the Right Hand: Psalm 110 in Early Christianity* (SBLMS 18; Nashville: Abingdon, 1973), 61.

eignty will constitute the new universe for human beings, not death and the other powers."[27]

What these statements preclude is *mutuality* between God and Jesus in the constitution of their fundamental identities. God as "Father" (15:24), God who will be all in all (v. 28), is the one whose identity underwrites and enables an affirmation of Jesus' lordship, but Jesus' identity as Christ and Son (v. 28) does not likewise determine the identity of God.[28] Strands of Paul's thought that seem to point in a different direction are frequently understood to be in tension with the "subordinationist" strands. So, for instance, Udo Schnelle remarks, "On the one hand, there is clear tendency toward subordination in Pauline Christology," evidenced in 1 Cor 3:23; 11:3; and 15:28 (cf. Phil 2:11). But then Schnelle adds: "At the same time, the Pauline formulations can be seen as the beginnings of thinking of God and Christ as equals."[29] No attempt is made to press for a deeper coherence; the dialectic is left standing, and the reader must puzzle over whether Paul was deliberately inconsistent or just unaware of the latent potential of his own constructions that would ultimately be realized in contradictory ways in the fourth-century trinitarian debates and beyond.

Yet if my readings of Phil 2:5-11 and 1 Cor 8:1-6 above are along the right lines, then the so-called elements indicating "subordination" and those indicating "oneness" are not meant to be played off one another, as in a zero-sum game whereby some elements must take priority and diminish the others. The question in relation to this text, however, is whether both elements are indeed present and how they may be said to cohere, since this is a text that on first reading appears to contain *only* subordination.

There is, however, reason to think that even here Paul explicates the divine identity as inclusive of both God (15:28) and Christ (v. 3 and *passim;*

27. Martinus C. de Boer, *The Defeat of Death: Apocalyptic Eschatology in 1 Corinthians 15 and Romans 5* (JSNTSup 22; Sheffield: JSOT, 1988), 126.

28. Wanamaker's comments on 1 Cor 8:6 could be read equally as his interpretation of the use of πατήρ for God in 15:24: "It appears as though the term 'Father' is used of God in order to spell out the relationship between the one God and the one Lord thereby insuring the subordination of Christ to God" ("Philippians 2.6-11," 192 n. 30).

29. Udo Schnelle, *Apostle Paul: His Life and Theology* (trans. M. Eugene Boring; Grand Rapids: Baker Academic, 2005), 395, 396. Compare Douglas A. Campbell's perspective that Paul has not allowed his "primitive trinitarianism" — inherently narrative and "egalitarian" — to eclipse the "subordinationist" strands of his thinking. Campbell attributes this failure of Paul to the situational, contingent character of the texts in question (1 Cor 3:23; 11:3; 15:28) (*The Quest for Paul's Gospel: A Suggested Strategy* [London: T&T Clark, 2005], 119 n. 26).

cf. ὁ υἱός, v. 28) and, hence, that this text discloses *both* the distinguishing of God and Jesus *and* their fundamental identity. My defense of that claim will proceed in three steps. First, I will argue that the allusion to Ps 110:1b in 15:25b is not simply a borrowing of scriptural language but a metalepsis that invites what the literary critic John Hollander calls "the recovery of the transumed material."[30] Second, I will argue that Christ is the subject of the verb "place" (τιθέναι) in the Ps 110:1b allusion in 15:25b. Finally, I will suggest that those two factors indicate an overlap of identity between Christ and God when read together with the "Father" (πατήρ) and "Son" (υἱός) titles in 15:24 and 28.

I turn first to the allusion to Ps 110:1b (109:1b LXX). The original scriptural text reads: "The Lord said to my lord, 'Sit at my right hand, until I put your enemies under your feet'" (Εἶπεν ὁ κύριος τῷ κυρίῳ μου Κάθου ἐκ δεξιῶν μου, ἕως ἂν θῶ τοὺς ἐχθρούς σου ὑποπόδιον τῶν ποδῶν σου). Paul has drawn selectively from the text without a citation formula and has introduced his own modifications: "For it is necessary for him to reign until he has placed all [his] enemies under his feet" (δεῖ γὰρ αὐτὸν βασιλεύειν ἄχρι οὗ θῇ πάντας τοὺς ἐχθροὺς ὑπὸ τοὺς πόδας αὐτοῦ, 15:25). At least two factors suggest that this fragmentary scriptural language is most aptly described as *allusive* or *resonant* rather than simply a Pauline creation that echoes early Christian traditional usage without regard for its scriptural context.[31] First, it is intertwined with Ps 8:7b. The "all" (πάντας) and "under his feet" (ὑπὸ τοὺς πόδας αὐτοῦ) are best explained as having their origin in that text, as 15:27 confirms. (The quotation of Ps 8:6b [LXX 7b] in 15:27 is introduced with a γάρ and is clearly intended as a citation, as the subsequent ὅταν δὲ εἴπῃ ὅτι makes obvious.) Ps 8:6b is here, then, brought in alongside the allusion to Ps 110:1b.[32] This pairing suggests a kind

---

30. John Hollander, *The Figure of Echo: A Mode of Allusion in Milton and After* (Berkeley: University of California Press, 1981), 115, as quoted in Richard B. Hays, *Echoes of Scripture in the Letters of Paul* (New Haven: Yale University Press, 1989), 20.

31. J. Lambrecht, "Paul's Christological Use of Scripture in 1 Cor. 15.20-28," *NTS* 28 (1982): 502-27, at 508-9, is misleading in framing the choice as one between a "proof text" and Paul's use of a "scripture verse — its vocabulary and concepts — to express his own ideas." Later, however, he rightly eschews this false alternative in favor of what Hollander would call *metalepsis*: "Free use, and deliberate, subtle allusion are here better terms than strict quotation" (509). Paul may be alluding to Ps 110:1b without citing the text.

32. The adjective πάντας derives from Ps 8:6, as Hay, *Glory at the Right Hand: Psalm 110 in Early Christianity*, 36-37 observes: "The word 'all' *(panta)* occurs in Ps 8:7 [LXX] and in 1 Cor 15:27, and the apostle's interpolation of it into his allusion to Ps 110:1 in 15:25 seems grounded on the supposition that the two psalm texts interpret one another. The word 'all'

of echo chamber of scriptural resonance, indicating that Paul is explicitly interpreting Scripture. Although these two texts were likely already being read as mutually interpreting prior to Paul's usage,[33] the fact that both remain detectable in Paul's artful paraphrase suggests that Paul has not lost sight of their scriptural origin, regardless of whether his Corinthian hearers themselves would have been able to pick up the wider LXX context.[34]

In addition to these considerations, there is a second reason for seeing a scriptural allusion here — namely, the introduction of 15:25 with "for it is necessary" (δεῖ γάρ). Elsewhere in Paul γάρ may function to point to the scriptural underpinnings of a Pauline affirmation (e.g., Rom 10:13; 1 Cor 2:16; 10:26)[35] without an accompanying γέγραπται (as in, e.g., Rom 12:19; 1 Cor 3:19; 9:9; Gal 4:22, 27), and it likely functions the same way here.[36] Some interpreters have explained the δεῖ as pointing to God's apocalyptic plan. In this account, the necessity of Christ's reign is explained from the necessity of death's defeat in light of Christ's resurrection.[37] Yet,

---

has great significance in Paul's argument, occurring no fewer than eleven times in 15:20-28. Here, then, he freely modifies Ps 110:1, but evidently justifies his freedom on the basis of a second scriptural text."

33. Their pairing elsewhere in the NT suggests a pre-formed, pre-Pauline tradition (Matt 22:44; Mark 12:36; Eph 1:20-23; Heb 1:13 and 2:6-9, with 1:14–2:5 intervening; 1 Pet 3:22). See Richard B. Hays, "Christ Prays the Psalms: Israel's Psalter as Matrix of Early Christology," in *The Conversion of the Imagination: Paul as Interpreter of Israel's Scripture* (Grand Rapids: Eerdmans, 2005), 101-18, at 109; Martinus C. de Boer, "Paul's Use of a Resurrection Tradition in 1 Cor 15,20-28," in *The Corinthian Correspondence* (ed. R. Bieringer; BETL; Leuven: Leuven University Press, 1996), 639-51, at 641-44.

34. Despite his considerably looser criteria for discerning an allusion compared to those of Christopher D. Stanley's study (see n. 36 below), Dieter-Alex Koch, *Die Schrift als Zeuge des Evangeliums: Untersuchungen zur Verwendung und zum Verständnis der Schrift bei Paulus* (BHT 69; Tübingen: Mohr Siebeck, 1986), 19-20, does not think the subtle references to Ps 110:1b warrant consideration as an allusion; cf. his overlook of 1 Cor 15:25-27 in "Beobachtungen zum christologischen Schriftgebrauch in den vorpaulinischen Gemeinden," *ZNW* 71 (1980): 174-91. De Boer, *The Defeat of Death*, 116-18, takes ὅταν δὲ εἴπῃ ὅτι as warrant for assuming the Corinthians' familiarity with Ps 110:1b and 8:6b, though perhaps not from the LXX.

35. Note the mention of Adam introduced with a γάρ in 15:21-22 and, of course, 15:27, already mentioned.

36. So Archibald Robertson and Alfred Plummer, *A Critical and Exegetical Commentary on the First Epistle of St. Paul to the Corinthians* (ICC; Edinburgh: T&T Clark, 1914), 356; Fee, *Pauline Christology,* 110. Pace Christopher D. Stanley, *Paul and the Language of Scripture: Citation Technique in the Pauline Epistles and Contemporary Literature* (SNTSMS 74; Cambridge: Cambridge University Press, 1992), 206-7.

37. Gordon D. Fee, *The First Epistle to the Corinthians* (NICNT; Grand Rapids: Eerd-

as Conzelmann has rightly argued,[38] any notion of apocalyptic necessity must not be played off against an understanding of specifically *scriptural* foreordination, as 15:3-4 already indicates. It is precisely *in Scripture* that the "divine purposes"[39] are disclosed (cf. κατὰ τὰς γραφὰς, v. 3), not least that of the overthrow of death (vv. 54-55), and it is for that reason that Christ must (δεῖ) reign.[40] These factors, taken together, make it likely that Paul intends a reference to Ps 110:1b in 15:25.

Turning from the source text to Paul's creative appropriation of it, we may ask who the subject of the actions described in 15:24-28 is. Significantly for our purposes, Paul has altered the first person singular θῶ in Ps 110:1b LXX to the third person θῇ in 15:25. This change introduces a subtle ambiguity. In the Psalm, God — or ὁ κύριος — is the subject who places the enemies of the psalmist's lord (also κύριος) under that lord's feet. Most interpreters have thought, despite the syntactical shift, that Paul keeps "God" as the subject in 1 Cor 15:25: "God" or "the Lord" remains the one who places the enemies of the psalmist's addressee — now Christ — under his feet.[41] But grammatically, Paul's adaptation of τιθέναι allows for either "God" or "Christ" to be the subject. Some interpreters have argued on theological grounds that the subject must be God. Tashio Aono, for example, maintains that Pauline theology uniformly attributes the destruction of God's enemies to God alone.[42] Taking this objection

mans, 1987), 755 n. 45; Richard Horsley, *1 Corinthians* (ANTC; Nashville: Abingdon, 1998), 205; Thiselton, *The First Epistle to the Corinthians*, 1233.

38. Conzelmann, *1 Corinthians*, 272.

39. Fee, *The First Epistle to the Corinthians*, 755 n. 45.

40. So James Moffatt, *The First Epistle of Paul to the Corinthians* (London: Hodder and Stoughton, 1938), 249; Fee, *Pauline Christology*, 110 (representing a shift from his earlier view?). On this, compare the remarks on predestination as determined for Paul by scriptural foreordination in Francis Watson, *Paul, Judaism, and the Gentiles: Beyond the New Perspective* (rev. ed.; Grand Rapids: Eerdmans, 2007), 323.

41. So F. W. Maier, "Ps 110,1 (LXX 109,1) in Zusammenhang von 1 Kor 15,24-26," *BZ* 20 (1932): 139-56; C. K. Barrett, *A Commentary on the First Epistle to the Corinthians* (2nd ed.; London: Black, 1971 [1968]), 358; Tashio Aono, *Die Entwicklung des paulinischen Gerichtsgedankens bei den Apostolischen Vätern* (Europäische Hochschulschriften XXIII/137; Bern/Frankfurt/Las Vegas: P. Lang, 1979), 26-28; U. Heil, "Theologische Interpretation von 1 Kor 15,23-28," *ZNW* 84 (1993): 27-35; C. Wolff, *Der erste Brief des Paulus an die Korinther* (THKNT 7; Leipzig: Evangelische Verlagsanstalt, 1996), 387-68; de Boer, *The Defeat of Death*, 117; Martin Hengel, "'Sit at My Right Hand!'," *Studies in Early Christology* (Edinburgh: T&T Clark, 1995), 119-225, at 165.

42. Aono, *Die Entwicklung des paulinischen Gerichtsgedankens bei den Apostolischen Vätern*, 26-28.

with full seriousness provides an entryway into the theological point I wish to argue.

Aono is correct to observe that the reign of God (βασιλεία, 15:24; βασιλεύειν, 15:25) is one of the standard means available to Paul to delineate the Creator-creature distinction.[43] The sovereignty of God over his enemies and over "all things" (πάντα, 15:27) distinguishes the one God from all else, as we have already seen in the exegesis of 1 Cor 8:6 above.[44] Furthermore, the texts in question — Ps 110:1b together with Ps 8:6b — depict the power of *God* to subject enemies and all things under the feet of whom he chooses, whether a messianic figure in Ps 110:1b or a representative human in Ps 8:6b. Read in their LXX context, the two psalms leave no doubt that although the human actors exercise sovereignty, they do so at the behest of the one God.[45] One might expect, then, that Paul's reading would emphasize Christ's reception of his sovereignty from God, as Paul does eventually affirm in 15:27-28. Yet there are grammatical as well as wider literary reasons to think that in vv. 24-25, before the picture is sharpened in vv. 27-28, Christ is not only the representative Messiah or Adamic ruler but also the one who exercises the role originally designated for God in Ps 110:1b. In addition to taking the unusual step of attributing Ps 110:1b to the Messiah's reign,[46] Paul now seems to have taken the additional, unprecedented step of attributing the cause of that reign to Christ himself.

What are the reasons for opting for this christological shift from the psalm's original subject? First, it is difficult to maintain that the subjects of the verbs "hand over" (παραδιδόναι) and "destroy" (καταργεῖν) are dif-

---

43. Jewish texts that emphasize the divine sovereignty (without necessarily employing the βασιλεία word group) as indicative of the divine uniqueness include: Dan 4:34-35; Bel 5; 3 Macc. 6:2; Sir 18:1-3; *Sib Or* 3.10, 19; Frag 1.7, 15, 17, 35; *2 Enoch* 33.7; *2 Bar* 54:13; Josephus, *Ant* 1.155-56. The only undisputed allusion to Ps 110:1b in extant literature is *Testament of Job* 33:3.

44. Jewish texts that employ πάντα to demarcate the sphere of the one God's sovereignty include: Isa 44:24; Jer 10:16; 51:19; Sir 43:33; Wis 9:6; 12:13; Add Est 13:9; 2 Macc 1:24; 3 Macc 2:3; *1 Enoch* 9.5; 84.3; *2 Enoch* 66.4; *Jub* 12.19; *Apoc Abr* 7.10; *Jos Asen* 12.1; *Sib Or* 3.20; 8.376; Frag 1.17; Josephus, *BJ* 5.218; 1QapGen 20.13; 4QD^b 18.5.9.

45. For discussion of these two texts in their OT and Jewish contexts, see N. T. Wright, "Adam, Israel and the Messiah," in *The Climax of the Covenant* (London: T&T Clark, 1991), 21-29; cf. Wright, *The Resurrection of the Son of God* (Christian Origins and the Question of God 3; Minneapolis: Fortress, 2003), 334-35.

46. Bauckham, *God Crucified,* 30-31 notes the lack of Jewish interest in Ps 110:1b as a messianic predication, though of course it was widespread in early Christianity, probably predating Paul.

ferent.[47] Given the syntactic parallelism,[48] it is far more likely that Christ is the subject of both actions. Second, grammar again lends weight to the supposition that Christ remains the subject of τιθέναι in 15:25, since there has been no new nominal reference inserted. "Had Paul intended 'God' at this point, it is almost demanded grammatically that he would have inserted a ὁ θεός."[49] Third, that v. 25 begins with δεῖ γάρ suggests — as we have already noted — that v. 25 grounds the affirmation of Christ's reign in v. 24 with scriptural undergirding.

Many commentators who see Christ as the subject of τιθέναι in 15:25 mention at this point as further evidence for their construal that Paul is not citing Ps 110:1b as such but only loosely paraphrasing it.[50] That periphrastic usage is then thought to strengthen the understanding that Christ is the subject, since Paul no longer has to worry about aligning his use of the psalm with the psalm's original subject, God. I have already argued above, however, that Paul is intentionally evoking Ps 110:1b and intends its resonances to reverberate here. If that is the case, and if Paul does take Christ as the subject of the psalm's verbal action, then Christ here assumes the role attributed to God in the original psalm. In other words, Paul is saying by way of the literary trope of metalepsis, "Jesus Christ is here doing what the psalm tells us God will do." As Larry Kreitzer explains: "It thus appears that Paul has reworked [Ps 110:1b] in order to serve his christological interest. We see quite clearly that an Old Testament function of God described in Ps. 110.1 (the subjugation of Israel's enemies) becomes the activity of Christ in 1 Cor. 15.25."[51]

47. The difficulty is indicated by appeals to incomplete redaction of traditional material; e.g., Ulrich Luz, *Das Geschichtsverständnis des Paulus* (Beiträge zur evangelischen Theologie 49; Munich: Kaiser, 1968), 343. Compare Fee, *The First Epistle to the Corinthians,* 754 n. 40: "nothing prepares the reader for such a radical shift in subjects."

48. The second ὅταν clause names an action prior to that named in the first, as the parallelism with 15:28 indicates; so Fee, *The First Epistle to the Corinthians,* 752.

49. Fee, *The First Epistle to the Corinthians,* 756 n. 50.

50. E.g., Lambrecht, "Paul's Christological Use of Scripture in 1 Cor. 15.20-28," 509; Thiselton, *The First Epistle to the Corinthians,* 1234.

51. Larry J. Kreitzer, *Jesus and God in Paul's Eschatology* (Sheffield: JSOT, 1987), 150. Cf. Fee, *Pauline Christology,* 111: "the 'citation' of Ps 110:1 in v. 25 is yet another place where, for Paul, Christ has assumed the role that God plays in the psalm itself. By changing from the first person, where Yahweh is speaking, to the third person, to conform to Paul's use of the psalm, he thus has attributed to Christ the role of 'putting the enemies under his (own) feet'"; Moffatt, *The First Epistle of Paul to the Corinthians,* 249: "In loosely quoting the hundred and tenth psalm he had seemed to make Christ do what God had promised to do for him." This conclusion finds support from Phil 3:20-21 in which Christ is the agent of resurrection (ὃς μετασχηματίσει τό σῶμα τῆς ταπεινώσεως ἡμῶν) and the one who is able

Having argued for an intended evocation of Ps 110:1b and having shown Christ's identification with God in the evocation, I turn now to one further reason for understanding the divine identity in this passage as inclusive of God (15:28) and Christ (v. 23): the commensurate designation of God as "Father" (v. 24) and Christ as "Son" (v. 28). The full designation of God in v. 24 is ὁ θεὸς καὶ πατήρ. Despite its popularity, "God the Father" is not the best English rendering of this phrase, unless, as Thiselton notes, the καί is taken as copulative or ascensive ("God, even the Father," as the KJV has it).[52] Weiss suggests that the definite article has the force of a demonstrative pronoun while the καί functions as a relative: so, in English, "that one, the one who is God and Father."[53] He also argues, in line with my discussion of the import of πατήρ in Phil 2:11, that πατήρ here takes as its reference point the sonship of Jesus. Weiss points to 2 Cor 1:3 (ὁ θεὸς καὶ πατὴρ τοῦ κυρίου ἡμῶν Ἰησοῦ Χριστοῦ) to strengthen this claim, but the primary evidence for this construal comes from the loosely chiastic structure of 1 Cor 15:24-28 itself:

A   When (ὅταν) Christ hands over the kingdom to the one who is God and Father (v. 24a),

    B   then Christ will have destroyed every rule, etc. (v. 24b).

        C   Christ must reign until all (πάντας) his enemies are placed under his feet (ὑπὸ τοὺς πόδας αὐτοῦ) (v. 25; Ps 110:1b).

            D   The last such enemy is death itself (v. 26).[54]

        C′   God subjected all things (πάντα) under Christ's feet (ὑπὸ τοὺς πόδας αὐτοῦ) (v. 27a; Ps 8:6b).[55]

---

to subject all things to himself (κατὰ τὴν ἐνέργειαν τοῦ δύνασθαι αὐτὸν καὶ ὑποτάξαι αὐτῷ τὰ πάντα). There is an allusion there in Phil 3 to Ps 8:6b, as in 1 Cor 15:27, in which Christ again performs actions reserved for God, both in resurrection — elsewhere in Paul the prerogative of God (Rom 4:24-25; 6:4 [cf. v. 9]; 8:11; 10:9; 1 Cor 6:14; 15:15 [2x], 38; 2 Cor 1:9; 4:14; 5:1; Gal 1:1; Eph 1:20; Col 2:12; 1 Thess 1:10) — and in subjecting τὰ πάντα (again, note the link with 1 Cor 8:6).

52. Thiselton, *The First Epistle to the Corinthians*, 1231.

53. J. Weiss, *Der erste Korintherbrief* (rev. ed.; Göttingen: Vandenhoeck & Ruprecht, 1910 [rpt. 1977]), 358-59.

54. Cf. de Boer, *The Defeat of Death*, 120: "Both formally and contextually, v. 26 represents the central claim of Paul's argument in vv. 23-28 — though when all is said and done it is subordinated (!) to the affirmation that God will be all in all."

55. Here I follow Kreitzer, *Jesus and God in Paul's Eschatology*, 149-54 and Fee, *Pauline Christology*, 112-13, against Lambrecht, "Paul's Christological Use of Scripture in 1 Cor. 15.20-

B′   After (ὅταν . . . τότε) Christ has had all things subjected to
him (by God) (v. 28a),

A′   then the Son will subject himself to God, so that God might be
all in all (v. 28b).[56]

The moment of Christ's handing over the kingdom to the one who is
God and Father in v. 24 is further described in v. 28; the Son's subordination to the one who subordinated all things to him (v. 28) does not
explicate a separate moment but is instead the expanded description of
the surrender of the kingdom already mentioned (v. 24). If that is the
case, then the description of God as ὁ θεὸς καὶ πατήρ and of Christ as ὁ
υἱός, despite the interval of three verses, belong together. The sonship
of Christ has as its explanatory counterpart the fatherhood of God. This
means that the identity of Christ in v. 28, although ordered asymmetrically with God's identity, is inseparable from that of God as his Father.
In N. T. Wright's fine summary, this motif of fatherhood and sonship is
"a way of predicating a relationship which, though differentiated, allows
Jesus to be seen *within,* and not outside, the Pauline picture of the One
God."[57] The Son is not who he is as the one who subjects himself[58] to
the Father without the Father. But conversely, the God who will be "all
in all" (v. 28) is the same one who is "God and Father" (v. 24). In that
way, God's eschatologically ultimate identity is inseparable from that
of Christ as his Son; God is, in a real way, *determined* as the God who
is all in all by the Son's glorification of him as such. The titles "Father"
and "Son" thus serve a dual, complementary purpose: to bind God and
Christ together in a relationship of mutuality whereby each of their distinct identities is inextricable from the other's, but also to distinguish

---

28," 510, in seeing a *Subjektwechsel* in 15:27 from Christ (15:25) to God. This seems demanded
by the fact that the subject of the passive ὑποτέτακται in 15:27b — itself an interpretation
(ὅταν δὲ εἴπῃ) of 15:27a — is clearly ὁ ὑποτάξας in the immediately following 15:27c, i.e.,
God. A minor difficulty with this reading, however, is that it requires αὐτοῦ to be reflexive
in 15:25 but not in 15:27a.

56. Since observing this structure independently, I have encountered a nearly identical structural analysis in Charles E. Hill, "Paul's Understanding of Christ's Kingdom in
1 Corinthians 15:20-28," *NovT* 30 (1988): 297-320, at 300.

57. Wright, "Adam, Israel and the Messiah," 30.

58. On ὑποταγήσεται as in the middle rather than the passive voice, see W. Larry
Richards, "ὑποταγήσεται in 1 Corinthians 15:28b," *Andrews University Seminary Studies* 38/2
(2000): 203-6.

them as irreducibly particular actors or agents on the eschatological stage.[59]

One further observation may strengthen my interpretation of an intertwining of unity and mutuality together with irreducible distinction here. In 15:27b, Paul offers an interpretive gloss on his citation of Ps 8:6b. When the psalm speaks of God subjecting all things under Christ's feet, "it is plain that this does not include the one who put all things in subjection under him" (δῆλον ὅτι ἐκτὸς τοῦ ὑποτάξαντος αὐτῷ τὰ πάντα). Commentators appear unsure what sense to give this phrase, other than to conjecture that it might reflect a Corinthian tendency to see Christ as having become "God" in a way that forces the one who subjects all things to him to abdicate his position of sovereignty.[60] Does Paul know he has approached a daring, potentially destabilizing conclusion? If so, perhaps Paul offers this corrective with the awareness that he has given his hearers room to picture God as having so totally surrendered his sovereignty to Christ that God himself is now in some way subordinate to Christ.[61] On this reading, Paul skates to the edge of that affirmation, only to back away at

---

59. Following Jürgen Moltmann, Miroslav Volf, *Exclusion and Embrace: A Theological Exploration of Identity, Otherness, and Reconciliation* (Nashville: Abingdon, 1996), 180, distinguishes between the "constitution" of the persons (which is asymmetrical) and the "life" of the persons (which is fully mutual). His comments on the Fourth Gospel (e.g., "The Father is first and the source of the [other persons]. But at the level of the unfolding of their relations, the Father gives all to the Son and glorifies the Son [John 13:1ff; 17:1]") are applicable, *mutatis mutandis*, to 1 Cor 15: God makes Jesus to be the eschatological sovereign, and Jesus, in turn, makes God the Father to be "all in all."

60. Barrett, *First Epistle to the Corinthians,* 359-60; David E. Garland, *1 Corinthians* (BECNT; Grand Rapids: Baker, 2003), 713, though both admit that there is no evidence for this conjecture. Godet, *First Epistle to the Corinthians,* 2:365-66, reads it only as rhetorical preparation for 15:28b. Thiselton, *The First Epistle to the Corinthians,* 1236, treats it with one cryptic sentence, and Fee, *Pauline Christology,* 113-14, overlooks it entirely.

61. For an interesting development of this tendency in the history of doctrine, one could compare the emphasis in Hans Urs von Balthasar, *Mysterium Paschale* (trans. Aidan Nichols; Edinburgh: T&T Clark, 1990), viii, on the Father's "self-giving" to and for the Son in the Spirit: "We shall never know how to express the abyss-like depths of the Father's self-giving, that Father who, in an eternal 'super-Kenosis', makes himself 'destitute' of all that he is and can be so as to bring forth a consubstantial divinity, the Son. Everything that can be thought and imagined where God is concerned is, in advance, included and transcended in this self-destitution which constitutes the person of the Father, and, at the same time, those of the Son and the Spirit." For discussion of this element of Balthasar's theology, see Edward T. Oakes, *Pattern of Redemption: The Theology of Hans Urs von Balthasar* (New York: Continuum, 2005 [1994]), 286-89.

the last minute and reaffirm the temporal limits of God's having entrusted his sovereignty to Christ. Although it may appear as if the mutuality between God and Christ is totally symmetrical, Paul says in effect, there do nonetheless remain eschatologically distinct roles for God and Christ. This conclusion might be strengthened if we observe the way this almost-total mutual self-giving appears in a letter designed to undermine factionalism and encourage unity.[62] What Paul *almost* affirms here — namely, a two-way submission of God to Christ and Christ to God — is anticipated in the earlier parts of the letter where hierarchical ordering subtly qualified or reinterpreted in a direction of mutuality.[63] Here in 15:28, in a kind of mirror image of that tendency, Paul resolves an apparently fully symmetrical relationship with a reemphasis on asymmetry — yet one that, for all that, does not abandon its bilateral character.

And here we return, finally, to the trinitarian conceptuality of "redoublement" as our hermeneutical aid. Many interpreters conclude that, whatever may be the import of Christ's exalted state in 15:24-25, by the time we arrive at v. 28, he has been decisively subordinated to God in such a way that a divine identity and sovereignty separate from Christ's is preserved. To quote C. A. Wanamaker again, 15:28 "demonstrates quite clearly that Paul did not believe in Christ's absolute equality with God."[64] Similarly, Kreitzer speculates that "this final theocentric affirmation may arise precisely because the christocentric content of the previous verses impinged upon the ontological territory of God so much that the note of subordination of Christ to God was thought to be necessary as a conclud-

---

62. Thus, Margaret M. Mitchell, *Paul and the Rhetoric of Reconciliation: An Exegetical Investigation of the Language and Composition of 1 Corinthians* (HUTh 28; Tübingen: Mohr Siebeck, 1992), 289 points to John Chrysostom's interpretation of 1 Cor 15:28 as a demonstration of the ὁμόνοια between God and Christ. Cf. Wayne A. Meeks, "The Temporary Reign of the Son: 1 Cor 15:23-28," in Tord Fornberg and David Hellholm (eds.), *Texts and Contexts: Biblical Texts in Their Textual and Situational Contexts* (Oslo: Scandinavian University Press, 1995), 801-11, who points to the lexical and thematic linkage of 15:2 and 15:58 as evidence of a rhetorical purpose of ensuring the harmonious effectiveness of the church (cf. 1:10).

63. That Χριστὸς . . . θεοῦ in 3:23 is intended to undermine one-upmanship and to ensure harmony is indicated by its relation to 3:21, just as 11:3 (κεφαλὴ δὲ τοῦ Χριστοῦ ὁ θεός), linked in immediate proximity to the affirmation that κεφαλὴ δὲ γυναικὸς ὁ ἀνήρ, is thereafter deprived of being the final word by the strongly egalitarian statements in 11:11-12, which are in turn deepened and not overturned by the surrounding instructions about head coverings (11:2-16). For exegesis along these lines, see Francis Watson, "The Authority of the Veil: A Theological Reading of 1 Cor 11.2-16," *NTS* 46 (2000): 520-36.

64. Wanamaker, "Philippians 2.6-11: Son of God or Adam Christology," 187-88.

ing remark."[65] These are telling statements, since in the terms of my argument in this chapter, these evaluations take two complementary aspects of 1 Cor 15:24-28 and construe them as competitive with one another. For Wanamaker and Kreitzer, the distinction between God and Christ in v. 28, whereby the Son subjects himself to God's final sovereignty, mitigates the *unity* or *identification* between God and Christ. More of one thing (distinction, subordination) means less of the other (oneness, unity). Yet this judgment mistakes the subordination of the Son to God in 15:28 as a point of conflict with Christ's sharing of God's unique prerogative of sovereignty in vv. 24-25 — a supposition that is not required by the text once we have learned to question the assumption of a necessary link between *distinction* and *disunity*. Although Christ assumes a different role after death has been defeated, this serves to distinguish him from the one who is "God and Father," not to qualify or draw back from the affirmation that the power he exerts in vv. 24-25 is identical with that of God. Rather, these two aspects of the text — his inclusion in the unique divine identity (vv. 24-25) and his irreducible difference from the one called "Father" — are non-overlapping, non-competitive, complementary aspects. They neither infringe on one another nor detract from one another.

Again, attending to the "Father"-"Son" language may help to underscore the point. The one who is "God and Father" (15:24) is not the one who comes to be designated "Son" (v. 28). Nor is there any doubt that the Son is the one who subordinates himself to God, and not vice versa. And yet the Son remains *the Son* in his subordination to the Father.[66] To conclude, in other words, from the Son's irreducible distinction from the Father that his inextricable identity *with* the Father is somehow mitigated or diminished is to confuse affirmations that belong on parallel rather than intersecting planes. The Son is still the Son when God is all in all, which means that the Father is still the Father when he at last enjoys full eschatological sovereignty. God and Christ remain basic to one another's identities, and so a "redoubled" form of speech is necessary to receive

---

65. Kreitzer, *Jesus and God in Paul's Eschatology,* 159.

66. Herman Ridderbos, *Paul: An Outline of His Theology* (trans. J. R. DeWitt; Grand Rapids: Eerdmans, 1975), 69: 1 Cor 15:28 "cannot mean the end of Sonship." Cf. Jürgen Moltmann, *The Trinity and the Kingdom* (trans. Margaret Kohl; Minneapolis: Fortress, 1993), 92: "The lordship of Christ, the risen One, as well as the kingdom of the One who is to come, is in an eschatological sense *provisional*. It is only completed when the universal kingdom is transferred to the Father by the Son. With this transfer the lordship of the Son ends. But it means the consummation of his sonship. . . . [T]he name of the Son remains to all eternity."

the theological pressure of 1 Cor 15:24-28. Explicating this text requires reference both to what unites God and Christ on the sovereign side of the Sovereign-ruled (or Creator-creature) divide as well as to what distinguishes God and Christ in terms of their personal uniqueness. Far from being a liability, as we have seen, trinitarian conceptualities enable recognition of both those aspects of the text and may serve as hermeneutical lenses for the interpretation of this text.

3. Conclusion

This chapter began as a continuation of the argument advanced in the previous chapter: God and Jesus are *identified* with one another at the level of the shared divine name κύριος and yet they are also irreducibly distinguished from one another in that God is πατήρ and Jesus Christ is the raised, exalted one (ὁ θεὸς αὐτὸν ὑπερύψωσεν, Phil 2:9). That twofold aspect of Phil 2:5-11, I suggested, invites two corresponding theological affirmations. First, the identification of God and Jesus and their distinction from one another are not in competition with one another, as if deeper or higher identification (but what would it mean for "identification" to be measured by degrees?) could take away from irreducible distinction or, conversely, as if absolute distinction could minimize identification. And second, such a "redoubled" discourse makes possible an understanding of what might be called *asymmetrical mutuality* between God and Jesus, whereby God is not who God is as "father" without Jesus and Jesus is not who he is as the raised and exalted one without God. This relationship is *mutual* in that the identities of God and Jesus are inseparably bound up with one another's. And yet it is asymmetrical insofar as God is determined in his relation to Jesus specifically as "father" (or "sender," "the one who raised . . .," etc.) while Jesus is determined in his relation to God specifically as the one who was "sent," "raised," and so on.[67]

This pattern or grammar of God- and Christ-discourse is confirmed when one turns to 1 Cor 8:6 and 15:20-28. Explicating the identity of the

---

67. Cf. the useful discussion of this dynamic in Peter J. Leithart, *Athanasius* (Foundations of Theological Exegesis and Christian Spirituality; Grand Rapids: Baker Academic, 2011), 87-88: "Dependence thus goes both ways, but the dependence is not symmetrical or identical. At least we can say that the Son depends 'filially' on the Father, and the Father 'paternally' on the Son. . . . The Father does not depend on the Son as one begetting him but depends on the Son for his status as Father."

divine Lord of the OT (Deut 6:4) requires reference to both "God" and "Christ"; or to say it the other way around, both God and Christ are identified at the level of the divine name and the unique divine prerogatives of creation (protology), salvation (1 Cor 8:6), and the subjugation of all things (15:24-28; eschatology). Correspondingly, Christ remains the one *through* whom God creates and the one who exercises sovereignty that has an eschatological terminus, after which point he surrenders that sovereignty back to God. There is, thus, an *identity* between God and Christ *and* an irreducible *distinction.* Such a pattern is obviously asymmetrical but not for that reason any less mutual: God is the one who is constituted as eschatological sovereign by "the Son," and Jesus is the one who is determined in his identity as "Son" by his relation to God as "Father." To speak of this grammatical pattern as an instance of "subordinationism" or "low" — or "high" — christology overlooks these subtle dynamics of asymmetrical mutuality. Finer conceptual tools are needed to do justice to these texts, and I have argued in the previous two chapters that trinitarian theologies provide better resources for this interpretive task than the categories of "christology," abstracted from a matrix of mutuality, have hitherto been able to do.

CHAPTER FIVE

The Spirit in Relation to God and Jesus

When it comes to the task of "picking out of the crowd" the God whom Paul preaches, I have argued, in the words of Robert Jenson, that "God the Father and Christ and the Spirit all demand dramatically coordinating mention."[1] To name the one is to name the three, since their identities mutually implicate one another's. But in the previous two chapters, I made a crucial qualification to that affirmation. The identities of God, Jesus, and the Spirit are mutually constituted by one another — but they are so implicated in an *asymmetrical* fashion. God is "the God and Father of our Lord Jesus Christ": who he is as God the Father is only specifiable by speaking of Jesus as his "Son." Insofar as God is the "Father" who "sends" and "raises" the Son, his identity is constituted *by* that relation to the Son. But precisely for that reason, the mutuality here is not entirely symmetrical: God is not "sent" or "fathered" by Jesus, and Jesus' identity, while it is constituted in relation to God as his Father, is, by the same token, constitutive for *God's* identity (as I argued in Chapter 2) insofar as he is God's *Son* without whom God is not "God the Father." Thus, I have argued for the full interdependence of "God the Father" and "Jesus Christ" on one another for the distinct identities of each but *not* their *interchangeability*. Put more succinctly: mutuality, yes; symmetry, no.

It might be objected at this point that no serious student of Paul has ever argued for perfect symmetry, as though God and Jesus were ciphers or placeholders whose roles in Paul's gospel could be traded without serious structural reconfiguration of Paul's theology. That is certainly true, and,

---

1. Robert W. Jenson, *Systematic Theology* (2 vols.; Oxford: Oxford University Press, 1997), 1:92.

PAUL AND THE TRINITY

as any reader of Paul's interpreters already knows, the catalog of options for interpreting Paul's God-talk and christology is rather the reverse. Very few Pauline scholars, it would appear, affirm the thesis that Paul's God- and Christ-discourses might exist in a relationship of mutuality. So in Chapters 1 and 2 I argued for such mutuality — that God's identity is not preformed from Paul's Jewish past, taken over wholesale into his "Christian" preaching, and then modified in light of the "addition" of christology to it as something to be fit in (rather uncomfortably?) alongside it. But in the course of making that argument, I had to show how my case could accommodate, and even *require,* a robust affirmation of asymmetrical relations between God and Jesus.

Turning to the Spirit, we find that this way of accounting for mutuality and asymmetry in the relations between God and Jesus provides the template for how to understand the Spirit's relation with both of them as well.[2] It will be the argument of this chapter that the Spirit is the Spirit *of* God and *of* Christ and that just so, concomitantly rather than competitively, the identities of God and Jesus are inseparable from the identity and activity of the Spirit. In short, I will be arguing for what C. Kavin Rowe has called "the relational determination of the Spirit's identity"[3] — the Spirit is who "he" is only by virtue of his relations to God and Jesus.[4] I will also be continuing my argument for the relational determination of God and Jesus'

2. On this strategy, compare the account in Lewis Ayres, *Nicaea and Its Legacy* (New York: Oxford University Press, 2004), 212, of how much of the fourth-century patristic specification of the Spirit's relation to "Father" and "Son" was dependent on prior theological accounts of the relation between Father and Son; see, e.g., Athanasius, *Ep. Serap.* 1.2, 14, 25; 2:11. This is not true, however, for all "pro-Nicene" pneumatologies, as Christopher A. Beeley, *Gregory of Nazianzus on the Trinity and the Knowledge of God: In Your Light We Shall See Light* (Oxford Studies in Historical Theology; New York: Oxford University Press, 2008), 281, argues: "The most pronounced difference [between Athanasius and Gregory] is that Gregory does not argue for the Spirit's divinity in connection with that of the Son."

3. C. Kavin Rowe, "The Trinity in the Letters of St. Paul and Hebrews," in Gilles Emery, O.P., and Matthew Levering (eds.), *The Oxford Handbook of the Trinity* (Oxford Handbooks in Religion and Theology; New York: Oxford University Press, 2011), 41-54, at 50.

4. The masculine pronoun, while it courts the charge of attributing more "personalism" to Paul's view of the Spirit than many scholarly treatments are inclined to do, seems closer to the mark than using "it"; cf. Volker Rabens, *The Holy Spirit and Ethics in Paul* (WUNT 2/283; Tübingen: Mohr Siebeck, 2010), 145 n. 77. On the theological problems with use of a feminine pronoun, having to do with an introduction of gender differentiation into the Godhead and thereby obscuring the analogical character of *both* masculine *and* feminine pronouns for God, see Francis Watson, *Agape, Eros, Gender: Towards a Pauline Sexual Ethic* (Cambridge: Cambridge University Press, 2004), 210.

respective identities, here with reference to the Spirit. The Spirit, most likely a "hypostatic" or "personal" reality for Paul, derives "his" character from God and Jesus;[5] and, by the same token, God and Jesus are disclosed in their self-identification by — and not apart from — the activity of the Spirit.

The chapter will proceed in two stages. First, I will argue that the Spirit conveys the presence and activity of the risen κύριος within the Pauline communities, which means that the Spirit's identity is specifically God- and Christ-determined. Here the focus will be on 1 Cor 12:3 and Gal 4:4-6 as representative texts, but the most important of the so-called "identification" texts — 2 Cor 3:17 — will also be examined briefly and the "identity thesis" will be rejected in favor of a version of the "hermeneutical" position (on the definition of which see below).[6] The Spirit, for Paul, is "picked out of the crowd" — named and determined as the unique agent he is — by means of reference to God and Jesus. Second, I will argue that

5. The brief discussion of the issue of the Spirit's "personalism" in Volker Rabens, "The Development of Pauline Pneumatology: A Response to F. W. Horn," *BZ* 43 (1999): 161-79, at 177 is judicious. Rabens observes that already in 1 Cor (and probably already in 1 Thess 5:19 as well), Paul is attributing a range of "personal traits" to the Spirit (e.g., 2:10-13; 3:16; 6:11; 12:11), which is in some tension with the developmental account in Friedrich W. Horn, *Das Angeld des Geistes: Studien zur paulinischen Pneumatologie* (Göttingen: Vandenhoeck & Ruprecht, 1992) in which it is only in Romans that Paul begins to conceive of the Spirit "hypostatically." These "personal traits" are similar to those elsewhere attributed to God and Jesus (note, e.g., the parallel construction in 1 Cor 12:4-6; cf. Rom 8:15-16 with 8:34; 2 Cor 3:6), but this similarity is maintained alongside differentiation between the three (1 Cor 2:10; 2 Cor 13:13). Cf. also the methodological comments in Rabens, *The Holy Spirit and Ethics in Paul,* 144-45, and the literature cited there. For the purposes of my thesis, it is important to emphasize that the "relational determination of the Spirit's identity" for which I will be arguing, although it is more compatible with Rabens's account of the Spirit's "personal" ontology, could perhaps still be maintained if one were to adopt the view of the Spirit as a "substance" as in, e.g., Troels Engberg-Pedersen, *Cosmology and Self in the Apostle Paul: The Material Spirit* (Oxford: Oxford University Press, 2011). Horn, *Das Angeld des Geistes,* 60, for instance, thinks Rom 5:5 shows the Spirit as both "hypostasis" and "Stoff." For a more robust defense of the Spirit's fully personal character, see Gordon D. Fee, *God's Empowering Presence: The Holy Spirit in the Letters of Paul* (Peabody, Mass.: Hendrickson, 1994), 830-31.

6. Famously, several "identification" texts have served as the basis for a fusion of the identities of the Spirit and the risen κύριος in, e.g., Hermann Gunkel, *Die Wirkungen des heiligen Geistes nach der populären Anschauung der apostolischen Zeit und der Lehre des Apostels Paulus* (Göttingen: Vandenhoeck & Ruprecht, 1909 [1888]); ET: *The Influence of the Holy Spirit: The Popular View of the Apostolic Age and the Teaching of the Apostle Paul* (Philadelphia: Fortress, 1979). For an extensive recent discussion also supporting a modified "identification" thesis ("eine funktionale Identität"), see Horn, *Das Angeld des Geistes.*

the divine self-identification in Jesus occurs through the agency of the Spirit, so that God's and Jesus' identities — who they are in the economy of redemption — are not specifiable without the Spirit. Here I will argue for a view that remains a minority report in New Testament scholarship, namely, that Jesus' sonship — and just so the fatherhood of God — is constituted in and through the Spirit's role in raising Jesus (and believers) from the dead (Rom 1:3-4; 8:9-11).

1. The Theologically- and Christologically-Determined Identity of the Spirit

In what way, then, is the Spirit's identity determined by his relations to God and Jesus?

i. "The Relational Determination of the Spirit's Identity"

In 1 Cor 12:3 we encounter a clear instance in which specifying the identity of the Spirit depends on an ability to grasp the Spirit's relation to God and Christ. Paul begins this new section of 1 Corinthians in 12:1 with a veiled criticism of the Corinthians' lack of understanding of the role τὰ πνευματικά ought to play in the life of the community: they are "ignorant" (οὐ θέλω ὑμᾶς ἀγνοεῖν) insofar as they conceive of the Spirit as enabling behaviors and postures that, Paul will argue, are out of step with the Spirit's true character.

Paul's response to the Corinthians' ignorance is double-edged. In the first place, he provides a negative criterion for assessing true Spirit-wrought activity from false: "No one speaking by the Spirit of God says, 'Jesus be cursed!'" (οὐδεὶς ἐν πνεύματι θεοῦ λαλῶν λέγει· Ἀνάθεμα Ἰησοῦς, 12:3a). The vast majority of interpreters take Ἰησοῦς as the subject of the utterance here and ἀνάθεμα as the predicate with an implied copulative verb, in parallel to the corresponding utterance in v. 3b, Κύριος Ἰησοῦς. Thus: "Jesus is cursed."[7] Probably this was an utterance the Corinthians

---

7. The alternative proposal in Bruce W. Winter, "Religious Curses and Christian Vindictiveness (1 Corinthians 12–14)," in *After Paul Left Corinth: The Influence of Secular Ethics and Social Change* (Grand Rapids: Eerdmans, 2001), 164-83 to take Ἰησοῦς as the subject and ἀνάθεμα as the object of an unstated verb of giving or pronouncing (e.g., "May Jesus enact a curse") is unlikely for two main reasons: first, the curse inscriptions from pagan contexts

had heard one or more of their members exclaim in the course of a gathering for worship, and they wrote to Paul to inquire about it. At least some of the Corinthians were apparently unsure of whether Ἀνάθεμα Ἰησοῦς and Κύριος Ἰησοῦς really were incompatible after all; perhaps, as Arnold Bittlinger has put it, they conceived of a split between "the historic Jesus" and "the pneumatic Christ" which enabled one to curse the former and pledge allegiance to the latter — and perhaps *only* so could one truly honor the latter.[8] Still, the phrase was evidently troubling enough to some that it prompted them to raise the issue with Paul. Would the Spirit have inspired some of the Corinthians to utter Ἀνάθεμα Ἰησοῦς?

Paul's response in 12:3b (καὶ οὐδεὶς δύναται εἰπεῖν· Κύριος Ἰησοῦς, εἰ μὴ ἐν πνεύματι ἁγίῳ) forces the Corinthians to confront the character and identity of the Spirit. Is the Spirit involved in constructing a *new* identity for Jesus, abstracted from his identity as the crucified and risen κύριος, in which case the way to determine what the Spirit is saying in the assembly does not depend on a prior grasp of the character of Jesus? Or is the test of the content of the Spirit's speech that prior identity of Jesus itself? Paul's answer is that there is "a *christological criterion* of what it is to experience the agency of the Spirit."[9] Discerning what the Spirit would say in the Corinthian assembly of believers depends on the Corinthians' ability to filter ostensible Spirit-utterances based on their agreement with the character and identity of Jesus.

D. A. Carson has objected that treating 12:3b as a criterion is unworkable, since, if it is such, "it is disturbingly broad and undiscriminating."[10] Yet this objection loses much of its force if we take v. 3b as the clarifying counterpart to v. 3a. The true Spirit is known not simply by the invocation of the syllables of Jesus' name, as if that, in and of itself, regardless of the posture of the one invoking it, were enough to guarantee spiritual authenticity; rather, "Jesus is Lord" entails a specific understanding of what it

---

(e.g., tablets, legal formulae) which he adduces as evidence are not really parallel to the public cry Ἀνάθεμα Ἰησοῦς in the context of a communal gathering for worship; and second, Winter's examples do not feature the *deity* enacting the curse but rather guaranteeing the human agent's curse's efficacy.

8. Arnold Bittlinger, *Gifts and Graces: A Commentary on 1 Corinthians 12–14* (London: Hodder and Stoughton, 1968), 17.

9. Anthony C. Thiselton, *The First Epistle to the Corinthians* (NIGTC; Grand Rapids: Eerdmans, 2000), 924.

10. D. A. Carson, *Showing the Spirit: A Theological Exposition of 1 Corinthians 12–14* (Carlisle: Paternoster, 1995), 27.

means for Jesus to be the κύριος. As we saw in Chapter 3 in our discussion of Phil 2:5-11, the giving of the divine name to Jesus is the culmination of his having humbled himself, so that κύριος must be understood here to bear a particular stamp. It is given to Jesus *by God* not in order to confer an equality with God that he hitherto did not enjoy but instead as the definitive indication that Jesus' course of humiliation was precisely the *expression of* that equality. As such, it is itself a relational designation — that is, to call Jesus κύριος is to speak of his relation to God — and the test of the authenticity of Spirit-experience becomes then, in 1 Cor 12:3, a grasp of Jesus' identity in terms of that relationship.

Paul contrasts two ways here. On the one hand, the Corinthians might be confused into thinking that the Spirit is known *first* and directly (but how?), and then *gives* the identity of Jesus as κύριος, in contrast, probably, to some inferior identity that they now, in their pneumatic enlightenment, know as ἀνάθεμα. On the other hand, the Corinthians might recognize that the true identity of the Spirit — the reliable way of picking the true Spirit out of the crowd of possible Spirit-utterances — is grasped by recognizing the Spirit as the one who enables recognition of Jesus as κύριος, that is, Jesus as uniquely endowed by God the Father with the divine name. Paul's point is that the confession of Jesus' identity in those terms is the way in which one is enabled to pick out the identity of the πνεῦμα θεοῦ.[11] And this, in turn, may be supported by noting that 12:1-3 constitutes the introduction to the whole of chs. 12–14, which are intended to undercut the division between the πνευματικοί who speak in tongues and the rest (those who merely acknowledge "the historic Jesus"?) who do not. By specifying that those who confess Κύριος Ἰησοῦς do so ἐν πνεύματι ἁγίῳ, "Paul undermines any pneumatic elitism. All Christians make this confession, thus all Christians, not a tongue-speaking few, are πνευματικοί."[12] The guarantee, in other words, that the Spirit is really

11. Cf. Michael J. Gorman, *Cruciformity: Paul's Narrative Spirituality of the Cross* (Grand Rapids: Eerdmans, 2001), 66; Rowe, "The Trinity in the Letters of St. Paul and Hebrews," 50: "the way to differentiate the true from the false is to see the connection of the Holy Spirit to God the Father and Jesus the Lord."

12. Jouette M. Bassler, "1 Cor 12:3 — Curse and Confession in Context," *JBL* 101 (1982), 415-18, at 416. Bassler sets this reading over against the understanding of 12:3 as a test of authentic Spirit-experience, as does Mehrdad Fatehi, *The Spirit's Relation to the Risen Lord in Paul* (WUNT 2/128; Tübingen: Mohr Siebeck, 2000), 230-32, on the grounds that 12:2 is better read as a rhetorical foil for 12:3 rather than as specifying the *Sitz im Leben* for the criterion of 12:3. Yet this overlooks the fact that genuine versus false remains the issue

present among *all* the Corinthians is the fact that the Corinthians confess Jesus as κύριος; the Spirit is known by invoking Jesus by the name — κύριος — he received from God the Father.

ii. *The Spirit of God's Son*

This "relational determination of the Spirit's identity" or what I have called the "theologically- and christologically-determined" character of the Spirit is most clearly seen, perhaps, in Gal 4:4-7. Since the work of Dunn and others arguing that this text does not imply the preexistence of Jesus,[13] there have been a number of studies that see Paul's "sending" language here, coupled with its contextual specifications (on which see below), as most probably pointing to preexistence.[14] Gordon Fee and Kavin Rowe have argued that the combination of "when the fullness of time had come" together with "born of a woman" makes it highly likely that Paul assumes the Son (v. 4) to have been present at that culminating moment and then freely (cf. 2:20) entering into or conforming himself to God's sending of him. But this sending is coordinated with a further sending in 4:6: "God sent the Spirit of his Son into our hearts." Here the same movement is attributed to the Spirit as was attributed earlier in v. 4 to the Son: "God" is the subject again, and the object of his sending is not simply the Spirit *of God* but the Spirit *of God's Son*. This language is nowhere else present in Paul as such, though Rom 8:9 (πνεῦμα Χριστοῦ) and Phil 1:19 (πνεῦμα

---

in chs. 12–14, since the hierarchical divisions of the supposed πνευματικοί from the rest of the Corinthians are precisely competing understandings of the God- and Christ-determined character of the Spirit (so R. W. L. Moberly, *Prophecy and Discernment* [Cambridge: Cambridge University Press, 2006], 179).

13. E.g., the brief treatment in James D. G. Dunn, *The Epistle to the Galatians* (BNTC; Peabody, Mass.: Hendrickson, 1993), 214-15; cf. J. Louis Martyn, *Galatians: A New Translation with Introduction and Commentary* (AB 33A; New York: The Anchor Bible/Doubleday, 1997), 407.

14. So C. Kavin Rowe, "Biblical Pressure and Trinitarian Hermeneutics," *Pro Ecclesia* 11 (2002): 295-312, at 304-5; Simon Gathercole, "Pre-Existence, and the Freedom of the Son in Creation and Redemption: An Exposition in Dialogue with Robert Jenson," *IJST* 7/1 (2005): 38-51, at 41. Richard B. Hays, "The Letter to the Galatians: Introduction, Commentary, and Reflections," *NIB* 11 (ed. Leander Keck; Nashville: Abingdon, 2000), 181-350, at 283; Ernest De Witt Burton, *The Epistle to the Galatians* (ICC; Edinburgh: T&T Clark, 1921), 217; Brendan Byrne, "Christ's Pre-existence in Pauline Soteriology," *Theological Studies* 58 (1997): 308-30, at 314.

Ἰησοῦ Χριστοῦ) come close to it. Here it is a striking indication that the kind of mutually determining language of the God who sends and Jesus as the υἱός who is sent — a reciprocal relationality that, as we have seen, likely extends in Paul's mind back to a time prior to the culminating moment of Gal 4:4 — is opened up to include a third, the Spirit, within its ambit. The result is that God, Jesus, and the Spirit are all implicated in a prior determination to effect the sonship of the Galatian believers (4:4-7 as the climax of a theme began in 3:1-5). As Rowe puts it,

> God the Father (*theos* is always the Father in Galatians) exists in rela-
> tion to his Son as well as in relation to the Spirit of his Son. The Spirit
> of the Father's Son, in turn, testifies (in the hearts of believers) to
> the Father of the Son. This relationship between the Father, his Son,
> and the Spirit of the Father's Son is mutually constitutive, which is
> to say that the economy of the one God, the creator of the world,
> is here spoken of in a way in which each of the three "persons" are
> immediately interrelated: the Father is the Father of his Son; the Son
> is, obviously, the Son of his Father; and the Spirit is the Spirit of the
> Son of the Father.[15]

Paul's specification of the Spirit's identity — his delineating who this Spirit is whom the Galatians have received — involves his referring the Galatians back to God and Jesus. However, he does not picture God and Jesus as enjoying a priority to which the Spirit is then *added* as a supplementary afterthought. If that were the case, then we would not be able to speak of *mutuality* in the constitution of the identities of God, Jesus, and the Spirit. Rather, Paul has in mind a fully reciprocal relationship whereby the Spirit's identity is intertwined with God's and Jesus' identities from the outset. *Both* in eternal priority *and* in the temporal outworking or "sending" *from* that eternal priority, the Spirit is identified here along with God and his Son in a web of inter-determinative relations. This matrix or web that exists between God, the Son, and the Spirit preexists their effecting of the Galatians' adoption described in 4:5;[16] and this relationship is demonstrated in a temporal pattern that is *both* successive or asymmetrical — insofar as the Spirit's historical sending is dependent on the Son's prior sending — and

---

15. Rowe, "Biblical Pressure and Trinitarian Hermeneutics," 304.

16. Rowe, "Biblical Pressure and Trinitarian Hermeneutics," 304: "the relationship between the Father, Son, and Spirit is eternal."

also mutual — insofar as the Spirit's sending *in the Galatians' experience* is coterminous with their experience of the Son's effecting of their adoption. The ὅτι clause that opens v. 6 is best read as introducing an explanation of what ὁ υἱοθεσία in the previous verse entails.[17] The Galatians' experience of the Spirit in v. 6b is coordinate with rather than consequent upon the Galatians' experience of sonship, which was effected by the sending of the Son (as the twofold use of ἵνα in v. 5 makes clear). The argument of 3:1-5 has already established that the Galatians "began" with the Spirit, so Paul does not have in mind a subjective *ordo salutis* in which the experience of adoption precedes the giving of the Spirit. Rather, here he means that the Galatians' experience (cf. εἰς τὰς καρδίας ἡμῶν, as well as the verb κράζειν, v. 6) of the Spirit is evidence or confirmation of their sonship.[18] Thereby Paul indicates that the Spirit belongs with the Son and the Father prior to their sending and that the Spirit also belongs with them in the effects which that sending was intended to accomplish.

The Spirit's identity is in this way understood to be "of the Son" (v. 6): "[Paul's] emphasis is on the reciprocal relation or correlational nature of sonship and the reception of the Spirit."[19] The Spirit is the one who joins in the Son's cry of "Abba, Father!"[20] and the Galatians, in turn, participate in that cry. The Spirit thus completes or confirms the sending of the Son. Or to put it in terms of the Galatians' experience, the Spirit is the corroborating evidence of their sonship, their adoptive relationship with the Father through the Son.

iii. "The Lord Is the Spirit"

Turning our attention to 2 Cor 3:17, we must now take a slight detour and address an objection to the foregoing discussion. This objection takes the following form: Paul appears in certain key texts to *identify* Jesus the κύριος with the Spirit, which means that Paul is not concerned with Jesus and the Spirit's relationship to one another as distinct persons but rather

---

17. The ὅτι is causal, not explanatory. But the entirety of v. 6 is best taken as an elucidation of v. 5.

18. So Martinus C. de Boer, *Galatians: A Commentary* (NTL; Louisville: Westminster/John Knox, 2011), 265-66.

19. Richard N. Longenecker, *Galatians* (WBC 41; Dallas: Word Books, 1990), 173.

20. The neuter participle κρᾶζον takes πνεῦμα for its subject; so, rightly, de Boer, *Galatians*, 266.

with the Spirit as the mode of Jesus' presence to believers. This objection depends on at least two major exegetical decisions.[21] First, those who see the Spirit as simply an extension of Jesus' presence or power or lordship take the use of Exod 34:34 in 2 Cor 3:16 as an appropriation of scriptural wording rather than a citation, to ensure that κύριος in v. 17 retains the same referent as in v. 16. And second, those adopting this view give κύριος its usual sense in Paul and take it as a reference to the risen Jesus rather than to YHWH as in the original source text.[22] The resulting conclusion is, to paraphrase v. 17, "The Lord Jesus is experienced among believers *as* the Spirit."

This way of interpreting 2 Cor 3:17 has been losing ground in recent years as a growing number of commentators have argued that the so-called equation of the Lord and the Spirit is better understood as an interpretive gloss on Exod 34:34. On this view, the linkage between the Lord and the Spirit is not an assertion of metaphysical or ontological sameness or even of *experiential* sameness — that the risen Lord has become, in some sense or other, the Spirit — but rather a *hermeneutical* claim. In the words of Richard Hays, "[T]he *kyrios* in the LXX of Exod. 34:34 is being read by Paul, for his present purposes, as a figure for the Spirit (i.e., the form in which God is regularly experienced in the Christian community), as over against the merely written covenant."[23] As both Hays and Dunn[24] point out, this reading is deftly rendered in the New English Bible translation,

21. For these objections, see James D. G. Dunn, "2 Corinthians 3:17 — 'The Lord is the Spirit'," in *The Christ and the Spirit; Volume 1: Christology* (Grand Rapids: Eerdmans, 1998), 115-25, at 120. To be clear, Dunn disagrees with these objections and attempts to address them in his discussion.

22. So J. Weiss, "Die Bedeutung des Paulus für den modernen Christ," *ZNW* 19 (1919/20): 127-42, at 139-40; Ingo Hermann, *Kyrios und Pneuma: Studien zur Christologie der paulinischen Hauptbriefe* (Munich: Kösel-Verlag, 1961), 17-58; Gunkel, *The Influence of the Holy Spirit,* 113; Wilhelm Bousset, *Kyrios Christos: A History of the Belief in Christ from the Beginnings of Christianity to Irenaeus* (trans. J. E. Steely; Nashville: Abingdon, 1970), 163. Dunn, "2 Corinthians 3:17 — 'The Lord is the Spirit'," 115 n. 1 provides a fuller bibliography.

23. Richard B. Hays, *Echoes of Scripture in the Letters of Paul* (New Haven: Yale University Press, 1989), 143. See also C. F. D. Moule, "2 Cor. 3:18b, καθάπερ ἀπὸ κυρίου πνεύματος," in *Neues Testament und Geschichte* (ed. H. Baltensweiler and R. Reicke; FS O. Cullmann; Tübingen: Mohr Siebeck, 1972), 231-37; Linda Belleville, *Reflections of Glory: Paul's Polemical Use of Moses-Doxa Tradition in 2 Corinthians 3.1-18* (JSNTSup 52; Sheffield: JSOT Press, 1991), 227-96; Fee, *God's Empowering Presence,* 309-20; Margaret Thrall, *A Critical and Exegetical Commentary on the Second Epistle to the Corinthians* (ICC; Edinburgh: T&T Clark, 1994), 261-97.

24. Dunn, "2 Corinthians 3:17," 122.

"However, as the Scripture says of Moses, 'whenever he turns to the Lord the veil is removed.' Now the Lord of whom this passage speaks is the Spirit." So, in response to the two exegetical decisions that buttress the "identification thesis" as enumerated above, Hays and others would contend, first, given the lack of a clear shift from Moses in 3:15 to a new subject in v. 16, Moses most likely remains the subject of the verb ἐπιστρέψῃ too, confirming that v. 16 is indeed an allusion to Exod 34:34, despite the changes Paul has introduced to it.[25]

In response to the second point in favor of an identification between the risen Lord and the Spirit — that κύριος must bear a christological reference here as it does uniformly elsewhere in Paul — Hays and others who opt for a theological referent would reply that κύριος in Paul (as we have already seen in previous chapters) is a multivalent term (or, better, a *name*) that requires a willingness to recognize more than one referent simultaneously. It is undisputed that most uses of κύριος in the Pauline corpus refer to Christ,[26] but it is also acknowledged that in the case of Paul's citations or allusions to the Old Testament, κύριος retains its reference to God/YHWH (see Rom 4:8; 9:28, 29; 10:16; 11:3, 34; 15:11; 1 Cor 1:31; 2:16; 3:20; 10:26; 14:21; 2 Cor 6:17-18; 8:21; 10:17; cf. 2 Thess 1:9; 2 Tim 2:19). But several of these uses of κύριος in the latter category (1 Cor 1:31; 2:16; 10:26; 2 Cor 10:17) demonstrate what C. Kavin Rowe has described

---

25. For discussion, see Horn, *Das Angeld des Geistes,* 320-21. Exodus 34:34a LXX: ἡνίκα δ᾽ ἂν εἰσεπορεύετο Μωυσῆς ἔναντι κυρίου λαλεῖν αὐτῷ, περιῃρεῖτο τὸ κάλυμμα ἕως τοῦ ἐκπορεύεσθαι. Paul omits the name Μωυσῆς as well as λαλεῖν αὐτῷ and ἕως τοῦ ἐκπορεύεσθαι. He also exchanges ἔναντι κυρίου for πρὸς κύριον and replaces the two imperfect indicatives with, respectively, an aorist subjunctive (ἐπιστρέψῃ) and a present indicative (περιαιρεῖται). Francis Watson, *Paul and the Hermeneutics of Faith* (London: T&T Clark, 2004), 297 notes, however, that these changes are less extensive than the ones that would be required if Moses were not in fact the referent of Paul's text (e.g., an indefinite pronoun would need to be inserted, and the active sense would need to be traded for a passive one: "Whenever anyone turns to the Lord, the veil is removed"). Watson cites the comment from Scott J. Hafemann, *Paul, Moses, and the History of Israel: The Letter/Spirit Contrast and Argument from Scripture in 2 Corinthians 3* (WUNT; Tübingen: Mohr Siebeck, 1995), 387: 3:16 is "the most explicit reference to Exod. 32–34 in our passage."

26. It is used by itself in reference to Jesus (e.g., Rom 10:12; 12:11; 14:6; 1 Cor 3:5; 4:4-5), together in compound phrases such as ὁ κύριος ἡμῶν Ἰησοῦς Χριστός (e.g., Rom 5:11; 2 Cor 1:2; Gal 1:3), and in prepositional phrases (e.g., ἐν κυρίῳ, Rom 16:2; 1 Cor 4:17; Gal 5:10; Phil 1:14). For full discussions of Pauline usage of κύριος, see Dieter-Alex Koch, *Die Schrift als Zeuge des Evangeliums: Untersuchungen zur Verwendung und zum Verständnis der Schrift bei Paulus* (BHT 69; Tübingen: Mohr Siebeck, 1986), 84-88; Gordon D. Fee, *Pauline Christology: An Exegetical-Theological Study* (Peabody, MA: Hendrickson, 2007), 25-27, 35.

as "kyriotic overlap,"[27] in which an Old Testament reference to God as κύριος is expanded to *include* Jesus. In these cases, κύριος does double duty, retaining its capacity to refer to God and gaining a capacity to refer to Jesus at the same time.[28] In the case of 2 Cor 3:17, a similar argument would be employed, as will be explained more fully below.

However, before going on, it should be noted that this apparently growing consensus — that the Lord is *not* identified ontologically but only *hermeneutically* with the Spirit — has been challenged once again recently and a form of identification between Jesus and the Spirit has been forcefully defended in Mehrdad Fatehi's revised doctoral thesis *The Spirit's Relation to the Risen Lord in Paul.*[29] It will be helpful to have Fatehi's argument in view before moving on to delineate my own understanding of the Spirit's relations to God and Jesus in 2 Cor 3:17.

Fatehi presents several pieces of evidence for seeing the κύριος of 3:17 as Christ. First, he notes that in v. 3 it is Christ who writes on believers' hearts by the Spirit, as the counterpart to YHWH's writing on tablets. Thus, since the reference to Exodus 31–34 begun here continues on through the end of the chapter, one would expect the relationship between Christ and Spirit adumbrated in v. 3 to remain the same in v. 17: Christ, the new covenant Lord, is now present and active by the Spirit.[30] Second, Fatehi suggests that τὸ τέλος τοῦ καταργουμένου in v. 13 is best read as the *goal* or *purpose* of the law that was concealed from Israel and is now seen as the veil is removed, that is, the Lord in v. 16. This reading finds contextual support, Fatehi suggests, from 4:3-4, where the removal of the veil enables seeing "the glory of Christ."[31] Third, Fatehi argues that the subject of καταργεῖται in 3:14 is the veil and not the old covenant, in which case the adverbial "in Christ" becomes the parallel to "to the Lord" in v. 16. And finally, he suggests that 4:1-6 becomes more intelligible if a christological interpretation of 3:16-18 is adopted. Paul speaks of the glory of Christ (4:4), the glory of God in the face of Christ (v. 6), and of that glory being veiled to unbelievers (v. 3). Moreover, he speaks in v. 4 of Christ as εἰκὼν

27. See discussion above in Chapters 3 and 4.

28. See David B. Capes, *Old Testament Yahweh Texts in Paul's Christology* (WUNT 2/47; Tübingen: Mohr Siebeck, 1992); cf. also Larry W. Hurtado, *Lord Jesus Christ: Devotion to Jesus in Earliest Christianity* (Grand Rapids: Eerdmans, 2003), 112; Fee, *Pauline Christology*, 127-34 and passim.

29. See note 12 above.

30. Fatehi, *The Spirit's Relation to the Risen Lord in Paul*, 290-91.

31. Fatehi, *The Spirit's Relation to the Risen Lord in Paul*, 291-92.

τοῦ θεοῦ, which can hardly be understood as anything other than an echo of τὴν αὐτὴν εἰκόνα (3:18) into which believers are being transformed, which is identified with τὴν δόξαν κυρίου. Furthermore, the progression from 4:4 to 4:5 indicates that Paul's gospel τῆς δόξης τοῦ Χριστοῦ has as its content Ἰησοῦν Χριστὸν κύριον, thus securing the link between δόξα and κύριος — the same link already made in 3:18.[32] For all these reasons, Fatehi thinks it is most likely that the κύριος of 3:17 is Jesus.

Fatehi supplements these positive arguments for seeing the Lord of 3:17 as Christ with negative reasons that v. 16 is most likely not a citation or allusion to Exod 34:34 as such. First, Paul is already, prior to 3:16, presenting a contemporized or Christianized reading of Exodus 31–34 (see, e.g., the reference to Christ in 3:14). Exod 34:34 "is already *an applied text* in which Paul basically and primarily *asserts something about his present situation,* in which case *κύριος* could hardly be taken as an undefined term to be explained by Paul in 17a."[33] Second, Fatehi argues that the δέ in 3:17a is not in itself an indication of an exegetical gloss on a cited text (i.e., v. 16) but rather picks up a word from the already modified text and shows that that word is a new point of departure for an expanded discussion.[34] Finally, Fatehi argues that ἐστιν is not truly parallel to Gal 4:25 and 1 Cor 10:4 as it is often alleged to be in discussions that take it as an exegetical *significat*.[35] The former uses ἀλληγορεῖν (Gal 4:24) and συστοιχεῖν (v. 25) to indicate the nature of the application of the Genesis text to the Galatians' situation, and ἐστιν merely aligns the terms of the allegory. Likewise, in 1 Cor 10:4 it is not clear that ἐστιν is an exegetical *significat* since Paul "may well have thought that the pre-existent Christ was actually involved in those key events of Israel's history," in which case ἐστιν could be a more or less straightforward statement of his personal pre-existence.[36]

For Fatehi, then, 2 Cor 3:17 means that the risen Lord Jesus is identified with the Spirit. But he understands the nature of this identification to be in line with the way Paul elsewhere speaks of the relationship between

---

32. Fatehi, *The Spirit's Relation to the Risen Lord in Paul,* 294-95.

33. Fatehi, *The Spirit's Relation to the Risen Lord in Paul,* 297. Emphasis original.

34. Fatehi, *The Spirit's Relation to the Risen Lord in Paul,* 300. This reading would allow for the definite article modifying κύριος to be understood as anaphoric, but then "Paul would be explaining *not* the '*κύριος*' of the cited text from Exodus, but the *κύριος to whom the Israelites turn* according to his *application* of that text in v. 16" (297-98, emphasis original).

35. Victor Paul Furnish, *II Corinthians* (AB 32A; New York: Doubleday, 1984), 212; Fee, *God's Empowering Presence,* 311.

36. Fatehi, *The Spirit's Relation to the Risen Lord in Paul,* 300-301.

Jesus and the Spirit.[37] The Spirit is *dynamically identified* with Christ: inseparable from Christ insofar as the Spirit is the way in which Christ "communicates his power, his life, his will, his very presence, to his people,"[38] and yet distinguishable from Christ — not reducible *to* Christ — insofar as the Spirit remains κυρίου (vv. 17b, 18). Fatehi's description of this dynamism is worth quoting in full:

> [T]he dynamic identification between Christ and the Spirit includes, most probably, also an *ontic* or *ontological* aspect, to use present day theological language and conceptual distinctions, which goes beyond a merely functional identification. In other words, one should not speak merely of the Spirit playing the role of Christ, or of the Spirit only representing Christ. Rather, there is a sense in which the risen Lord himself is actually present and active through the Spirit which is hardly imaginable without there being some ontic or ontological connection between the two. . . . Nevertheless, the risen Lord is not reduced to the Spirit. The exalted Christ has for Paul a real existence as the Son in relation to God the Father which is clearly distinct from the Spirit's relation to God. . . . But neither is the Spirit reduced to the risen Lord, even in the believer's experience. This is because the Spirit retains for Paul its primary characteristic of being the Spirit *of God,* and in so far as for Paul this "God" remains primarily "the Father of our Lord Jesus Christ," one simply cannot say that "Paul defines the Spirit as no more and no less than the Spirit of Jesus," or that "one cannot experience the Spirit except as Christ."[39]

We thus are faced with two contrasting readings of 2 Cor 3:17. To recapitulate, in the Hays et al. line of interpretation, the role of the Lord of the "old covenant" — YHWH — is assigned to the Spirit among the believers in Corinth. When Moses turned to YHWH, the veil over his face was removed; so also, when a person (Jew or Gentile) turns to the Lord

---

37. A useful summary of Fatehi's monograph may be found in Max Turner, "'Trinitarian' Pneumatology in the New Testament? — Towards an Explanation of the Worship of Jesus," *Asbury Theological Journal* 58/1 (2003): 167-86, at 180-82.

38. Fatehi, *The Spirit's Relation to the Risen Lord in Paul,* 304.

39. Fatehi, *The Spirit's Relation to the Risen Lord in Paul,* 305-6. The quotations near the end are from James D. G. Dunn, *Jesus and the Spirit: A Study of the Religious and Charismatic Experience of Jesus and the First Christians as Reflected in the New Testament* (London: SCM, 1975), 325 and 323 respectively.

(κύριος) through Paul's ministry (cf. vv. 1-3), the Lord to whom they turn is the Spirit. By contrast, in the Fatehi line of interpretation, the risen Lord is present in the unveiling of unbelievers in and as the Spirit — *his* Spirit (v. 17b). It is difficult to decide which of these readings is the stronger — or whether there is another, different option that is stronger than either of them. Given the obscurity and intractability of the interpretive problems v. 17 raises — it has been referred to as "the Mount Everest of Pauline texts as far as difficulty is concerned"[40] — I will not base any firm conclusions in this chapter on this text alone. However, I do want to explore briefly how my argument for the "relational determination of the Spirit's identity" would look in a modified form of the "hermeneutical" perspective. In the course of my discussion, I hope that that perspective will gain plausibility and that its persuasive power will be enough to tip the scales in that direction, in contrast to Fatehi's case.

If Hays and others who see 3:17 as an interpretive gloss are right, then we have what amounts to another "kyriotic overlap," this one not between the κύριος of the LXX and Jesus but rather between the κύριος of Exod 34:34 specifically and the Spirit. As we saw in Chapter 3, in Phil 2:6-11 the divine name — κύριος — became the medium for asserting both the oneness between God and Jesus (their "unity" or "identity") and their distinction (their irreducible personal uniqueness, since Jesus receives the name κύριος from God the πατήρ). God and Jesus *together* constitute the identity of the κύριος; or, to say it the other way around, if we ask who is the κύριος of the LXX (or, specifically, in the case of Phil 2:6-11, the κύριος of Isa 45:23) to whom believers now turn, the answer is "God and Jesus." In a similar way, we have in 2 Cor 3:17 both an indication of the Spirit's unity or oneness or "identification" with God — the Spirit is κύριος insofar as the Spirit is identified for the Corinthians with the κύριος of Exod 34:34 — and also an indication of the Spirit's personal distinction from God insofar as the Spirit is also "of" the Lord (τὸ πνεῦμα κυρίου). As Kavin Rowe puts it:

> Paul's Spirit-identifying gloss on *kyrios* [in Exod 34:34] subsumes the Spirit under the divine name *kyrios* which is used both of the Father and of Jesus the Son. . . . [T]he Spirit is not Jesus, nor is Jesus the Spirit, but both are "the Lord" *(ho kyrios)*. The very next phrase con-

---

40. Anthony T. Hanson, "The Midrash in II Corinthians 3: A Reconsideration," *JSNT* 9 (1980): 2-28, at 19.

firms such a differentiation within the identity of the Lord: "and where the Spirit of the Lord *(to pneuma kyriou)* — freedom!" (2 Cor 3:17b). Read canonically, then, the full unity of God as expressed through his name *kyrios* is that of Father, Son, and Spirit: the *kyrios heis* (one Lord) of Deut 6:4 is in the New Testament differentiated into *kyrios pater* (Father), *kyrios iesous* (Son), and *kyrios pneuma* (Spirit). Thus the oneness and unity of God is not impaired but is dynamically upheld through the use of his name *kyrios* for the Father, Son, and Spirit, the one Lord God.[41]

On this view, if we are to "pick out" the Spirit to whom Paul refers — if we are to ask, "Who is this Spirit you, Paul, are speaking of?" — then Paul's answer is, "The Spirit who is of the Lord, the Spirit whom you know because he is *God's* Spirit."

This view may receive support from renewed attention to Exod 34:34 and its context, to which Paul alludes here, as we have already seen. In what follows, I want to suggest that "the Lord is the Spirit" is best read as Paul's statement not only of what is true for the Corinthians as they turn to the Lord (2 Cor 3:16) but as what was true for *Moses* in Exodus: the Lord to whom Moses turned in the tent of meeting was the Spirit.[42]

In the Exodus text Paul references, Moses meets with God on an ongoing basis, assuming an office of mediation, presumably at the site of the tent of meeting.[43] In the preceding chapter, Moses' meeting with God is described in some detail (33:7-11 LXX):

> And Moses took his tent and pitched it outside the camp, at a distance from the camp; and it was called the tent of testimony: and it happened that every one that sought the Lord went out to the tent that was outside the camp. And whenever Moses went into the tent outside the camp, all the people stood each one watching by the doors of his tent; and when Moses departed, they observed [him] until he entered into the tent. And when Moses entered into the tent, the pillar of the cloud descended, and stood at the door of the tabernacle, and he [the Lord] spoke to Moses. And all the people saw the pillar of the cloud standing

41. Rowe, "Biblical Pressure and Trinitarian Hermeneutics," 303-4.

42. For what follows I am indebted to a conversation with Francis Watson.

43. For these points, see Brevard Childs, *Exodus: A Commentary* (OTL; London: SCM, 1974), 356.

by the door of the tent, and all the people stood and worshiped each one at the door of his tent. And the Lord spoke to Moses face to face, as if one should speak to his friend; and he retired into the camp, but his servant Joshua the son of Naue, a young man, did not depart from the tent.[44]

Here, then, prior to the description of Moses' going "in" to speak "before" the Lord in 34:34, we have a fuller description of those repeated meetings, as well as a mechanism to explain the glory on Moses' face: it comes from the presence of the Lord speaking face to face with Moses, symbolized by the cloud that descends on the tent as a marker of that presence. It is when Moses is speaking with the Lord that the cloud is present (33:9).[45] Does Paul, picking up on this feature of the Exodus text, envision a link between the *cloud* as the mediation of the Lord's presence to Moses and the *Spirit*? If so, that could easily explain why the Spirit, in addition to the expected κύριος, is mentioned here.

Elsewhere in the Corinthian correspondence, Paul not only shows interest in identifying distinct features of the Pentateuchal narratives as prefigurements of contemporary Christian realities but also specifically shows an interest in the cloud. He mentions it twice in 1 Cor 10:1-2: "For I do not want you to be ignorant, brothers, that our fathers were all under the cloud and all passed through the sea and all accepted baptism[46] in the cloud and in the sea." It is easy enough to see the link between baptism and the waters of the sea,[47] but the cloud is a startling feature of Paul's typo-

---

44. Compare the same tradition of the cloud's presence at the tent of meeting in Numbers 12.

45. William H. C. Propp, *Exodus 19–40* (AB 2A; New York: Doubleday, 2006), 600 suggests that 33:18-23 may indicate that YHWH speaks from within the cloud and not in the midst of the tent with Moses.

46. The aorist middle here is likely the original, later changed to ἐβαπτίσθησαν to bring it in line with 12:13. *Pace* Thiselton, *1 Corinthians*, 722, however, the middle does not so much indicate self-interest ("all of them had themselves baptized") as it does a receptive sense ("accepted baptism"; so my translation); cf. Georg Heinrici, *Kritisch exegetisches Handbuch über den ersten Brief an die Korinther* (KEK 5; 7th ed.; Göttingen: Vandenhoeck & Ruprecht, 1888), 269, 271.

47. Alexander J. M. Wedderburn, *Baptism and Resurrection: Studies in Pauline Theology against Its Greco-Roman Background* (WUNT 44; Tübingen: Mohr Siebeck, 1987), 59 suggests that the preposition εἰς in the phrase "into Moses" may carry connotations of plunging into water, thus ruling out a strictly metaphorical or "spiritual" meaning for βαπτίζειν. On the problem of separating "Spirit baptism" from "water baptism," see the

logical reading here; it is not immediately clear why he speaks of baptism being "in the cloud." If we see, however, that elsewhere Paul connects Christ and the Spirit to baptism (6:11),[48] the likelihood increases that he has in mind here the cloud as a figure of the Spirit.[49] In the same way that the Israelites encountered Christ as the rock that followed them (10:4), so they also encountered the Spirit in the event of their journey through the sea in the exodus. In Paul's reading, they encountered the cloud *as* the divine presence just as the Corinthians encountered the Spirit in their baptism — a baptism not in the cloud and the sea but in water.

Returning to 2 Cor 3:17, we can see that Paul's link between the Lord of Exod 34:34 and the Spirit to whom believers turn and behold (2 Cor 3:18) may also be owing to Paul's typological or figural reading of the cloud in Exodus 33. The Lord who met with Moses signaled his presence by the cloud, and that cloud is the Spirit.[50] Furthermore, having made this link,

---

nuanced discussion in Rabens, *The Holy Spirit and Ethics in Paul*, 106-8, at, e.g., 106: "[Paul] can remind the Corinthians of their common experience of (water-)baptism by which the Spirit has united them in the body of Christ and in this way calls attention to their experience of the one Spirit at the outset of their new life."

48. 1 Cor 6:11 is usually paired with 1 Cor 12:13 in sacramental readings of water-baptism. In my judgment, Rabens, *The Holy Spirit and Ethics in Paul*, 98-109 has argued cogently that ἐν ἑνὶ πνεύματι in 12:13 is instrumental, in which case it would not be parallel to 10:2 where the cloud is the *substance* into which the Israelites are baptized.

49. So Kilian McDonnell and George T. Montague, *Christian Initiation and Baptism in the Holy Spirit: Evidence from the First Eight Centuries* (Collegeville, Minn.: Liturgical, 1991), 45. Cf. James D. G. Dunn, *Baptism in the Holy Spirit: A Re-Examination of the New Testament Teaching on the Gift of the Spirit in Relation to Pentecostalism Today* (2nd ed.; London: SCM, 2010 [1970]), 127 n. 34: "Paul may have mentioned the cloud first because he is thinking of the whole as baptism in the Spirit, since according to Ex. 13:21; 14:24 the Lord was in the cloud"; also Hans Conzelmann, *1 Corinthians* (Philadelphia: Fortress, 1975), 166: "apparently the cloud is the sign of the divine presence, and to this the Spirit in baptism corresponds." Compare on this Gerhard Delling, *Die Taufe im Neuen Testament* (Berlin: Evangelische, 1963), 112 n. 405. Athanasius, *Ep. Serap.*, 1.19.1 interprets the "drinking of the spiritual rock" in 1 Cor 10:4 as a drinking of the Spirit; cf. Origen, *Homilies on Exodus* 5:1 and *Commentary on John* 6.227-29, both of which take the cloud in 1 Cor 10:2 as the Spirit.

50. Interpreters who think Paul refers to Moses' meeting with the Spirit, though without necessarily equating the cloud with the Spirit, include C. J. A. Hickling, "The Sequence of Thought in II Corinthians, Chapter Three," *NTS* 21/3 (1975): 380-95, at 394 n. 3: "when Moses ascended Sinai it was in fact the Spirit himself, the source of freedom, that he met"; Bernardin Schneider, "*Dominus autem Spiritus est*" (*II. Cor. 3,17a): Studium Exegeticum* (Rome: Catholic Book Agency, 1951), 102-5; J. B. Nisius, "Zur Erklärung von 2 Kor 3,16ff.," *ZKT* 40 (1916): 617-75. The Targum of Pseudo-Jonathan discusses the Spirit as the voice that spoke with Moses at the tent of meeting in Num 7:89. For discussion, see

we can then draw out the trinitarian implications of this hermeneutical identification of "Lord" and "Spirit" even more sharply. Paul's point is not simply, as Hays and Rowe emphasize, that the Lord of Exodus 34 now corresponds to the Spirit active among the Corinthians; rather, Paul's claim is stronger: the Lord whom Moses met at the tent of meeting *was already* the Spirit, the *same* Spirit whom Paul's addressees are encountering when they behold "the glory of the Lord" (2 Cor 3:18). Ruled out here is any modalist conceptuality whereby the Lord *becomes* the Spirit for Paul in a way he was not before. Instead, the Spirit who appeared to Moses, the Spirit who was the Lord (κύριος, YHWH), is now who he has been in the past: the Lord whose glory is transforming the Corinthians is that Spirit.

2. The Spirit's Role in Determining the Identities of God and Jesus

We have now seen that Paul traces the identity of the Spirit back to the identities and actions of God and Jesus, and he does this more often than he does the reverse. The Spirit is the Spirit "of God" (Rom 8:9, 14; 15:19; 1 Cor 2:11; 6:11; 7:40; 12:3; Phil 3:3; cf. Rom 8:11, "the Spirit of him who raised Jesus from the dead," and 2 Cor 3:3, "the Spirit of the living God"). And, since "Paul sees Christ as having conveyed the life and activity of God, . . . now the Spirit is defined by Christ" as well.[51] Hence, Paul uses the designations "the Spirit of Christ" (Rom 8:9), "the Spirit of his Son" (Gal 4:6), and "the Spirit of Jesus Christ" (Phil 1:19) to indicate this dual relationality.[52] The Spirit's identity is, in a sense, *governed* or *delimited by* his relation to God and Jesus. He receives his identity from being sent by God and assuming the character of Jesus. "Paul's Christology everywhere provides the context for his *pneuma*tology."[53]

M. McNamara, *The New Testament and the Palestinian Targum to the Pentateuch* (AnBib 27a; Rome: Editrice Pontificio Istituto Biblico, 1966), 184, 187. Compare also Watson, *Paul and the Hermeneutics of Faith,* 297.

51. John Ziesler, *Paul's Letter to the Romans* (TPINTC; Philadelphia: Trinity Press International, 1989), 210.

52. On these genitives as most probably genitives of relationship rather than genitives of source, see Andrew K. Gabriel, "Pauline Pneumatology and the Question of Trinitarian Presuppositions," in *Paul and His Theology* (ed. Stanley E. Porter; Pauline Studies vol. 3; Leiden: Brill, 2006), 347-62, at 355-57.

53. Paul W. Meyer, "The Holy Spirit in the Pauline Letters," *Interpretation* 33 (1979): 3-18, at 13.

Yet there are two prominent passages in Romans that appear to speak of the Spirit as the agent of God whereby God raises Jesus and just so designates him as his Son. If that is in fact what those passages indicate, then we have grounds for speaking of *a return movement* in the identity-constituting relations that exist between God, Jesus, and the Spirit. Not only is the Spirit's identity traceable back to the identities of God and Jesus as the persons or agents who determine the Spirit's character but also the Spirit's identity affects the identities of God and Jesus, constituting them in their character as specifiable agents. With this question of the Spirit's role in "marking out" or "identifying" God and Jesus in mind, we may turn to the texts themselves. The first is Rom 1:3-4, and the second is Rom 8:11. One would be hard pressed to think of two passages that have been examined with more care and thoroughness in NT scholarship,[54] yet if my argument is going to stand I have to deal with them again here, however briefly.

i. The Spirit Identifies Jesus as Son-of-God-in-Power

In Rom 1:3-4, God's Son is said to be "declared" (or "appointed," ὁρίζειν) "Son-of-God-in-power[55] according to the Spirit of holiness by the resurrection of the dead" (κατὰ πνεῦμα ἁγιωσύνης ἐξ ἀναστάσεως νεκρῶν). Virtually every aspect of this text is disputed, so space does not permit me to offer anything like an adequate treatment of all the exegetical conundrums here. Yet the dispute that is most interesting for my purposes — namely, the import of the prepositional phrase κατὰ πνεῦμα ἁγιωσύνης — has, until recently, been discussed less frequently than the other matters of contention in this text. Most scholars have taken the phrase as prime evidence that we have here a pre-Pauline formula, since the role it attributes to the Spirit — an apparently active role that places the Son in a correspondingly passive position — is not well attested elsewhere in Paul. Käsemann, for example, maintains that "[f]or the apostle the Spirit proceeds from Christ or represents him, but the Spirit does not act upon him.

---

54. For a full discussion with up-to-date bibliography, see Robert Jewett, *Romans: A Commentary* (Hermeneia; Minneapolis: Fortress, 2007), 103-8.

55. C. E. B. Cranfield, *The Epistle to the Romans* (2 vols.; ICC; Edinburgh: T&T Clark, 1975), 1:62, is almost certainly correct to take ἐν δυνάμει with υἱοῦ θεοῦ rather than ὁρισθέντος in view of the fact the two mentions of υἱός in vv. 3 and 4 respectively need to be distinguished from one another; so also Douglas J. Moo, *The Epistle to the Romans* (NICNT; Grand Rapids: Eerdmans, 1996), 48.

It seems, then, that the statement is pre-Pauline and must be part of the original formula."[56] Regardless of the origins of the formula, however, we must assume that Paul's lifting it from its original context and placing it into his own text indicates his satisfaction with it in its altered form.[57] The question then becomes, What is its meaning in the context of the opening of Romans?

Mehrdad Fatehi has offered the most extensive answer to this question in recent scholarship. His conclusion is that the phrase does *not* refer to the Spirit's action for or upon Jesus but rather to Jesus' own presence and action as mediated or effected *through* the Spirit.

> *Κατὰ πνεῦμα ἁγιωσύνης* is best understood as defining the power that distinctively characterises Christ's condition of existence and operation [as the risen Lord that] originat[es] from his resurrection. The *κατά* clause affirms in a general way, that Jesus' power in his post-resurrection condition *has to do with* and *is according to* the Spirit and its work. . . . Romans 1:4 is basically a confession of Christ's lordship, and when Paul characterises this lordship as being *κατὰ πνεῦμα ἁγιωσύνης* he essentially affirms that *Christ exercises his function as lord κατὰ πνεῦμα,* i.e. the risen Christ is present and active as the lord of the new covenant community through the Spirit.[58]

Fatehi's support for this reading comes from several considerations. First, he rejects the thought that κατὰ πνεῦμα could denote the heavenly sphere in which the risen Lord now exists post-resurrection or a "new age" characterized by the Spirit's work, since neither of these meanings enjoys support from Jewish sources. These sources employ πνεῦμα-language to describe the characteristics of but not to *denote* the new age or heavenly sphere. Second, Fatehi suggests that the placement of κατὰ πνεῦμα ἁγιωσύνης prior to ἐξ ἀναστάσεως νεκρῶν indicates the resurrection event is not in view so much as the *effect of* the resurrection; Jesus' becoming υἱὸς θεοῦ ἐν δυνάμει κατὰ πνεῦμα ἁγιωσύνης, with κατὰ πνεῦμα ἁγιωσύνης being

---

56. Ernst Käsemann, *Commentary on Romans* (trans. G. W. Bromiley; Grand Rapids: Eerdmans, 1980), 11.

57. See Douglas A. Campbell, *The Deliverance of God: An Apocalyptic Rereading of Justification in Paul* (Grand Rapids: Eerdmans, 2009), 634-36; cf. James M. Scott, *Adoption as Sons of God: An Exegetical Investigation into the Background of ΥΙΟΘΕΣΙΑ in the Pauline Corpus* (WUNT II/48; Tübingen: Mohr Siebeck, 1992), 227-36.

58. Fatehi, *The Spirit's Relation to the Risen Lord in Paul,* 254, 256. Emphasis original.

taken as adjectival modifier in parallel to ἐν δυνάμει, is *a result of* his resurrection. Third, Fatehi points to the frequent connection between πνεῦμα and δύναμις elsewhere in Paul (1 Thess 1:5; 1 Cor 2:4; 12:9-10; 15:43-44; Gal 3:5; Rom 15:13, 19) as evidence for the claim that "the power spoken of here [in Rom 1:4] refers to Jesus' post-resurrection power which is in fact contrasted with his pre-resurrection condition, a condition which would be characterised by Paul as being 'in weakness' in comparison."[59] Fourth, Fatehi argues for a connection between Rom 1:3-4 (and on through v. 6) and 15:15-20, so that the prepositional phrase in 15:19, ἐν δυνάμει πνεύματος, designating the work of the risen Christ in and through Paul (15:18, οὐ γὰρ τολμήσω τι λαλεῖν ὧν οὐ κατειργάσατο Χριστὸς δι' ἐμοῦ), should be seen as illuminating the κατὰ πνεῦμα ἁγιωσύνης in 1:4. And finally Fatehi suggests that the κατὰ σάρκα/κατὰ πνεῦμα contrast in 1:3-4 must be understood in light of the whole letter in which it becomes clear that there are two halves to Jesus' saving work, the first concerning his death (which is explicitly linked to his σάρξ in 8:3) and the second concerning his risen life, in which he continues to save by means of the Spirit (note the double-sided constructions in 4:23-25; 5:10; 8:3-4). Thus, Fatehi presents a cumulative case, none of whose steps is sufficient on its own to establish his position but which gain their persuasive power when considered together.

I wish to challenge Fatehi's reading and argue that the Spirit does act upon Jesus in the resurrection. In keeping with the character of Fatehi's case, however, my approach will similarly depend for its effectiveness on its cumulative force. That is, I will offer an alternative reading that should be evaluated not only or primarily on the basis of whether it provides specific rebuttals to each of Fatehi's points but mainly on the basis of whether it possesses a coherence and persuasive power on its own. My conclusion is that Jesus is appointed or determined as "Son of God in power" *by* the action of the Spirit of holiness in raising him from the dead. In defense of that conclusion, I make several observations.

First, the rhetorical progression of Rom 1:3-4 enables us to assign two different meanings to the preposition κατά in vv. 3 and 4 respectively. The formal similarity between the two κατά-phrases does not constitute sufficient reason to take them as materially parallel. The ἐκ-phrases in vv. 3 (ἐκ σπέρματος Δαυίδ) and 4 (ἐξ ἀναστάσεως νεκρῶν), for instance, are not materially parallel: that Jesus is "from the seed of David" is a statement

---

59. Fatehi, *The Spirit's Relation to the Risen Lord in Paul*, 255.

of his original ancestry, but that he is Son of God in power "from the resurrection of the dead" is a temporal marker — he became Son-in-power *at* the resurrection.[60] Assigning a temporal meaning to ἐκ σπέρματος Δαυίδ results in strained exegesis, while taking ἐξ ἀναστάσεως νεκρῶν as causal, although possible, seems less plausible than seeing it as an indicator of the time at which Jesus became Son of God in power.[61] Seeing this structural parallelism but material differentiation may, in turn, provide the vantage point from which to see the κατά-phrases as formally related but materially distinguishable. In the first instance, κατὰ σάρκα in v. 3, Paul uses the preposition to indicate genealogy. As in 9:5, the thought here is of Jesus' human nature: he is Son of David insofar as his earthly lineage is concerned. But in the second instance, it is likely that the thought is of the *instrument by which* he is determined as "Son of God in power." That supposition is strengthened when we note the passive form of ὁρίζειν in 1:4. Commentators are quick to label this as a "divine passive."[62] Given its proximity to κατὰ πνεῦμα ἁγιωσύνης, however, it is much more likely that it takes the Spirit as its implied subject.[63]

Second, the likelihood of this reading increases if we place it in parallel with 1 Cor 12:8-9.[64] There κατὰ τὸ αὐτὸ πνεῦμα is paired with the passive verb δίδοται and is placed in parallel with two other instrumental phrases. I have rearranged the word order slightly in order to bring out the parallels more clearly:

A ᾧ μὲν γὰρ	B διὰ τοῦ πνεύματος	C δίδοται λόγος σοφίας,
A ἄλλῳ δὲ	B κατὰ τὸ αὐτὸ πνεῦμα	C λόγος γνώσεως
A ἑτέρῳ	B ἐν τῷ αὐτῷ πνεύματι	C πίστις
A ἄλλῳ δὲ	B ἐν τῷ ἑνὶ πνεύματι	C χαρίσματα ἰαμάτων

The verb δίδοται is implied in each clause, and the (B) phrases indicate the subject of the verb who is performing the action of "giving": the same

---

60. For the second ἐκ-phrase as temporal, see Gerhard Schneider, "ὁρίζω," *Exegetical Dictionary of the New Testament* (ed. Horst Balz and Gerhard Schneider, 3 vols.; Grand Rapids: Eerdmans, 1990-93), 2:532.

61. So Cranfield, *Romans*, 1:62.

62. E.g., Joseph A. Fitzmyer, *Romans* (AB 33; New York: Doubleday, 1992), 235.

63. So Martin Hengel, *Der Sohn Gottes: Die Entstehung der Christologie und die jüdisch-hellenistische Religiongeschichte* (2nd ed.; Tübingen: Mohr Siebeck, 1977), 97; Ulrich Wilckens, *Der Brief an die Römer* (third ed.; 3 vols.; EKKNT 6; Zurich: Benziger, 1997), 1:65.

64. Scott, *Adoption as Sons of God*, 242.

Spirit who gave the word of wisdom is the one who gave the word of knowledge, etc. This makes it virtually certain that κατά is functioning to indicate instrumentality. If it does not bear a fully or straightforwardly instrumental sense, it likely means something akin to "on the basis of," denoting the Spirit as the one *because of whom* the word of knowledge is given, which is materially close to denoting the Spirit as the one *through whom* that gift is given.[65]

This usage lends plausibility to the claim that κατὰ πνεῦμα ἁγιωσύνης in Rom 1:4 functions similarly. Either translation — "through the Spirit of holiness" or "because of [the action of] the Spirit of holiness" — amounts to the same thing.[66] Jesus is the Son of God in power *by means of* the Spirit of holiness, rather than, as Fatehi maintains, exercising his power as Son of God *through* the Spirit of holiness.

A third observation that may serve to buttress further this reading is that the Spirit's agency in the resurrection of Jesus is asserted elsewhere in the New Testament, most notably in 1 Pet 3:18: "Christ . . . put to death in/by the flesh but made alive in/by the Spirit" (Χριστὸς . . . θανατωθεὶς μὲν σαρκὶ ζῳοποιηθεὶς δὲ πνεύματι). The verb ζῳοποιεῖν is regularly used to refer to the resurrection (John 5:21; Rom 4:17; 8:11; 1 Cor 15:22; cf. Eph 2:5; Col 2:13), in addition to the more usual Pauline use of ἐγείρειν (e.g., Rom 4:24), and it is virtually certain that it refers to the resurrection here. Whether the dative πνεύματι denotes sphere, manner, or instrumental agency is more difficult to decide, but the fact that it occurs with the passive participle ζῳοποιηθείς would seem to tip the scales in favor of its being a dative of instrument. The parallel σαρκί could also be given an instrumental sense, so that the contrast becomes one in which Christ, while put to death by sinful humanity ("flesh"), was nonetheless made alive through the agency of God's Spirit.[67]

---

65. H. Lietzmann, *An die Korinther I, II* (HNT; fifth ed.; Tübingen: Mohr Siebeck, 1969), 61; C. K. Barrett, *A Commentary on the First Epistle to the Corinthians* (London: Black, 1968), 284; G. R. Beasley-Murray, *Baptism in the New Testament* (London: Macmillan, 1962), 167. For the causal or "on the basis of" use of κατά, see BDAG. Raymond F. Collins, *First Corinthians* (Sacra Pagina 7; Collegeville, Minn.: Liturgical, 1999), 453, comments: "No substantial difference in meaning appears to result from Paul's use of different prepositions. In the popular *koine* Greek of his time prepositions tended to lose their specific meaning and were readily interchangeable with one another. The various prepositions in Paul's list of charisms provide the list with stylistic variation."

66. Cf. Käsemann, *Romans*, 12: "The Spirit of holiness is the power in virtue of which Jesus is appointed the Son of God."

67. So Paul J. Achtemeier, *1 Peter* (Hermeneia; Minneapolis: Fortress, 1996), 250-51,

Fourth, one may observe that assigning this meaning to Rom 1:4 — that Jesus was designated Son through the agency of the Spirit — coheres with the Old Testament and Jewish understanding that the Spirit is the one through whom God will raise the dead, most notably in Ezek 37:5, 14.[68]

Finally, the parallel with Rom 8:11 may help to resolve the apparent problem of the Spirit's role in 1:4 — as well as to contribute to the argument I am making for the Spirit's role in marking out Jesus and God in their respective identities by his own action. So, turning now to Romans 8, I intend what follows both to further strengthen the conclusion offered above with regard to 1:4 as well as to further solidify the wider case I am making for the Spirit as an agent in the resurrection of Jesus, thereby playing a role in the identification of God and Jesus.

ii. The One Who Raised, Jesus Who Was Raised, and the Spirit

Rom 8:11 may constitute Paul's richest, densest triadic formulation: "But if the Spirit of the one who raised Jesus from the dead dwells in you, the one who raised Christ from the dead will give life to your mortal bodies through his Spirit who dwells in you" (εἰ δὲ τὸ πνεῦμα τοῦ ἐγείραντος τὸν Ἰησοῦν ἐκ νεκρῶν οἰκεῖ ἐν ὑμῖν, ὁ ἐγείρας Χριστὸν ἐκ νεκρῶν ζῳοποιήσει καὶ τὰ θνητὰ σώματα ὑμῶν διὰ τοῦ ἐνοικοῦντος αὐτοῦ πνεύματος ἐν ὑμῖν).[69] Despite the intermingling and intertwining of the agencies of God, Jesus, and the Spirit here, however, some exegetes have seen in the passage

---

who comments: "Such a construal has the advantage of allowing us to understand Christ's resurrection in the second member of the parallel phrase in its normal form, as a bodily resurrection, since the resurrection is being described in terms of the one who brought it about (Spirit), not in terms of the sphere within which it occurred (spirit). Such a construal would therefore allow the interpretation of the phrase to remain within the normal boundaries of NT tradition. One need no longer posit here some unique affirmation about Christ's resurrection that is at odds with the remainder of such tradition."

68. Cf. Scott, *Adoption as Sons of God*, 243 n. 81. This point has now been argued extensively in John W. Yates, *The Spirit and Creation in Paul* (WUNT 2/251; Tübingen: Mohr Siebeck, 2008). It should also be noted that the Niceno-Constantinopolitan Creed's article on the Holy Spirit, designating him as "the Lord, the Giver of Life," is based on this tradition, likely including Rom 8:2 and 1 Cor 15:45.

69. We have already had occasion to note Robert Jenson's comment that Rom 8 is the "most remarkable trinitarian passage in the New Testament" and 8:11 is its "conceptual and argumentative heart" (*The Triune Identity: God According to the Gospel* [Philadelphia: Fortress, 1982], 44).

a deliberate exclusion of the Spirit's agency from the resurrection of Jesus. Gordon Fee has made the point with greater clarity and forcefulness than most:

> [D]espite much that is asserted or argued to the contrary, Paul neither says nor does the logic of the sentence demand that God raised Christ by means of the Spirit. In fact, despite the prevalence of this idea . . . , Paul nowhere explicitly suggests as much; it is doubtful whether it is implicit in the few texts — including this one — that are often read this way. One can understand how this sentence might easily be misread, but such an idea is quite beside Paul's point. His reason for identifying the Spirit as "the Spirit of him who raised Christ from the dead" is not to say something about the role of the Spirit in Christ's having been raised, but to make the closest possible connection between Christ's resurrection and ours. For Paul the presence in our lives of the Spirit of the God who raises the dead does not imply agency, but rather expresses certainty about our future, predicated on the Risen Christ and by the already present Spirit; that, after all, is quite the point of the repeated "who dwells in you," and especially in its second instance, "*because of* the Spirit who *indwells* in you."[70]

Two steps are implied or asserted here. First, Fee rightly notes that the "one" (ὁ ἐγείρας) who raised Jesus from the dead is explicitly said to be God and not the Spirit, since the Spirit is "of" the one who so raises (τὸ πνεῦμα τοῦ ἐγείραντος τὸν Ἰησοῦν). Second, Fee opts for the διά + accusative reading for the final phrase of v. 11, διὰ τὸ ἐνοικοῦν αὐτοῦ πνεῦμα,[71] which removes any thought of even a secondary agency for the Spirit. The resultant position is that Paul means to say that *God the Father* raised Jesus and will raise believers as well because believers now have the indwelling Spirit as a guarantee of their relation to Jesus.

In response to this, we need to say first that the case for the διά + accusative reading at the end of v. 11 is not as assured as Fee suggests. If we grant that the external evidence is inconclusive and turn to internal considerations, we note immediately that v. 11 may be read as an expansion of the highly compressed formulation at the end of v. 10: πνεῦμα ζωὴ διὰ

---

70. Fee, *God's Empowering Presence*, 553.

71. As read by B D F G K Ψ 33 181 1241 1739 1881 lat MajT Origen. Fee, *God's Empowering Presence*, 543 n. 205.

δικαιοσύνην. In keeping with the immediate context in which the Spirit has been described as τὸ πνεῦμα τῆς ζωῆς (v. 2; cf. v. 6, τὸ δὲ φρόνημα τοῦ πνεύματος ζωὴ καὶ εἰρήνη), this is most likely an abbreviated way of attributing resurrecting agency to the Spirit — that is, the Spirit *will give* life to believers' bodies on the basis of their having become "righteous," as v. 11 goes on to explain.[72] On the basis of the righteousness believers already possess (their "justification"), the Spirit will grant eschatological life.[73] Although Paul is able to think of the life of the resurrection as experienced already in the present (e.g., 6:11), he has in view primarily the *bodily* life of *the* "resurrection of the dead," as the contrast with σῶμα indicates. Thus, contra Fee, the Spirit has already been described in terms that suggest his life-giving capacity in v. 10, so we are prepared for the Spirit to assume that role again in v. 11.[74]

But also in response to Fee, we may ask whether the assurance he thinks Paul offers in 8:11 really *is* assurance if the resurrection of believers does not correspond to that of Christ. Fee wants the indwelling Spirit to function as the basis on which believers may have confidence that they will be raised as Christ was raised. Assuming that this was indeed Paul's aim, but (contra Fee) adopting the genitive reading of the final clause of v. 11, διὰ τοῦ ἐνοικοῦντος αὐτοῦ πνεύματος, we may pose the question this way: If believers will be raised through the agency of the Spirit, and if Paul's point is to draw a parallel between Jesus' resurrection and that of believers, for the purpose of providing confidence to believers that they will be raised *as* Jesus was raised, is it not best to assume that Paul thinks *Jesus* also was

---

72. So Douglas A. Campbell, *The Quest for Paul's Gospel: A Suggested Strategy* (London: T&T Clark, 2005), 78.

73. So Cranfield, *Romans,* 1:390; Moo, *Romans,* 492.

74. It may be, however, that the same thought could be expressed with the accusative τὸ ἐνοικοῦν αὐτοῦ πνεῦμα, as Käsemann, *Romans,* 225 ("Materially it makes no difference"), Wilckens, *Römer,* 2:134 n. 551 ("keine inhaltliche Differenz"), and J. Lionel North, "The Transformation of Some New Testament Texts in Fourth- and Fifth-Century Disputes about Πνεῦμα: *Disputando Inclarescet Veritas,*" in *The Holy Spirit and Christian Origins: Essays in Honor of James D. G. Dunn* (ed. G. N. Stanton, B. W. Longenecker, and S. C. Barton; Grand Rapids: Eerdmans, 2004), 335-48, at 343, suggest, *pace* Otto Michel, *Der Brief an die Römer* (Göttingen: Vandenhoeck & Ruprecht, 1955), 255. Scott, *Adoption as Sons of God,* 256 n. 122, says, "A case can be made that both readings express the idea of agency," presumably since the accusative rendering — "On account of the Spirit, [God] will give life" — could be filled out to mean that God depends on the Spirit ("on the basis of") to grant resurrection life. In any case, elsewhere in the undisputed Paulines, διά + accusative πνεῦμα is not used while διά + πνεύματος does recur (Rom 5:5; 15:30; 1 Cor 2:10; 12:8; cf. Eph 3:16).

raised through the agency of the Spirit? Certainly Paul does not say this directly. Fee is right that God (the Father) remains the explicit ultimate cause of Jesus' resurrection: ὁ ἐγείρας Χριστὸν ἐκ νεκρῶν ζῳοποιήσει κτλ. But what Fee cannot really explain is why Paul would not have simply said θεός will raise the dead. If Fee is right, why would Paul have resorted to the elaborate circumlocution in v. 11b if he did not intend it to recall the identifying description in v. 11a and thereby draw God and the Spirit together? My answer is that Paul references God and the Spirit together in this way precisely in order to *unite* their agencies: God raises Jesus *by means of* the Spirit. If the parallel between believers' future resurrection and Jesus' resurrection is to function as Paul means for it to function, the thought must be that the Spirit who will be the means of believers' resurrection was also active alongside God as he raised Jesus.[75] And vice versa: the same Spirit who raised Jesus, who now indwells believers, will in the future be the means — again — by which God raises the dead. As F. X. Durrwell puts it, "The Holy Spirit appears as an agent of the Resurrection; the glorification of the faithful is explicitly attributed to him and that of Christ *indirectly*. The Father is behind the action of resurrecting, but it becomes effective by means of the Spirit."[76]

We have here, then, both a confirmation of my wider argument about the Spirit's role in identifying Jesus and God by means of raising Jesus from the dead and also a confirmation that my exegesis of Rom 1:4 was along

75. Scott Brodeur, *The Holy Spirit's Agency in the Resurrection of the Dead: An Exegetico-Theological Study of 1 Corinthians 15,44b-49 and Romans 8,9-13* (Rome: Editrice Pontificia Università Gregoriana, 1996), 214. Yates, *The Spirit and Creation in Paul*, 149: "In v. 11 God himself is directly involved as the one who raises Christ from the dead. It is also clear that the spirit is intimately involved in this act in some way. If Paul does not intend to attribute agency to the spirit then the final phrase of v. 11 is very odd indeed. In v. 11a Paul has already established that the spirit is God's guarantee of future resurrection: 'If the spirit indwells you, God will give you life' is the simplest paraphrase of v. 11a-b. However, Paul adds the final phrase 'through his Spirit who dwells in you' (v. 11c) in an evident desire to underscore the fact of the spirit's activity in the resurrection. Otherwise, v. 11c becomes an unnecessary repetition of v. 11a."

76. F. X. Durrwell, *The Resurrection: A Biblical Study* (New York: Sheed & Ward, 1960), 91-92. Italics added. Durwell's whole discussion of Paul's account of the Spirit's role in the resurrection (91-107) is especially rich. Compare Neill Q. Hamilton, *The Holy Spirit and Eschatology in Paul* (SJTOP 6; Edinburgh: Oliver & Boyd, 1957), 18: "Whereas in [Rom] 1.4 Jesus' resurrection was attributed directly to the agency of the Spirit, and the general resurrection only indirectly, in 8.11 the general resurrection is attributed directly to the agency of the Spirit, while Christ's resurrection is attributed indirectly to the Spirit." Cf. Wilckens, *Römer*, 2:133.

the right lines. According to these two texts from Romans, Paul not only thinks of the Spirit as dispatched by God and Jesus and thus deriving his identity from their identities and actions; Paul also conceives of God and Jesus as being determined in their identities and actions in part from the Spirit. Insofar as God raises Jesus by the Spirit, it is difficult to escape the conclusion that the identities determined for God and Jesus in that act of resurrection — namely, as the Father who exalts and glorifies and the Son who becomes Son of God in power and exalted Lord — are determined precisely in and through the Spirit's agency. No one in recent scholarship has put the point more forcefully than Douglas Campbell:

> The Father will not be a Father without a Son to send and to sacrifice; the Son not a Son without a Father who has sent and surrendered (and whom presumably he also obeys). Moreover, Christ is not resurrected merely at the behest of the Father but by the Spirit. Indeed, the Spirit is consistently in this story a Spirit *of life* who creates life (so vv. 2, 6, 10, 11, 13b, and 16-17; cf. esp. 4:17, 19). Hence the story is also incomplete without Him. To speak of the Father's relationship to the Son or vice versa is to speak of the Spirit's role in re-establishing that (so that, perhaps, we can therefore speak easily of a Spirit associated both with the Father, God, and with the Son, Christ, as in vv. 9 and 11).[77]

The Spirit raises Jesus at God's initiative, thereby binding God and Jesus together in such a way that their relationship may be said to involve his agency. God and Jesus are who they are only in relation to this action of the Spirit, just as the Spirit is who the Spirit is only as the Spirit of God and of Jesus.

3. Against "Binitarianism"

What we have seen, then, is clear reciprocity in how the identities of God, Jesus, and the Spirit are constituted. The Spirit is who he is only insofar as he is sent by God to be the Spirit of God's Son; but, in a movement of mutuality, the Spirit is the agent by which God raises Jesus from the dead, constituting himself as Jesus' Father and Jesus as the "Son of God in power." In the light of this triune relationality, we must ask briefly what

---

77. Campbell, *The Quest for Paul's Gospel*, 78.

it might mean, therefore, for Paul's theology to be called "binitarian."[78] Is such a description really viable? This claim, frequently met in the literature of Pauline scholarship, is not always placed in opposition to "trinitarian," although occasionally it is. Sometimes the term is used to speak of Jesus' highly exalted status vis-à-vis God, but at other times it appears to be employed for a polemical purpose — to assert that Paul's theology is *not* trinitarian but instead focused on only two (God and Jesus) as holding priority or together constituting the "divine identity" to the exclusion of a third (the Spirit). C. F. D. Moule is representative of this latter usage when he writes,

> The Incarnation has led Christians to a binitarian conception of the Deity; but is there anything in the phenomena of the Spirit comparably cogent for an essentially trinitarian differentiation in this pluriform unity? The idea of the sending of the Spirit . . . does not seem to secure more than that God's activity impinges on his world through or because of Christ.[79]

Moule seems to be concerned about whether the Spirit may rightly be described as *personal* for Paul, that is, irreducibly distinct from and yet also united with God. Since Moule thinks the Spirit may not be so distinguished, he is doubtful whether the later fourth-century conceptualities of "persons" and "relations" can offer any insight into the dynamics of Paul's pneumatology, and in this he is not alone.

Such a perspective goes hand in hand with the decision to evaluate Paul's christology as either "high" or "low," as I argued in Chapter 1. There I attempted to show that the regular pattern among Paul's interpreters is to begin by identifying Paul's God, followed by seeing Jesus as placed somewhere along a spectrum of closeness to or distance from that God. On this account, the Spirit becomes the means whereby Jesus mediates his power or presence to and among believers but does not thereby enjoy a role in identifying God or Jesus by means of his mutual relations with them. God

78. Note the refrain in Hurtado, *Lord Jesus Christ,* 50, 51, 64, 74, 134-53, especially 151-53; cf. Larry W. Hurtado, "The Binitarian Shape of Early Christian Worship," in *The Jewish Roots of Christological Monotheism: Papers from the St Andrews Conference on the Historical Origins of the Worship of Jesus* (ed. C. C. Newman, J. Davila, G. Lewis; Leiden: Brill, 1999), 187-213.

79. C. F. D. Moule, "The New Testament and the Doctrine of the Trinity: A Short Report on an Old Theme," *ExpTim* 88 (1976): 16-20, at 18.

and Jesus are *who they are* initially without the Spirit and simply mediate their identities *through* deploying the Spirit in their redemptive actions.

In contrast to these perspectives, I have argued for a matrix of relationality in which God and Jesus together determine the character and action of the Spirit, while the Spirit, in turn, impinges upon and just so helps identify God and Jesus in their personal uniqueness in the "economy" of their actions with and among believers.[80] The Spirit is only identifiable as a unique agent in the drama of God's saving work if one speaks of the Spirit as the Spirit of God and the Spirit of Christ. Concomitantly, God and Jesus are only specifiable as the unique agents they are if one speaks of Jesus as raised through the agency of the Spirit and thereby also speaks of God as the one who raised him according to that Spirit. Such a perspective suggests that Moule's and other scholars' language of "binitarianism" is drastically misleading. The "binitarian" descriptor implies (or overtly asserts) that the Spirit is not essential to the story of God and Jesus' identities. It suggests that Paul's theology is better limned by keeping the Spirit's identity and action in a secondary, derivative place from those of God and Jesus. But that, as we have seen, is a perspective exegesis will not support.

---

80. This careful statement is meant to signal my reticence to claim too much for Paul. In contrast to, e.g., Thomas Weinandy, *The Father's Spirit of Sonship: Reconceiving the Trinity* (Edinburgh: T&T Clark, 1995), 32, who claims that Rom 8:11 indicates that "within the immanent Trinity the Father begets (eternally establishes and confirms) the Son in divine glory and power by the Holy Spirit," I am saying that for Paul the identities of God, Jesus, and the Spirit *in the economy of redemption* are mutually constitutive. To pick out God, Jesus, or the Spirit as distinguishable, unique identities or agents in the story of their interaction with humanity requires reference to the three of them together; as Hans Urs von Balthasar, *Theo-Drama* (vol. III; trans. Graham Harrison; San Francisco: Ignatius Press, 1992), 508, puts it, "theological persons cannot be defined apart from their dramatic action." My argument has concerned these *dramatis personae* in the economy. Asking what implications Pauline theology has for a doctrine of the immanent trinity is a question that has largely, though not entirely, been ignored in this thesis. For interesting reflections on the "person-constituting" role of the Spirit in the *immanent* trinity, see, in addition to Weinandy's study, Peter J. Leithart, *Athanasius* (Foundations of Theological Exegesis and Christian Spirituality; Grand Rapids: Baker Academic, 2011), 87: "As the one by whom the Father begets the Son, the Spirit gives fatherhood to the Father and sonship to the Son, so that the Father and the Son are both dependent on the Spirit, but asymmetrically"; and Mark A. McIntosh, *Mystical Theology: The Integrity of Spirituality and Theology* (Challenges in Contemporary Theology; Oxford: Blackwell, 1998), 159-60: "Thus God the Holy Spirit, I am suggesting, might be thought of as the Love who . . . is not simply a 'bond' of love between the Father and the Son but who truly marks the Father and Son as who they are, as Persons, by drawing them into . . . mutual ecstasy."

For Paul, the Spirit is necessary if we are to identify God and Jesus, just as we must have recourse to God's and Jesus' identities if we are to identify the Spirit. To invoke again Campbell's felicitous way of putting the point, "the story is . . . incomplete" without the Spirit.[81]

81. Campbell, *The Quest for Paul's Gospel,* 78.

Conclusion

*If it be acknowledged that appeals to [the doctrine of the] Trinity
. . . may in practice sometimes function as anachronistic impositions
which distort true historical understanding, it does not follow that
this is their sole function. May they not be insights of an ultimate
kind into the nature of God and humanity, focused in Jesus Christ,
whose role is to enable understanding of God and humanity in any
context, not least within the Bible . . . ?*

R. W. L. Moberly[1]

Describing the theology of Athanasius of Alexandria, Khaled Anatolios
speaks of "the very character of God as christological." For Athanasius,
"The patterns of scriptural co-naming of God and Christ lead us to conceive of the God-Christ relation as intrinsically constitutive of God."[2] Add
the Spirit to this equation, and one might expand Anatolios's description
as follows: the patterns of New Testament speech about God, Christ, and
the Spirit lead us to understand that triune, reciprocal web of relations as
constitutive of the identities of each of the three. God the Father, the Son
of God, and the Holy Spirit are constituted by and in their relations to and
with one another.

Many scholars of early Christianity are happy to affirm something

---

1. R. W. L. Moberly, *The Bible, Theology, and Faith: A Study of Abraham and Jesus* (Cambridge Studies in Christian Doctrine; Cambridge: Cambridge University Press, 2000), 6.

2. Khaled Anatolios, *Retrieving Nicaea: The Development and Meaning of Trinitarian
Doctrine* (Grand Rapids: Baker Academic, 2011), 156.

like this as an accurate description of certain fourth-century pro-Nicene theological trajectories. Most of those same scholars, however, are wary of affirming that the first-century apostle Paul thought in conceptually equivalent terms. Rejecting trinitarian categories of thought, Pauline scholars have developed newer, allegedly more "historical" descriptors to capture Paul's theological discourse. I have outlined in detail the theological conceptualities that have replaced the Nicene language when it comes to the interpretation of Pauline God-, Christ-, and Spirit-talk. Across a wide range of scholarship, the language of "high" and "low" christologies has come to dominate the description of the theology found in Paul's letters. This conceptuality offers the image of a vertical axis (rather than the picture of a web or a matrix that a more Nicene, trinitarian model suggests). With "God" at the top of the axis, the interpretive question becomes, How close or how distant are "Jesus" and "the Spirit" from God? At what point should they be plotted on the vertical axis? For many self-consciously "orthodox" interpreters, Jesus and the Spirit come very close indeed to God, perhaps even, after the fashion of certain Jewish angelic or intermediary figures, taking on the divine titles and prerogatives. For other readers, less concerned to preserve a connection between Pauline and later Christian theologies, Jesus and the Spirit are not so close to the one God after all; they are "lower" on the scale of being. Regardless of how they differ, though, all these interpreters — the more "orthodox" and the less so — share a commitment to the vertical axis approach. "High" or "low" christologies, and "high" or "low" pneumatologies, represent the primary (or only) options in the debate.

Such a perspective, however, has left a few interpreters dissatisfied. As we have seen, there *has* been a minority report in the guild of Pauline scholars, pushing back against the "high" versus "low" debate. Nils Dahl, Leander Keck, Kavin Rowe, and others, while not explicitly and thoroughly rejecting the language and conceptuality of "high" versus "low" christologies, have nonetheless advocated for a more complex, dynamic, "relational" approach. Instead of starting with God and attempting to fit Jesus and the Spirit in alongside or underneath him somewhere on an axis of nearness, it is better — these interpreters have posited — to see neither God, Jesus, nor the Spirit as enjoying primacy on their own but to see them all as equally primal, mutually determinative, relationally constituted. "God," on this account, is unspecifiable apart from Jesus and the Spirit; likewise, "Jesus" is unknowable apart from his relations with God and the Spirit; and "the Spirit" is impossible to identify without God and

Jesus. Together, all three exist in a web or skein of relationality that makes each of the three who they are.

Such a perspective, of course, is not really a "minority report." It is simply the perspective of the mainstream of mature fourth-century (and later) trinitarian doctrine. Dahl, Keck, Rowe, and others are aware of this but have not exploited it in the way that they might have done. Taking up their hunch about the contours of Pauline theology, I have tried to allow some of the conceptualities of trinitarian doctrine to serve as a hermeneutical lens for rereading Paul's letters and thereby put the Dahl/Keck/Rowe hunch to the test. Is it possible, I asked, that a kind of broad, pluriform trinitarian perspective, far from being an anachronistic imposition on the texts of Paul, may instead prove genuinely insightful in a fresh look at Paul? With that question in mind, I turned to exegesis.

In Chapter 2, I demonstrated that Paul's God-discourse, at several key moments (Rom 4:24; 8:11; Gal 1:1), bears a distinctly christological shape. In other words, Paul identifies God — picks God out of the crowd, as it were — by referring to Jesus. And this, in turn, means that the vertical axis model — whereby "God" is known first apart from Jesus and only then, subsequently, as Jesus is brought into relation to God — finds itself under severe theological strain. If Paul's God-discourse is permeated with christological references, if it is stamped with a christological imprint, then it is better to speak of mutuality between God and Jesus. In short, a web, not an axis, is a better metaphor for describing the relationship between God and Jesus in Paul's letters. This led, in turn, in Chapters 3 and 4, to a discussion of the *theo*logical shape of Paul's christology. Jesus, in other words, is determined in his unique identity by his relationship to God. The mutuality and reciprocity that obtains between God and Jesus was thus confirmed from the opposite angle: not only is God who God is only in relation to Jesus, but also Jesus is who he is only in relation to God.

At this point, however, I confronted an objection. The latter half of the reciprocal movement is so obvious in Paul's letters — Jesus is so evidently *dependent* on God for his identity — that it has led many interpreters to speak of Jesus' "subordination" to God and to see that "subordination" as out of step with trinitarian theology. This apparent problem for my thesis of relational mutuality had to be confronted. Hence, Chapters 3 and 4, in addition to speaking of the mutuality between God and Jesus, also explored in greater depth the concept of "asymmetry" (which had already been treated briefly in Chapter 2). As I interpreted Phil 2:5-11 and 1 Cor 8:6 and 15:24-28, I concluded that Jesus and God mutually constitute one another's identities, but those identities are not thereby interchangeable. God remains "Father," and Jesus remains "Son."

One might think that this asymmetry simply *confirms* subordination; Jesus is subordinate to God, and *that is what* asymmetry *means*. Facing this objection and using the trinitarian conceptual resource of *redoublement* (covering the same ground twice over), I argued that God and Jesus share the divine identity — they each bear the same divine name (unity) — but their personal uniqueness is not thereby impaired (distinction). If that is the case, then two affirmations emerge that call into question the usefulness of the "subordination" rubric. First, God's and Jesus' identities are constituted in and by their differing ways of relating to one another: God sends and exalts, Jesus is sent and exalted. But second, those differing relations are one perspective on God and Jesus that must be held together with a second perspective which sees them as fundamentally one or unified: God and Jesus share the divine name; they are both together "the Lord."

This led, finally, to a discussion of the identity of the Spirit in Paul's letters and to a confrontation with those interpreters who view Paul's theology as "binitarian" but not fully "trinitarian." Chapter 5 began with a discussion of "the relational determination of the Spirit's identity"[3] in 1 Cor 12:3; Gal 4:4-6; and 2 Cor 3:17. There I argued that the Spirit's identity is grasped by recognizing his personal identity to be derived from God and Jesus. In a reciprocal movement, however, I went on to argue that Rom 1:4 and 8:9-11 give the Spirit a role in identifying God as the one who raised Jesus from the dead and, just so, Jesus as the Son of God in power. The mutually constituted identity of God as Father and Jesus as Son is, therefore, inclusive of the Spirit: God and Jesus would not be who they are in the drama of salvation if it were not for the Spirit's agency in the resurrection of Jesus at the behest of God the Father.

What I tried to demonstrate in the course of these chapters, in addition to the limitations of the categories of "high" and "low" christology, is what might be called the hermeneutical fruitfulness of trinitarian theology. Scholarship is well served with a variety of studies displaying how the biblical texts were used in the construction of trinitarian doctrine. These studies are rightly concerned to respect the linear unfolding of historical

---

3. C. Kavin Rowe, "The Trinity in the Letters of St. Paul and Hebrews," in Gilles Emery, O.P. and Matthew Levering (eds.), *The Oxford Handbook of the Trinity* (Oxford Handbooks in Religion and Theology; New York: Oxford University Press, 2011), 41-54, at 50.

development, rather than anachronistically imposing later theologies back onto Paul's letters. But my thesis, while it may have contributed indirectly to that historical-critical project, has been mostly taken up with demonstrating the converse: that trinitarian doctrine may be used *retrospectively* to shed light on and enable a deeper penetration of the Pauline texts in their own historical milieu, and that it is not necessarily anachronistic to allow later Christian categories to be the lens through which one reads Paul. Borrowing the language of R. R. Reno, I have treated trinitarian doctrine as "a clarifying agent, an enduring tradition of theological judgments that amplifies the living voice" of Paul.[4] If, as Rowe thinks, "there is (or can be) a profound continuity, grounded in the subject matter itself, between the biblical text and traditional Christian exegesis and theological formulation,"[5] then it should be possible to trace out some of that "profound continuity." I have tried to do some of that tracing — to show that the conceptual categories of "persons in relation," developed so richly in the fourth century and in the following theological eras, may enable those who live with them to live more deeply and fruitfully with the first-century apostle himself.

The results of such an endeavor may, it is hoped, lead to further examination of the interdependence of biblical exegesis and dogmatic theology. If trinitarian theology comes to the assistance of the exegete grappling with Paul's theology, then that reader of Paul may in turn remind trinitarian theology of its own exegetical roots. As we have seen, there are tensions and trajectories in Paul's letters that lead to the construction of trinitarian conceptualities, and, as we have also seen, those conceptualities are then able retrospectively to assist in the rereading of the Pauline texts. If that is the case, then we are dealing with a reciprocal, mutual relationship between exegesis and theology. Exegesis of Paul does not reach its full potential without trinitarian theology, I have argued, and, likewise, trinitarian theology is impoverished if it neglects biblical exegesis in general and exegesis of Paul in particular. Such a symbiosis should come as no surprise to stewards of the history of trinitarian doctrine, nor to those cultivating the vineyard of Pauline studies. That it is surprising to many today need lead us not to despair but instead to a renewed commitment to

---

4. R. R. Reno, "Series Preface," in Joseph L. Mangina, *Revelation* (Brazos Theological Commentary on the Bible; Grand Rapids: Brazos, 2010), 9-14, at 11.

5. C. Kavin Rowe, "Biblical Pressure and Trinitarian Hermeneutics," *Pro Ecclesia* 11 (2002): 295-312, at 308.

cultivate both fields simultaneously. Theology and the reading of Scripture belong together. And that belonging is both a description of the history of Pauline and trinitarian studies *and* a summons to practice those disciplines in a renewed form today.

Bibliography

PRIMARY SOURCES

Aquinas, Thomas. *Summa theologiae*. Edited by T. Gilby and T. C. O'Brien. Blackfriars. 60 vols. London: Eyre and Spottiswoode; New York: McGraw-Hill, 1964-73.

Athanasius of Alexandria. *Werke I/1. Die dogmatischen Schriften. 4. Lieferung. Epistulae I-IV ad Serapionem*. Edited by Dietmar Wyrwa and Kyriakos Savvidis. Berlin/New York: Walter de Gruyter, 2010.

Athanasius the Great and Didymus the Blind. *Works on the Spirit*. Translated by Mark DelCogliano, Andrew Radde-Gallwitz, and Lewis Ayres. Popular Patristics Series. Yonkers, NY: St. Vladimir's Seminary Press, 2011.

Augustine of Hippo. *On the Trinity*. Edited by W. J. Mountain and F. Glorie. 2 vols. CCSL 50-50A. Turnhout: Brepols, 1968. ET E. Hill. *The Trinity*. Hyde Park, NY: New City Press, 1991.

Augustine. *Tractates on John 28-54*. Translated by John W. Rettig. Washington, DC: Catholic University of America Press, 1993.

Augustine. *Commentary on the Letter to the Galatians*. CSEL 84. Translated by Eric Plumer. Oxford: Clarendon Press, 2003.

Basil of Caesarea. *Against Eunomius*. Edited by B. Sesboüé, with G.-M. Durand and L. Doutreleau. *Basile de Césarée: Contre Eunome suive de Eunome Apologie*. SC 299, 305. Paris: Cerf, 1982-83.

Gregory of Nazianzus. *Theological Orations 27-31*. Edited by P. Gallay, with M. Jourjon. *Grégoire de Nazianze: Discours 27-31 (Discours Théologiques)*. SC 250. Paris: Cerf, 1978. ET: L. Wickham and F. W. Norris. *Faith Gives Fullness to Reasoning: The Five Theological Orations of Gregory Nazianzus*. Leiden: Brill, 1991.

Gregory of Nyssa. *Against Eunomius*. Edited by W. Jaeger. *Contra Eunomium Libri*. GNO 1-2. Leiden: Brill, 1960. ET: NPNF[2] 5:35-314.

Gregory of Nyssa. *To Ablabius, On Not Three Gods.* Edited by F. Müller. *Opera Dogmatica Minora.* GNO 3.1. Leiden: Brill, 1958. ET: C. Richardson. *Christology of the Later Fathers.* Philadelphia: Westminster, 1954.

Origen. *Homilies on Genesis and Exodus.* Translated by R. E. Heine. The Fathers of the Church 71. Washington, D.C.: Catholic University of America, 1982.

Origen. *Commentary on the Gospel according to John Books 1-10.* Translated by R. E. Heine. The Fathers of the Church 80. Washington, D.C.: Catholic University of America, 1989.

Richard of St.-Victor, *La Trinité.* Edited by G. Salet. SC 63. Paris: Cerf, 1999. ET: Richard of St. Victor. *De Trinitate.* In *The Twelve Patriarchs: The Mystical Ark, Book Three of the Trinity.* Translated by G. A. Zinn. New York: Paulist Press, 1979.

SECONDARY SOURCES

Achtemeier, Paul J. *1 Peter.* Hermeneia. Minneapolis: Fortress, 1996.

Anatolios, Khaled. *Retrieving Nicaea: The Development and Meaning of Trinitarian Doctrine.* Grand Rapids: Baker Academic, 2011.

Andrews, Elias. *The Meaning of Christ for Paul.* Nashville: Abingdon, 1949.

Aono, Tashio. *Die Entwicklung des paulinischen Gerichtsgedankens bei den Apostolischen Vätern.* Europäische Hochschulschriften 23/137. Bern/Frankfurt/Las Vegas: P. Lang, 1979.

Ayres, Lewis. "Augustine, the Trinity and Modernity." *Augustinian Studies* 26/2 (1995): 127-33.

———. *Nicaea and Its Legacy: An Approach to Fourth-Century Trinitarian Theology.* Oxford: Oxford University Press, 2004.

———. "A Response to the Critics of *Nicaea and Its Legacy.*" *HTR* 100/2 (2007): 159-71.

———. *Augustine and the Trinity.* Cambridge: Cambridge University Press, 2010.

Badiou, Alain. *Saint Paul: The Foundation of Universalism.* Translated by Roy Brassier. Stanford: Stanford University Press, 2003.

Baird, W. "New Testament Criticism." Pages 730-36 in *Anchor Bible Dictionary.* Volume 1. Edited by David Noel Freedman. New York and London: Doubleday, 1992.

Bakhtin, Mikhail M. "Response to a Question from the *Novy Mir* Editorial Staff." Pages 1-9 in *Speech Genres and Other Late Essays.* Edited by Caryl Emerson and Michael Holquist. Translated by Vern W. McGee. Austin: University of Texas Press, 1986.

Barclay, John M. G. "Paul's Story: Theology as Testimony." Pages 133-56 in *Narrative Dynamics in Paul: A Critical Assessment.* Edited by Bruce W. Longenecker. Louisville/London: Westminster John Knox, 2002.

———. "'By the Grace of God I Am What I Am': Grace and Agency in Philo and

Paul." Pages 140-57 in *Divine and Human Agency in Paul and His Cultural Environment*. Edited by John M. G. Barclay and Simon Gathercole. LNTS 335. London: T&T Clark, 2006.

———. "Paul, the Gift and the Battle over Gentile Circumcision: Revisiting the Logic of Galatians." *Australian Biblical Review* 58 (2010): 36-56.

Barnes, Michel René. "Augustine in Contemporary Trinitarian Theology." *Theological Studies* 56/2 (1995): 237-50.

———. "De Régnon Reconsidered." *Augustinian Studies* 26 (1995): 51-79.

Barrett, C. K. *A Commentary on the First Epistle to the Corinthians.* 2nd edition. London: Black, 1971 (1968).

———. *The Epistle to the Romans.* Revised edition. BNTC. Peabody: Hendrickson, 1991 (1957).

Barth, Karl. *Church Dogmatics.* Translated by G. W. Bromiley, et al. Edinburgh: T&T Clark, 1956-75.

———. *The Epistle to the Philippians.* Louisville: Westminister John Knox, 2002 (1962).

Barton, John. *The Nature of Biblical Criticism.* Louisville: Westminster John Knox, 2007.

Bassler, Jouette M. "1 Cor 12:3 — Curse and Confession in Context." *JBL* 101 (1982): 415-18.

Bauckham, Richard J. *God Crucified: Monotheism and Christology in the New Testament.* Grand Rapids: Eerdmans, 1998.

———. "The Worship of Jesus in Philippians 2:9-11." Pages 128-39 in *Where Christology Began: Essays on Philippians 2.* Edited by Ralph P. Martin and Brian J. Dodd. Louisville: Westminster John Knox, 1998.

———. *Jesus and the God of Israel:* God Crucified *and Other Studies on the New Testament's Christology of Divine Identity.* Grand Rapids: Eerdmans, 2008.

Baur, F. C. *Die christliche Lehre von der Dreieinigkeit und Menschwerdung Gottes in ihrer geschichtlichen Entwicklung.* Tübingen: Osiander, 1843.

Beasley-Murray, G. R. *Baptism in the New Testament.* London: Macmillan, 1962.

Beeley, Christopher A. *Gregory of Nazianzus on the Trinity and the Knowledge of God: In Your Light We Shall See Light.* Oxford Studies in Historical Theology; New York: Oxford University Press, 2008.

Beker, J. Christiaan. *Paul the Apostle: The Triumph of God in Life and Thought.* Philadelphia: Fortress, 1980.

Belleville, Linda. *Reflections of Glory: Paul's Polemical Use of Moses-Doxa Tradition in 2 Corinthians 3.1-18.* JSNTSup 52. Sheffield: JSOT Press, 1991.

Betz, H. D. *Galatians.* Hermeneia. Philadelphia: Fortress, 1979.

Bittlinger, Arnold. *Gifts and Graces: A Commentary on 1 Corinthians 12–14.* London: Hodder and Stoughton, 1968.

Blaising, Craig A. "Creedal Formulation as Hermeneutical Development: A Reexamination of Nicaea." *Pro Ecclesia* 19/4 (2010): 371-88.

Bockmuehl, Markus. "'The Form of God' (Phil. 2:6): Variations on a Theme of Jewish Mysticism." *JTS* 48/1 (1997): 1-23.

―――. *Seeing the Word: Refocusing New Testament Study*. Studies in Theological Interpretation. Grand Rapids: Baker Academic, 2006.

Boer, Martinus C. de. *The Defeat of Death: Apocalyptic Eschatology in 1 Corinthians 15 and Romans 5*. JSNTSup 22. Sheffield: JSOT, 1988.

―――. "Paul's Use of a Resurrection Tradition in 1 Cor 15,20-28." Pages 639-51 in *The Corinthian Correspondence*. Edited by R. Bieringer. BETL. Leuven: Leuven University Press, 1996.

―――. *Galatians: A Commentary*. NTL. Louisville: Westminster John Knox, 2011.

Boring, M. Eugene. "The Voice of Jesus in the Apocalypse of John." *NovT* 34 (1992): 334-59.

Bousset, Wilhelm. *Kyrios Christos. Geschichte des Christusglaubens von den Anfängen des Christentums bis Irenaeus*. Göttingen: Vandenhoeck & Ruprecht, 1913; revised edition, 1921. ET: *Kyrios Christos: A History of the Belief in Christ from the Beginnings of Christianity to Irenaeus*. Translated by J. E. Steely. Nashville: Abingdon, 1970.

Brodeur, Scott. *The Holy Spirit's Agency in the Resurrection of the Dead: An Exegetico-Theological Study of 1 Corinthians 15,44b-49 and Romans 8,9-13*. Rome: Editrice Pontificia Università Gregoriana, 1996.

Brown, Raymond E. *An Introduction to New Testament Christology*. New York: Paulist Press, 1994.

Brunner, Emil. *The Christian Doctrine of God*. Philadelphia: Westminster, 1950.

Bultmann, Rudolf. "Bekenntnis- und Liedfragmente im ersten Petrusbrief." Pages 1-14 in ConNT in Honorem Antonii Fridrichsen. Lund: C. W. K. Gloerup, 1947.

―――. *Theology of the New Testament*. 2 volumes. New York: Scribner's, 1951-55.

Burchard, C. "Joseph and Asenath: A New Translation and Introduction." Pages 177-247 in *The Old Testament Pseudepigrapha*. Volume 2. Edited by James H. Charlesworth. New York: Doubleday, 1985.

Burk, Denny. "On the Articular Infinitive in Philippians 2:6: A Grammatical Note with Christological Implications." *Tyndale Bulletin* 55/2 (2004): 253-74.

Burton, E. D. *A Critical and Exegetical Commentary on the Epistle to the Galatians*. ICC. New York: Scribner's, 1920.

Byassee, Jason. "Closer than Kissing: Sarah Coakley's Early Work." *Anglican Theological Review* 90/1 (2007): 139-55.

Byrne, Brendan. *"Sons of God" — "Seed of Abraham."* AnBib 83. Rome: Biblical Institute, 1979.

―――. *Romans*. Sacra Pagina 6. Collegeville, MN: Liturgical Press, 1996.

―――. "Christ's Pre-Existence in Pauline Soteriology." *Theological Studies* 58 (1997): 308-30.

Caird, G. B. *New Testament Theology*. Edited and completed by L. D. Hurst. Oxford: Clarendon, 1994.

Calvin, John. "Acts 14–28 and Romans 1–6." In *Calvin's Commentaries Volume 19.* Translated by J. Owen. Grand Rapids: Baker, 2003.

Campbell, Douglas A. *The Rhetoric of Righteousness in Romans 3:21-26.* JSNTSup 65. Sheffield: JSOT Press, 1992.

————. *The Quest for Paul's Gospel: A Suggested Strategy.* London: T&T Clark, 2005.

————. *The Deliverance of God: An Apocalyptic Rereading of Justification in Paul.* Grand Rapids: Eerdmans, 2009.

Capes, David B. *Old Testament Yahweh Texts in Paul's Christology.* WUNT 2/47. Tübingen: Mohr Siebeck, 1992.

Carson, D. A. *Showing the Spirit: A Theological Exposition of 1 Corinthians 12–14.* Carlisle: Paternoster, 1995.

Casey, Maurice. *From Jewish Prophet to Gentile God: The Origins and Development of New Testament Christology.* Louisville: Westminster John Knox, 1991.

————. "Monotheism, Worship and Christological Developments in Pauline Churches." Pages 214-33 in *The Jewish Roots of Christological Monotheism: Papers from the St Andrews Conference on the Historical Origins of the Worship of Jesus.* Edited by C. C. Newman, J. Davila, and G. Lewis. Leiden: Brill, 1999.

Cerfaux, L. "Hymne au Christ — Serviteur de Dieu (Phil., II,6-11 = Is., LII,13–LIII,12)." Pages 425-37 in *Receuil Lucien Cerfaux. Études d'Exégèse et d'Histoire Religieuse.* Volume 2. BETL 6-7. Gembloux: Duculot, 1954.

Christoph, Monika. *Pneuma und das neue Sein der Glaubenden. Studien zur Semantik und Pragmatik der Rede von Pneuma in Röm 8.* Europäische Hochschulschriften 28/813. Frankfurt am Main: Peter Lang, 2005.

Ciampa, Roy E. *The Presence and Function of Scripture in Galatians 1 and 2.* WUNT 2/102. Tübingen: Mohr Siebeck, 1998.

Coakley, Sarah. "God as Trinity: An Approach through Prayer." Pages 104-21 in *We Believe in God: A Report by the Doctrine Commission of the General Synod of the Church of England.* Wilton, CN: Morehouse-Barlow, 1987.

————. "Why Three? Some Further Reflections on the Origins of the Doctrine of the Trinity." Pages 29-56 in *The Making and Remaking of Christian Doctrine.* FS Maurice Wiles. Edited by Sarah Coakley and David Pailin. Oxford: Clarendon Press, 1993.

————. "Living into the Mystery of the Holy Trinity: Trinity, Prayer, and Sexuality." *Anglican Theological Review* 80/2 (1998): 223-32.

————. "*Kenōsis* and Subversion: On the Repression of 'Vulnerability' in Christian Feminist Writing." Pages 3-39 in *Powers and Submissions: Spirituality, Philosophy and Gender.* Challenges in Contemporary Theology. Oxford: Blackwell, 2002.

————. "'Persons' in the 'Social' Doctrine of the Trinity: Current Analytic Discussion and 'Cappadocian' Theology." Pages 109-29 in *Powers and Submissions: Spirituality, Philosophy and Gender.* Challenges in Contemporary Theology. Oxford: Blackwell, 2002.

Collins, Raymond F. *First Corinthians.* Sacra Pagina 7. Collegeville, MN: Liturgical, 1999.

Congar, Yves M. J. *I Believe in the Holy Spirit.* 2 volumes. Translated by David Smith. New York: Seabury, 1983.

Congdon, David W. "The Trinitarian Shape of πίστις: A Theological Exegesis of Galatians." *JTI* 2/2 (2008): 231-258.

Conzelmann, Hans. *1 Corinthians.* Translated by James W. Leitch. Hermeneia. Philadelphia: Fortress, 1975.

Cranfield, C. E. B. *The Epistle to the Romans.* 2 volumes. ICC. Edinburgh: T&T Clark, 1975.

Dahl, Nils Alstrup. "Christ, Creation, and the Church." Pages 422-43 in *The Background of the New Testament and Its Eschatology.* Edited by W. D. Davies and D. Daube. Cambridge: Cambridge University Press, 1964.

———. "Promise and Fulfillment." Pages 121-36 in *Studies in Paul.* Minneapolis: Augsburg, 1977.

———. "The One God of Jews and Gentiles." Pages 178-91 in *Studies in Paul.* Minneapolis: Augsburg, 1977.

———. "The Atonement: An Adequate Reward for the Akedah?" Pages 137-51 in *Jesus the Christ: The Historical Origins of Christological Doctrine.* Edited by Donald H. Juel. Minneapolis: Fortress, 1991.

———. "The Neglected Factor in New Testament Theology." Pages 153-63 in *Jesus the Christ: The Historical Origins of Christological Doctrine.* Edited by Donald H. Juel. Minneapolis: Fortress, 1991.

———. "Trinitarian Baptismal Creeds and New Testament Christology." Pages 165-86 in *Jesus the Christ: The Historical Origins of Christological Doctrine.* Edited by Donald H. Juel. Minneapolis: Fortress, 1991.

Daley, Brian E. " 'One Thing and Another': The Persons in God and the Person of Christ in Patristic Theology." *Pro Ecclesia* 15 (2006): 17-46.

Davis, Carl Judson. *The Name and Way of the Lord: Old Testament Themes, New Testament Christology.* JSNTSup 129. Sheffield: Sheffield Academic Press, 1996.

Dawson, John David. *Christian Figural Reading and the Fashioning of Identity.* Berkeley: University of California, 2002.

Deissmann, Adolf. *St. Paul: A Study in Social and Religious History.* Translated by L. R. M. Strachan. London: Hodder & Stoughton, 1912.

Del Colle, Ralph. " 'Person' and 'Being' in John Zizioulas' Trinitarian Theology: Conversations with Thomas Torrance and Thomas Aquinas." *SJT* 54/1 (2001): 70-86.

Delling, Gerhard. *Die Taufe im Neuen Testament.* Berlin: Evangelische, 1963.

———. "Partizipiale Gottesprädikationen in den Briefen des Neuen Testaments." *Studia Theologica* 17 (1963): 1-59.

———. "Der Bezug der christlichen Existenz auf das Heilshandeln Gottes nach dem ersten Petrusbrief." Pages 95-113 in *Neues Testament und christliche Ex-*

istenz. FS Herbert Braun. Edited by H. D. Betz and L. Schottroff. Tübingen: Mohr Siebeck, 1973.

Denaux, Adelbert. "Theology and Christology in 1 Cor 8,4-6: A Contextual-Redactional Reading." Pages 593-606 in *The Corinthian Correspondence.* Edited by R. Bierenger. BETL. Leuven: Leuven University Press, 1996.

Dodd, C. H. *According to the Scriptures: The Sub-Structure of New Testament Theology.* London: Nisbet, 1952.

Donfried, Karl P. "Alien Hermeneutics and the Misappropriation of Scripture." Pages 19-45 in *Reclaiming the Bible for the Church.* Edited by Carl E. Braaten and Robert W. Jenson. Grand Rapids: Eerdmans, 1995.

Dorner, I. A. *Entwickelungsgeschichte der Lehre von der Person Christi.* 2 volumes. Stuttgart: Verlag von Samuel Gottlieb Liesching, 1845-53. ET: *History of the Development of the Doctrine of the Person of Christ.* 5 volumes. Edinburgh: T&T Clark, 1861-63.

Dunn, James D. G. *Jesus and the Spirit: A Study of the Religious and Charismatic Experience of Jesus and the First Christians as Reflected in the New Testament.* London: SCM, 1975.

———. *Romans 1–8.* WBC 38A. Dallas: Word, 1988.

———. *Christology in the Making: A New Testament Inquiry into the Origins of the Doctrine of the Incarnation.* 2nd edition. London: SCM, 1989.

———. *The Epistle to the Galatians.* BNTC. Peabody, MA: Hendrickson, 1993.

———. "In Quest of Paul's Theology: Retrospect and Prospect." Pages 95-115 in *Pauline Theology,* Volume IV: *Looking Back, Pressing On.* Edited by E. Elizabeth Johnson and David M. Hay. Atlanta: Scholars Press, 1997.

———. "2 Corinthians 3:17 — 'The Lord is the Spirit.'" Pages 115-25 in *The Christ and the Spirit;* Volume 1: *Christology.* Grand Rapids: Eerdmans, 1998.

———. "Pauline Christology: Shaping the Fundamental Structures." Pages 229-38 in *The Christ and the Spirit;* Volume 1: *Christology.* Grand Rapids: Eerdmans, 1998.

———. "Christology as an Aspect of Theology." Pages 377-87 in *The Christ and the Spirit;* Volume 1: *Christology.* Grand Rapids: Eerdmans, 1998.

———. "The Making of Christology: Evolution or Unfolding?" Pages 388-404 in *The Christ and the Spirit;* Volume 1: *Christology.* Grand Rapids: Eerdmans, 1998.

———. *The Theology of Paul the Apostle.* Grand Rapids: Eerdmans, 1998.

———. "When Was Jesus First Worshipped? In Dialogue with Larry Hurtado's *Lord Jesus Christ: Devotion to Jesus in Earliest Christianity.*" *ExpTim* 116 (2005): 193-96.

Dunn, James D. G., and Maurice Wiles. "M. Wiles on *Christology in the Making* and Responses by the Author." Pages 257-69 in *The Christ and the Spirit;* Volume 1: *Christology.* Grand Rapids: Eerdmans, 1998.

Durrwell, F. X. *The Resurrection: A Biblical Study.* New York: Sheed & Ward, 1960.

Eastman, Susan Grove. "Philippians 2:6-11: Incarnation as Mimetic Participation." *Journal for the Study of Paul and His Letters* 1/1 (2010): 1-22.

Emery, Gilles, O.P. "Essentialism or Personalism in the Treatise on God in Saint Thomas Aquinas?" *The Thomist* 64 (2000): 521-64.

———. *The Trinitarian Theology of St. Thomas Aquinas.* Translated by Francesca Aran Murphy. Oxford: Oxford University Press, 2007.

———. *Trinity, Church, and the Human Person: Thomistic Essays.* Naples, FL: Sapientia Press, 2007.

Engberg-Pedersen, Troels. *Cosmology and Self in the Apostle Paul: The Material Spirit.* Oxford: Oxford University Press, 2011.

Eriksson, Anders. *Traditions as Rhetorical Proof: Pauline Argumentation in 1 Corinthians.* ConBNT 29. Stockholm: Almqvist & Wiksell, 1998.

Eskola, Timo. *Messiah and the Throne: Jewish Merkabah Mysticism and Early Christian Exaltation Discourse.* WUNT 2/142. Tübingen: Mohr Siebeck, 2001.

Fatehi, Mehrdad. *The Spirit's Relation to the Risen Lord in Paul.* WUNT 2/128. Tübingen: Mohr Siebeck, 2000.

Fay, Ron C. "Was Paul a Trinitarian? A Look at Romans 8." Pages 327-45 in *Paul and His Theology.* Edited by Stanley E. Porter. Pauline Studies 3. Leiden: Brill, 2006.

Fee, Gordon D. *The First Epistle to the Corinthians.* NICNT. Grand Rapids: Eerdmans, 1987.

———. "Christology and Pneumatology in Romans 8:9-11 — and Elsewhere: Some Reflections on Paul as a Trinitarian." Pages 312-31 in *Jesus of Nazareth: Lord and Christ.* Edited by Joel B. Green and Max Turner. Grand Rapids: Eerdmans, 1994.

———. *God's Empowering Presence: The Holy Spirit in the Letters of Paul.* Peabody, MA: Hendrickson, 1994.

———. *Paul's Letter to the Philippians.* NICNT. Grand Rapids: Eerdmans, 1995.

———. "Paul and the Trinity: The Experience of Christ and the Spirit for Paul's Understanding of God." Pages 49-72 in *The Trinity: An Interdisciplinary Symposium on the Trinity.* Edited by S. T. Davis, D. Kendall, and G. O'Collins. Oxford: Oxford University Press, 1999.

———. *Pauline Christology: An Exegetical-Theological Study.* Peabody, MA: Hendrickson, 2007.

Fitzmyer, Joseph A., S.J. "The Semitic Background of the New Testament *Kyrios*-Title." Pages 115-42 in *A Wandering Aramean: Collected Aramaic Essays.* Chico, CA: Scholars Press, 1979.

———. "New Testament *Kyrios* and *Maranatha* and Their Aramaic Background." Pages 218-35 in *To Advance the Gospel: New Testament Studies.* New York: Crossroad, 1981.

———. *The Gospel according to Luke.* 2 volumes. AB 28-28A. Garden City, NY: Doubleday, 1981, 1985.

———. *Romans.* AB 33. New York: Doubleday, 1992.

Bibliography

Flebbe, Jochen. *Solus Deus. Untersuchungen zur Rede von Gott im Brief des Paulus an die Römer.* BZNW 158. Berlin/New York: Walter de Gruyter, 2008.

Fletcher-Louis, Crispin. "A New Explanation of Christological Origins: A Review of the Work of Larry W. Hurtado." *TynBul* 60/2 (2009): 161-205.

Foley, Grover. "Ritschls Urteil über Zinzendorfs Christozentrismus." *Evangelische Theologie* 20 (1960): 314-26.

Ford, David F., and Frances Young. *Meaning and Truth in 2 Corinthians.* London: SPCK, 1987.

Fossum, Jarl E. "The New *Religionsgeschichtliche Schule:* The Quest for Jewish Christology." Pages 638-46 in *SBLSP 1991.* Edited by E. Lovering. Atlanta: Scholars, 1991.

Frei, Hans. *The Identity of Jesus Christ: The Hermeneutical Bases of Dogmatic Theology.* Reprint. Eugene, OR: Wipf & Stock, 1997.

Fuller, Reginald H. *The Foundations of New Testament Christology.* London: Lutterworth Press, 1965.

Furnish, Victor Paul. *II Corinthians.* AB 32A. New York: Doubleday, 1984.

Gabriel, Andrew K. "Pauline Pneumatology and the Question of Trinitarian Presuppositions." Pages 347-62 in *Paul and His Theology.* Edited by Stanley E. Porter. Pauline Studies 3. Leiden: Brill, 2006.

Garland, David E. *1 Corinthians.* BECNT. Grand Rapids: Baker, 2003.

Gathercole, Simon J. "Pre-Existence, and the Freedom of the Son in Creation and Redemption: An Exposition in Dialogue with Robert Jenson." *IJST* 7/1 (2005): 38-51.

———. *The Preexistent Son: Recovering the Christologies of Matthew, Mark, and Luke.* Grand Rapids: Eerdmans, 2006.

Gaventa, Beverly. "Galatians 1 and 2: Autobiography as Paradigm." *NovT* 28 (1986): 309-26.

Gioia, Luigi. *The Theological Epistemology of Augustine's* De Trinitate. Oxford: Oxford University Press, 2008.

Glöel, Johannes. *Der heilige Geist in der Heilsverkündigung des Paulus. Eine biblisch-theologische Untersuchung.* Halle: Numeyer, 1888.

Godet, F. *Commentary on St. Paul's First Epistle to the Corinthians.* 2 volumes. Translated by A. Cusin. Edinburgh: T&T Clark, 1886-87.

Gorman, Michael J. *Cruciformity: Paul's Narrative Spirituality of the Cross.* Grand Rapids: Eerdmans, 2001.

Greenwood, David. "The Lord Is Spirit: Some Considerations of 2 Cor 3:17." *CBQ* 34 (1972): 467-72.

Groot, Aart de. "L'antitrinitarisme socinien." *Études théologiques et religieuses* 61/1 (1986): 51-61.

Gunkel, Hermann. *Die Wirkungen des heiligen Geistes nach der populären Anschauung der apostolischen Zeit und der Lehre des Apostels Paulus.* Göttingen: Vandenhoeck & Ruprecht, 1909 (1888). ET: *The Influence of the Holy Spirit:*

The Popular View of the Apostolic Age and the Teaching of the Apostle Paul. Philadelphia: Fortress, 1979.

Gunton, Colin E. "Augustine, the Trinity, and the Theological Crisis of the West." *SJT* 43 (1994): 33-58.

————. *The Promise of Trinitarian Theology.* 2nd edition. Edinburgh: T&T Clark, 1997 (1991).

————. *Act and Being: Towards a Theology of the Divine Attributes.* London: SCM, 2002.

Habermann, J. *Präexistenzaussagen im Neuen Testament.* Europäische Hochschulschriften; Frankfurt am Main: Peter Lang, 1990.

Hafemann, Scott J. *Paul, Moses, and the History of Israel: The Letter/Spirit Contrast and Argument from Scripture in 2 Corinthians 3.* WUNT. Tübingen: Mohr Siebeck, 1995.

Hahn, Ferdinand. *Theologie des Neuen Testaments.* Vol. II: *Die Einheit des Neuen Testaments.* Tübingen: Mohr Siebeck, 2005.

Hamilton, Neill Q. *The Holy Spirit and Eschatology in Paul.* SJTOP 6. Edinburgh: Oliver & Boyd, 1957.

Hanson, Anthony T. "The Midrash in II Corinthians 3: A Reconsideration." *JSNT* 9 (1980): 2-28.

Hanson, R. P. C. *The Search for the Christian Doctrine of God: The Arian Controversy 318-381 AD.* Edinburgh: T&T Clark, 1988.

Harris, Harriet A. "Should We Say That Personhood Is Relational?" *SJT* 51 (1998): 214-34.

Hart, David Bentley. "The Angel at the Ford of the Jabbok: On the Theology of Robert Jenson." Pages 156-69 in *In the Aftermath: Provocations and Laments.* Grand Rapids: Eerdmans, 2009.

Hart, Hendrick. *Understanding Our World: An Integral Ontology.* Lanham, MD: University Press of America, 1984.

Hay, David M. *Glory at the Right Hand: Psalm 110 in Early Christianity.* SBLMS 18. Nashville: Abingdon, 1973.

Haykin, Michael A. G. *The Spirit of God: The Exegesis of 1 and 2 Corinthians in the Pneumatomachian Controversy of the Fourth Century.* Leiden: Brill, 1994.

Hays, Richard B. *The Faith of Jesus Christ: An Investigation of the Narrative Substructure of Galatians 3:1–4:11.* SBL Dissertation Series 56. Chico, CA: Scholars Press, 1983.

————. *Echoes of Scripture in the Letters of Paul.* New Haven: Yale University Press, 1989.

————. *First Corinthians.* Interpretation; Louisville: Westminster John Knox, 1997.

————. "The Letter to the Galatians: Introduction, Commentary, and Reflections." Pages 181-350 in *NIB* 11. Edited by Leander Keck. Nashville: Abingdon, 2000.

————. "The God of Mercy Who Rescues Us from the Present Evil Age." Pages

123-43 in *The Forgotten God: Perspectives in Biblical Theology*. Edited by A. Andrew Das and Frank J. Matera. Louisville: Westminster John Knox, 2002.

———. "Abraham as Father of Jews and Gentiles." Pages 61-84 in *The Conversion of the Imagination: Paul as Interpreter of Israel's Scripture*. Grand Rapids: Eerdmans, 2005.

———. "Christ Prays the Psalms: Israel's Psalter as Matrix of Early Christology." Pages 101-18 in *The Conversion of the Imagination: Paul as Interpreter of Israel's Scripture*. Grand Rapids: Eerdmans, 2005.

———. "Spirit, Church, Resurrection: The Third Article of the Creed as Hermeneutical Lens for Reading Romans." *JTI* 5/1 (2011): 35-48.

Heil, U. "Theologische Interpretation von 1 Kor 15,23-28." *ZNW* 84 (1993): 27-35.

Hengel, Martin. *Der Sohn Gottes. Die Entstehung der Christologie und die jüdisch-hellenistische Religiongeschichte*. 2nd edition. Tübingen: Mohr Siebeck, 1977. ET: *The Son of God*. London: SCM Press, 1976.

———. "'Sit at My Right Hand!'" Pages 119-225 in *Studies in Early Christology*. Edinburgh: T&T Clark, 1995.

Héring, J. *La seconde épître de saint Paul aux Corinthiens*. Neuchatel: Delachaux et Niestle, 1958.

Hermann, Ingo. *Kyrios und Pneuma. Studien zur Christologie der paulinischen Hauptbriefe*. Munich: Kösel-Verlag, 1961.

Hickling, C. J. A. "The Sequence of Thought in II Corinthians, Chapter Three." *NTS* 21/3 (1975): 380-95.

Hill, Charles E. "Paul's Understanding of Christ's Kingdom in 1 Corinthians 15:20-28." *NovT* 30 (1988): 297-320.

Hofius, Otfried. "Eine Altjüdische Parallele zu Röm. IV.17b." *NTS* 18 (1971): 93-94.

———. "'Einer ist Gott — Einer ist Herr.' Erwägungen zu Struktur und Aussage des Bckcnntnisses 1 Kor 8,6." Pages 167-80 in *Paulusstudien II*. WUNT 143. Tübingen: Mohr Siebeck, 2002.

———. "Christus als Schöpfungsmittler und Erlösungsmittler. Das Bekenntnis 1 Kor 8,6 im Kontext der paulinischen Theologie." Pages 181-92 in *Paulusstudien II*. WUNT 143. Tübingen: Mohr Siebeck, 2002.

Holl, Karl. "Die iustitia dei in der vorlutherischen Bibelauslegung des Abendlandes." Pages 171-88 in *Gesammelte Aufsätze zur Kirchengeschichte. Der Westen*. Volume 3. Tübingen: Mohr, 1928.

Hollander, John. *The Figure of Echo: A Mode of Allusion in Milton and After*. Berkeley: University of California Press, 1981.

Holtz, Traugott. "Theo-logie und Christologie bei Paulus." Pages 105-21 in *Glaube und Eschatologie*. Edited by E. Grässer and O. Merk. FS W. G. Kümmel. Tübingen: Mohr Siebeck, 1985.

Hooker, Morna. "Philippians 2.6-11." Pages 88-100 in *From Adam to Christ: Essays on Paul*. Cambridge: Cambridge University Press, 1990.

Hoover, R. W. "The *Harpagmos* Enigma: A Philological Solution." *HTR* 64 (1971): 95-119.

Horn, Friedrich W. *Das Angeld des Geistes. Studien zur paulinischen Pneumatologie.* Göttingen: Vandenhoeck & Ruprecht, 1992.

Horsley, R. A. "The Background of the Confessional Formula in 1 Kor 8:6." *ZNW* 69 (1978): 130-5.

———. *1 Corinthians.* ANTC. Nashville: Abingdon, 1998.

Hunsinger, George. "Election and the Trinity: Twenty-Five Theses on the Theology of Karl Barth." *Modern Theology* 24/2 (2008): 179-98.

Hurtado, Larry W. *One God, One Lord: Early Christian Devotion and Ancient Jewish Monotheism.* Philadelphia: Fortress, 1988.

———. "Pre-Existence." Pages 743-46 in *Dictionary of Paul and His Letters.* Edited by G. F. Hawthorne, R. P. Martin, and D. G. Reid. Downers Grove, IL: InterVarsity Press, 1993.

———. "The Binitarian Shape of Early Christian Worship." Pages 187-213 in *The Jewish Roots of Christological Monotheism: Papers from the St Andrews Conference on the Historical Origins of the Worship of Jesus.* Edited by C. C. Newman, J. Davila, and G. Lewis. Leiden: Brill, 1999.

———. *Lord Jesus Christ: Devotion to Jesus in Earliest Christianity.* Grand Rapids: Eerdmans, 2003.

———. "Paul's Christology." Pages 185-98 in *The Cambridge Companion to St Paul.* Edited by James D. G. Dunn. Cambridge: Cambridge University Press, 2003.

———. *How on Earth Did Jesus Become a God? Historical Questions about Earliest Devotion to Jesus.* Grand Rapids: Eerdmans, 2005.

———. *God in New Testament Theology.* Library of Biblical Theology. Nashville: Abingdon, 2010.

———. "The Origins of Jesus-Devotion: A Response to Crispin Fletcher-Louis." *TynBul* 61/1 (2010): 1-20.

Jenson, Robert W. *The Triune Identity: God according to the Gospel.* Philadelphia: Fortress, 1982.

———. *Systematic Theology.* 2 volumes. Oxford: Oxford University Press, 1997.

———. "A Reply" [to Paul Molnar]. *SJT* 52/1 (1999): 132.

———. "Response to Watson and Hunsinger." *SJT* 55/2 (2002): 225-32.

———. "Identity, Jesus, and Exegesis." Pages 43-59 in *Seeking the Identity of Jesus: A Pilgrimage.* Edited by Beverly Roberts Gaventa and Richard B. Hays. Grand Rapids: Eerdmans, 2008.

Jewett, Robert. *Romans.* Hermeneia. Minneapolis: Fortress, 2007.

Jonge, Marinus de. "Monotheism and Christology." Pages 225-37 in *Early Christian Thought in Its Jewish Context.* Edited by John Barclay and John Sweet. Cambridge: Cambridge University Press, 1996.

———. *God's Final Envoy: Early Christology and Jesus' Own View of His Mission.* Grand Rapids: Eerdmans, 1998.

Juel, Donald H. "The Trinity in the New Testament." *Theology Today* 54/3 (1997): 312-24.

Jüngel, Eberhard. *The Doctrine of the Trinity: God's Being Is in Becoming.* Translated by Horton Harris. Edinburgh: Scottish Academic Press, 1976.

———. *God as the Mystery of the World.* Translated by Darell L. Guder. Grand Rapids: Eerdmans, 1983.

———. *Justification: The Heart of the Christian Faith.* Translated by Jeffrey F. Cayzer. London: T&T Clark, 2001.

Kammler, Hans-Christian. "Die Prädikation Jesu Christi als 'Gott' und die paulinische Christologie. Erwägungen zur Exegese von Röm 9,5b." *ZNW* 95/3-4 (2003): 164-80.

Käsemann, Ernst. "Kritische Analyse von Phil. 2, 5-11." *Zeitschrift für Theologie und Kirche* 47 (1950): 313-60.

———. *Commentary on Romans.* Translated by G. W. Bromiley. London: SCM, 1980.

Kasper, Walter. *The God of Jesus Christ.* Translated by Matthew J. O'Connell. London: SCM, 1984.

Keck, Leander E. "Toward the Renewal of New Testament Christology." *NTS* 32 (1986): 362-77.

Kerst, R. "1 Kor 8.6 — Ein vorpaulinisches Taufbekenntnis?" *ZNW* 66 (1975): 130-39.

Kilby, Karen. "Perichoresis and Projection: Problems with Social Doctrines of the Trinity." *New Blackfriars* 81 (2000): 432-45.

Kim, Seyoon. *The Origin of Paul's Gospel.* Grand Rapids: Eerdmans, 1982.

Kirk, J. R. Daniel. *Unlocking Romans: Resurrection and the Justification of God.* Grand Rapids: Eerdmans, 2008.

Klumbies, Paul-Gerhard. *Die Rede von Gott bei Paulus in ihrem zeitgeschichtlichen Kontext.* Göttingen: Vandenhoeck & Ruprecht, 1992.

Koch, Dieter-Alex. "Beobachtungen zum christologischen Schriftgebrauch in den vorpaulinischen Gemeinden." *ZNW* 71 (1980): 174-91.

———. *Die Schrift als Zeuge des Evangeliums. Untersuchungen zur Verwendung und zum Verständnis der Schrift bei Paulus.* BHT 69. Tübingen: Mohr Siebeck, 1986.

Kramer, Werner. *Christ, Lord, Son of God.* Translated by Brian Hardy. Studies in Biblical Theology 50. London: SCM, 1966 (1963).

Kreitzer, Larry J. *Jesus and God in Paul's Eschatology.* JSNTSup 19. Sheffield: JSOT, 1987.

———. "'When He at Last Is First!' Philippians 2:9-11 and the Exaltation of the Lord." Pages 111-27 in *Where Christology Began: Essays on Philippians 2.* Edited by Ralph P. Martin and Brian J. Dodd. Louisville: Westminster John Knox, 1998.

Kümmel, W. G. *The New Testament: The History of the Investigation of Its Prob-*

lems. Translated by S. M. Gilmour and H. C. Kee. Nashville: Abingdon, 1972 (1970).

Lafont, Ghislain. *Peut-on Connaître Dieu en Jésus-Christ?* Paris: Cerf, 1969.

Lambrecht, J. "Paul's Christological Use of Scripture in 1 Cor. 15.20-28." *NTS* 28 (1982): 502-27.

Langkammer, P. H. "Literarische und theologische Einzelstücke in 1 Kor VIII:6." *NTS* 17 (1970-71): 193-97.

Lash, Nicholas. "Up and Down in Christology." Pages 31-46 in *New Studies in Theology*, I. Edited by S. W. Sykes and J. D. Holmes. London: Duckworth, 1979.

Leenhardt, F. J. *The Epistle to the Romans*. London: Lutterworth Press, 1961.

Leithart, Peter J. *Athanasius*. Foundations of Theological Exegesis and Christian Spirituality. Grand Rapids: Baker Academic, 2011.

Levering, Matthew. *Scripture and Metaphysics: Aquinas and the Renewal of Trinitarian Theology*. Challenges in Contemporary Theology. Oxford: Blackwell, 2004.

Liddon, H. P. *The Divinity of Our Lord and Saviour Jesus Christ; Eight Lectures Preached Before the University of Oxford, in the Year 1866, on the Foundation of the Late Rev. John Bampton, M.A. Canon of Salisbury*. Lansing: Scholarly Publishing Office, University of Michigan Library, 2005 (1866).

Lietzmann, Hans. *An die Römer*. HNT 8. Tübingen: Mohr Siebeck, 1933.

————. *An die Korinther I, II*. 5th edition. HNT. Tübingen: Mohr Siebeck, 1969.

Lincicum, David. *Paul and the Early Jewish Encounter with Deuteronomy*. WUNT 2/284. Tübingen: Mohr Siebeck, 2010.

Lindbeck, George A. *The Nature of Doctrine: Religion and Theology in a Postliberal Age*. Philadelphia: Westminster, 1984.

Lindemann, Andreas. "Die Rede von Gott in der paulinische Theologie." *Theologie und Glaube* 69 (1979): 357-76.

Linebaugh, Jonathan A. "Debating Diagonal Δικαιοσύνη: The Epistle of Enoch and Paul in Theological Conversation." *Early Christianity* 1 (2010): 107-28.

————. "Announcing the Human: Rethinking the Relationship Between *Wisdom of Solomon* 13-15 and Romans 1.18–2.11." *NTS* 57 (2011): 214-37.

Linnemann, Eta. "Tradition und Interpretation in Röm 1,3f." *Evangelische Theologie* 31 (1971): 264-76.

Lohmeyer, E. *Kyrios Jesus. Eine Untersuchung zu Phil 2,5-11*. 2nd edition. Sitzungsberichte der Heidelberger Akademie der Wissenschaften. Heidelberg: Carl Winter, Universitätsverlag, 1961 (1927/28).

Lohse, Eduard. *Der Brief an die Römer*. KEK 4. Göttingen: Vandenhoeck & Ruprecht, 2003.

Longenecker, Bruce W. *The Triumph of Abraham's God: The Transformation of Identity in Galatians*. Edinburgh: T&T Clark, 1998.

————. "On Israel's God and God's Israel: Assessing Supersessionism in Paul." *JTS*, n.s. 58 (2007): 26-44.

Longenecker, Richard N. *Galatians*. WBC 41. Dallas: Word Books, 1990.

Lossky, Vladimir. *The Mystical Theology of the Eastern Church.* London: James Clarke, 1957.

Luther, Martin. *D. Martin Luthers Werke Kritische Gesamtausgabe.* Volume 10. Weimar: Herman Bohlaus Nachfolger, 1883ff. ET: *Luther's Works.* Vol. 25. St. Louis: Concordia and Philadelphia: Fortress, 1955-86.

Luz, Ulrich. *Das Geschichtsverständnis des Paulus.* Beiträge zur evangelischen Theologie 49. Munich: Chr. Kaiser, 1968.

MacDonald, Nathan. "The Origin of 'Monotheism.'" Pages 204-15 in *Early Jewish and Christian Monotheism.* Edited by Loren T. Stuckenbruck and Wendy E. S. North. JSNTSup 263. London: T&T Clark, 2004.

Madec, G. *"Inquisitione proficiente.* Pour une lecture 'saine' du *De Trinitate* d'Augustin." Pages 53-78 in *Gott und sein Bild. Augustinus De Trinitate im Spiegel gegenwärtiger Forschung.* Edited by J. Brachtendorf. Paderborn: Schöning, 2000.

Maier, F. W. "Ps 110,1 (LXX 109,1) in Zusammenhang von 1 Kor 15,24-26." *BZ* 20 (1932): 139-56.

Maleparampil, Joseph. *The "Trinitarian" Formulae in St. Paul: An Exegetical Investigation into the Meaning and Function of Those Pauline Sayings Which Compositely Make Mention of God, Christ and the Holy Spirit.* European University Studies Series 23 Theology 546. New York and Frankfurt am Main: Peter Lang, 1995.

Marshall, Bruce D. "Christ and the Cultures: The Jewish People and Christian Theology." Pages 81-100 in *The Cambridge Companion to Christian Doctrine.* Edited by Colin E. Gunton. Cambridge: Cambridge University Press, 1997.

———. *Trinity and Truth.* Cambridge Studies in Christian Doctrine. Cambridge: Cambridge University Press, 2000.

———. "Trinity." Pages 183-203 in *The Blackwell Companion to Modern Theology.* Edited by Gareth Jones. Oxford: Blackwell, 2004.

Marshall, I. Howard. "Incarnational Christology in the New Testament." Pages 1-16 in *Christ the Lord: Studies in Christology Presented to Donald Guthrie.* Edited by H. H. Rowdon. Leicester: InterVarsity Press.

Martin, Ralph P. *Carmen Christi: Philippians ii.5-11 in Recent Interpretation and in the Setting of Early Christian Worship.* Revised edition. Grand Rapids: Eerdmans, 1983 (1967).

Martyn, J. Louis. *Galatians: A New Translation with Introduction and Commentary.* AB 33A. New York: Doubleday, 1997.

———. "John and Paul on the Subject of Gospel and Scripture." Pages 209-30 in *Theological Issues in the Letters of Paul.* Nashville: Abingdon, 1997.

Mauser, Ulrich. "One God and Trinitarian Language in the Letters of Paul." *HBT* 20/2 (1998): 99-108.

McCall, Thomas H. *Which Trinity? Whose Monotheism? Philosophical and Systematic Theologians on the Metaphysics of Trinitarian Theology.* Grand Rapids: Eerdmans, 2010.

McCormack, Bruce L. "Grace and Being: The Role of God's Gracious Election in Karl Barth's Theological Ontology." Pages 92-110 in *The Cambridge Companion to Karl Barth*. Edited by John Webster. Cambridge: Cambridge University Press, 2000.

————. "Seek God Where He May Be Found: A Response to Edwin Chr. van Driel." *SJT* 60/1 (2007): 62-79.

————. "Election and the Trinity: Theses in Response to George Hunsinger." *SJT* 63/2 (2010): 203-24.

McDonnell, Kilian, and George T. Montague. *Christian Initiation and Baptism in the Holy Spirit: Evidence from the First Eight Centuries*. Collegeville, MN: Liturgical Press, 1991.

McGrath, James F. *The Only True God: Early Christian Monotheism in Its Jewish Context*. Urbana and Chicago: University of Illinois Press, 2009.

McIntosh, Mark A. *Mystical Theology: The Integrity of Spirituality and Theology*. Challenges in Contemporary Theology; Oxford: Blackwell, 1998.

McNamara, M. *The New Testament and the Palestinian Targum to the Pentateuch*. AnBib 27a. Rome: Editrice Pontificio Istituto Biblico, 1966.

Meeks, Wayne A. "The Temporary Reign of the Son: 1 Cor 15:23-28." Pages 801-11 in *Texts and Contexts: Biblical Texts in Their Textual and Situational Contexts*. Edited by Tord Fornberg and David Hellholm. Oslo: Scandinavian University Press, 1995.

Meyer, Paul W. "The Holy Spirit in the Pauline Letters." *Interpretation* 33 (1979): 3-18.

————. "'The Father': The Presentation of God in the Fourth Gospel." Pages 255-73 in *Exploring the Gospel of John*. Edited by R. A. Culpepper and C. C. Black. Louisville: Westminster John Knox, 1996.

Michel, Otto. *Der Brief an die Römer*. Göttingen: Vandenhoeck & Ruprecht, 1955.

Mitchell, Margaret M. *Paul and the Rhetoric of Reconciliation: An Exegetical Investigation of the Language and Composition of 1 Corinthians*. HUTh 28. Tübingen: Mohr Siebeck, 1992.

Moberly, R. W. L. *The Bible, Theology, and Faith: A Study of Abraham and Jesus*. Cambridge Studies in Christian Doctrine. Cambridge: Cambridge University Press, 2000.

————. "How Appropriate Is 'Monotheism' as a Category for Biblical Interpretation?" Pages 216-34 in *Early Jewish and Christian Monotheism*. Edited by Loren T. Stuckenbruck and Wendy E. S. North. JSNTSup 263. London: T&T Clark, 2004.

————. *Prophecy and Discernment*. Cambridge Studies in Christian Doctrine. Cambridge: Cambridge University Press, 2006.

Moffatt, James. *The First Epistle of Paul to the Corinthians*. London: Hodder and Stoughton, 1938.

Moltmann, Jürgen. *The Trinity and the Kingdom*. Minneapolis: Fortress, 1993 (1981).

Bibliography

Moo, Douglas J. *The Epistle to the Romans*. NICNT. Grand Rapids: Eerdmans, 1996.

Moule, C. F. D. "2 Cor. 3:18b, καθάπερ ἀπὸ κυρίου πνεύματος." Pages 231-37 in *Neues Testament und Geschichte*. Edited by H. Baltensweiler and R. Reicke. FS O. Cullmann. Tübingen: Mohr Siebeck, 1972.

———. "The New Testament and the Doctrine of the Trinity: A Short Report on an Old Theme." *ExpTim* 88 (1976): 16-20.

Moulton, J. H., and G. Milligan. *The Vocabulary of the Greek New Testament*. Peabody, MA: Hendrickson, 1995 (1930).

Moxnes, Halvor. *Theology in Conflict: Studies in Paul's Understanding of God in Romans*. NovTSup 53. Leiden: Brill, 1980.

Nagata, Takeshi. "Philippians 2:5-11: A Case Study in the Shaping of Early Christology." Ph.D. thesis, Princeton Theological Seminary, 1981.

Newman, Carey C. *Paul's Glory-Christology: Tradition and Rhetoric*. NovTSup 69. Leiden: Brill, 1992.

Nicolson, Marjorie Hope, and Sarah Hutton. *The Conway Letters: The Correspondence of Anne, Viscountess Conway, Henry More and Their Friends, 1642-1684*. Oxford: Oxford University Press, 1992.

Nisius, J. B. "Zur Erklärung von 2 Kor 3,16ff.." *ZKT* 40 (1916): 617-75.

North, J. Lionel. "The Transformation of Some New Testament Texts in Fourth- and Fifth-Century Disputes about Πνεῦμα: *Disputando Inclarescet Veritas*." Pages 335-48 in *The Holy Spirit and Christian Origins: Essays in Honor of James D. G. Dunn*. Edited by G. N. Stanton, B. W. Longenecker, and S. C. Barton. Grand Rapids: Eerdmans, 2004.

Oakes, Edward T. *Pattern of Redemption: The Theology of Hans Urs von Balthasar*. New York: Continuum, 2005 (1994).

O'Brien, Peter T. *The Epistle to the Philippians*. NIGTC. Grand Rapids: Eerdmans, 1991.

———. "The Gospel and Godly Models in Philippians." Pages 273-84 in *Worship, Theology and Ministry in the Early Church: Essays in Honor of Ralph P. Martin*. Edited by Michael J. Wilkins and Terence Page. JSNTSup 87. Sheffield: Sheffield Academic Press, 1992.

Ohlig, Karl-Heinz. *Ein Gott in drei Personen? Vom Vater Jesu zum "Mysterium" der Trinität*. Mainz: Matthias-Grünewald-Verlag, 1999.

Pannenberg, Wolfhart. *Jesus — God and Man*. Philadelphia: Westminster, 1968.

———. *Systematic Theology*. Volume 1. Translated by G. W. Bromiley. Grand Rapids: Eerdmans, 1991.

Paulsen, Henning. *Überlieferung und Auslegung in Römer 8*. WMANT 43. Neukirchen-Vluyn: Neukirchener Verlag, 1974.

Peters, Ted. *God as Trinity: Relationality and Temporality in Divine Life*. Louisville: Westminster John Knox, 1993.

Powell, Samuel M. *The Trinity in German Thought*. Cambridge: Cambridge University Press, 2001.

Propp, William H. C. *Exodus 19–40*. AB 2A. New York: Doubleday, 2006.

Rabens, Volker. "The Development of Pauline Pneumatology: A Response to F. W. Horn." *BZ* 43 (1999): 161-79.

———. *The Holy Spirit and Ethics in Paul.* WUNT 2/283. Tübingen: Mohr Siebeck, 2010.

Radde-Gallwitz, Andrew. *Basil of Caesarea, Gregory of Nyssa, and the Transformation of Divine Simplicity.* Oxford Early Christian Studies. Oxford: Oxford University Press, 2009.

Rahner, Karl. *The Trinity.* Translated by J. Donceel. 2nd edition. New York: Crossroad, 1997 (1967).

Rainbow, Paul A. "Jewish Monotheism as the Matrix for New Testament Christology: A Review Article." *NovT* 33 (1991): 78-91.

Reumann, John. *Philippians: A New Translation with Introduction and Commentary.* AB 33B. New Haven and London: Yale University Press, 2008.

Richard, E. "Polemics, Old Testament, and Theology: A Study of II Cor., III,I–IV,6." *Revue Biblique* 88 (1981): 340-67.

Richards, Jay Wesley. "Truth and Meaning in George Lindbeck's *The Nature of Doctrine.*" *Religious Studies* 33 (1997): 33-53.

Richards, W. Larry. "ὑποταγήσεται in 1 Corinthians 15:28b." *Andrews University Seminary Studies* 38/2 (2000): 203-6.

Richardson, Neil. *Paul's Language about God.* JSNTSup 99. Sheffield: Sheffield Academic Press, 1994.

Ricoeur, Paul. "Interpretative Narrative." Pages 237-57 in *The Book and the Text: The Bible and Literary Theory.* Edited by Regina M. Schwartz. Cambridge, MA: Basil Blackwell, 1990.

———. "Philosophical Hermeneutics and Biblical Hermeneutics." Pages 89-101 in *From Text to Action: Essays in Hermeneutics II.* London: Athlone Press, 1991.

Ridderbos, Herman. *Paul: An Outline of His Theology.* Translated by J. R. DeWitt. Grand Rapids: Eerdmans, 1975.

Robertson, Archibald, and Alfred Plummer. *A Critical and Exegetical Commentary on the First Epistle of St. Paul to the Corinthians.* ICC. Edinburgh: T&T Clark, 1914.

Rogers, Eugene F., Jr. *After the Spirit: A Constructive Pneumatology from Resources outside the Modern West.* Grand Rapids: Eerdmans, 2005.

Rowe, C. Kavin. "Romans 10:13: What Is the Name of the Lord?" *HBT* 22/2 (2000): 135-73.

———. "Biblical Pressure and Trinitarian Hermeneutics." *Pro Ecclesia* 11 (2002): 295-312.

———. "Luke and the Trinity: An Essay in Ecclesial Biblical Theology." *SJT* 56/1 (2003): 1-26.

———. *Early Narrative Christology: The Lord in the Gospel of Luke.* Grand Rapids: Baker Academic, 2009.

———. "The Trinity in the Letters of St. Paul and Hebrews." Pages 41-54 in *The Oxford Handbook of the Trinity.* Edited by Gilles Emery, O.P. and Matthew

Levering. Oxford Handbooks in Religion and Theology. New York: Oxford University Press, 2011.

Royse, James R. "Philo, Kyrios, and the Tetragrammaton." *Studia Philonica Annual* 3 (1991): 167-83.

Sanday, William, and Arthur C. Headlam. *The Epistle to the Romans.* ICC. Edinburgh: T&T Clark, 1895.

Sanders, E. P. *Paul and Palestinian Judaism.* London: SCM, 1977.

———. *Paul, the Law, and the Jewish People.* Philadelphia: Fortress, 1983.

Sanders, Fred. "Entangled in the Trinity: Economic and Immanent Trinity in Recent Theology." *Dialog: A Journal of Theology* 40/3 (2001): 175-82.

———. *The Image of the Immanent Trinity: Rahner's Rule and the Theological Interpretation of Scripture.* Issues in Systematic Theology 12. New York and Frankfurt am Main: Peter Lang, 2005.

Sandys-Wunsch, J., and L. Eldredge. "On the Proper Distinction between Biblical and Dogmatic Theology and the Specific Objectives of Each." *SJT* 33 (1980): 133-58.

Schlier, Heinrich. *Der Brief an die Galater.* KEK 7. Göttingen: Vandenhoeck & Ruprecht, 1971.

Schließer, Benjamin. *Abraham's Faith in Romans 4.* WUNT 2/224. Tübingen: Mohr Siebeck, 2007.

Schneider, Bernardin. *"Dominus autem Spiritus est" (II. Cor. 3,17a). Studium Exegeticum.* Rome: Catholic Book Agency, 1951.

———. "Κατὰ Πνεῦμα Ἁγιωσύνης (Romans 1,4)." *Biblica* 48 (1967): 359-87.

Schneider, Gerhard. "ὁρίζω," *Exegetical Dictionary of the New Testament.* 3 volumes. Edited by Horst Balz and Gerhard Schneider. Grand Rapids: Eerdmans, 1990-93.

Schnelle, Udo. *Apostle Paul: His Life and Theology.* Translated by M. Eugene Boring. Grand Rapids: Baker Academic, 2005.

Scholder, Klaus. *The Birth of Modern Critical Theology: Origins and Problems of Biblical Criticism in the Seventeenth Century.* Translated by John Bowden. London: SCM, 1990.

Schrage, Wolfgang. *Die Erste Briefe an die Korinther (1 Kor. 6,12–11,16).* EKKNT 7/2. Solothurn and Düsseldorf: Benziger; Neukirchen-Vluyn: Neukirchener, 1995.

Schweizer, E. "υἱός, υἱοθεσία, κτλ." *TDNT* 8:334-99.

Schwöbel, Christoph. "Christology and Trinitarian Thought." Pages 113-46 in *Trinitarian Theology Today: Essays on Divine Being and Act.* Edited by Christoph Schwöbel. Edinburgh: T&T Clark, 1995.

———. "Christologie und trinitarische Theologie." Pages 257-91 in *Gott in Beziehung.* Tübingen: Mohr Siebeck, 2002.

———. "God as Conversation: Reflections on a Theological Ontology of Communicative Relations." Pages 43-67 in *Theology and Conversation: Towards a Relational Theology.* Edited by J. Haers and P. De Mey. Leuven: Peeters, 2003.

Scmidbaur, H. C. *Personarum Trinitas. Die trinitarische Gotteslehre des heiligen Thomas von Aquin.* St. Ottilien: Eos Verlag, 1995.

Scott, James M. *Adoption as Sons of God: An Exegetical Investigation into the Background of ΥΙΟΘΕΣΙΑ in the Pauline Corpus.* WUNT 2/48. Tübingen: Mohr Siebeck, 1992.

Scroggs, Robin. *Christology in Paul and John: The Reality and Revelation of God.* Philadelphia: Fortress, 1988.

Seifrid, Mark A. *Christ, Our Righteousness: Paul's Theology of Justification.* NSBT 9. Leicester: Apollos, 2000.

Seitz, Christopher R. Review of Richard Bauckham, *God Crucified. IJST* 2/1 (2000): 112-16.

———. "Handing Over the Name: Christian Reflection on the Divine Name YHWH." Pages 131-44 in *Figured Out: Typology and Providence in Christian Scripture.* Louisville: Westminster John Knox, 2001.

Staniloae, Dumitru. *The Experience of God.* Orthodox Dogmatic Theology 1. Translated and edited by Ioan Ionita and Robert Barringer. Brookline, MA: Holy Cross Orthodox Press, 1994.

Stanley, Christopher D. *Paul and the Language of Scripture: Citation Technique in the Pauline Epistles and Contemporary Literature.* SNTSMS 74. Cambridge: Cambridge University Press, 1992.

Steenburg, David. "The Case against the Synonymity of Morphê and Eikôn." *JSNT* 34 (1988): 77-86.

Sterling, Gregory E. "Prepositional Metaphysics in Jewish Wisdom Speculation and Early Christian Liturgical Texts." *Studia Philonica Annual* 9 (1997): 219-38.

Strawson, P. F. *Individuals: An Essay in Descriptive Metaphysics.* London: Methuen, 1964.

Stuhlmacher, Peter. *Der Brief an die Römer.* NTD 6. Göttingen: Vandenhoeck & Ruprecht, 1989.

———. "Christus Jesus ist hier, der gestorben ist, ja vielmehr, der auch auferweckt ist, der zur Rechten Gottes ist und uns vertritt." Pages 351-61 in *Auferstehung-Resurrection: The Fourth Durham-Tübingen Research Symposium.* Edited by F. Avemarie and H. Lichtenberger. Tübingen: Mohr Siebeck, 2001.

Tanner, Kathryn. *Christ the Key.* Current Issues in Theology. Cambridge: Cambridge University Press, 2010.

Thiselton, Anthony C. *The First Epistle to the Corinthians.* NIGTC. Grand Rapids: Eerdmans, 2000.

Thrall, Margaret. *A Critical and Exegetical Commentary on the Second Epistle to the Corinthians.* ICC. Edinburgh: T&T Clark, 1994.

Thüsing, Wilhelm. *Per Christum in Deum. Das Verhältnis der Christozentrik zur Theozentrik.* Volume 1. Münster: Aschendorff, 1965.

———. *Erhöhungsvorstellung und Parousieerwartung in der ältesten nachösterlichen Christologie.* SBS 42. Stuttgart: KBW, 1979.

Torrance, Thomas F. *The Christian Doctrine of God: One Being, Three Persons.* Edinburgh: T&T Clark, 1996.

Turcescu, Lucian. "'Person' versus 'Individual,' and Other Modern Misreadings of Gregory of Nyssa." *Modern Theology* 18/4 (2002): 527-39.

Turner, Geoffrey. "Review: *Lord Jesus Christ: Devotion to Jesus in Earliest Christianity* by Larry W. Hurtado." *Heythrop Journal* 47 (2006): 453-54.

Turner, Max. "'Trinitarian' Pneumatology in the New Testament? — Towards an Explanation of the Worship of Jesus." *Asbury Theological Journal* 58/1 (2003): 167-86.

Vanhoozer, Kevin J. *Remythologizing Theology: Divine Action, Passion, and Authorship.* Cambridge Studies in Christian Doctrine. Cambridge: Cambridge University Press, 2010.

Volf, Miroslav. *Exclusion and Embrace: A Theological Exploration of Identity, Otherness, and Reconciliation.* Nashville: Abingdon, 1996.

Von Balthasar, Hans Urs. *Mysterium Paschale.* Translated by Aidan Nichols. Edinburgh: T&T Clark, 1990.

———. *Theo-Drama.* Volume III. Translated by Graham Harrison. San Francisco: Ignatius Press, 1992.

Waaler, Erik. *The Shema and the First Commandment in First Corinthians: An Intertextual Approach to Paul's Re-Reading of Deuteronomy.* WUNT 2/253. Tübingen: Mohr Siebeck, 2008.

Wagner, J. Ross. *Heralds of the Good News: Isaiah and Paul "In Concert" in the Letter to the Romans.* Leiden: Brill, 2002.

Wallace, Daniel B. *Greek Grammar beyond the Basics: An Exegetical Syntax of the New Testament.* Grand Rapids: Zondervan, 1996.

Wanamaker, C. A. "Philippians 2.6-11: Son of God or Adam Christology." *NTS* 33 (1987): 179-93.

Watson, Francis. "Trinity and Community: A Reading of John 17." *IJST* 1/2 (1999): 168-84.

———. "The Triune Divine Identity: Reflections on Pauline God-language, in Disagreement with J. D. G. Dunn." *JSNT* 80 (2000): 99-124.

———. "The Authority of the Veil: A Theological Reading of 1 Cor 11.2-16." *NTS* 46 (2000): 520-36.

———. "The Quest for the Real Jesus." Pages 156-69 in *The Cambridge Companion to Jesus.* Edited by M. Bockmuehl. Cambridge: Cambridge University Press, 2001.

———. "'America's Theologian': An Appreciation of Robert Jenson's *Systematic Theology,* with Some Remarks about the Bible." *SJT* 55/2 (2002): 201-23.

———. *Agape, Eros, Gender: Towards a Pauline Sexual Ethic.* Cambridge: Cambridge University Press, 2004.

———. *Paul and the Hermeneutics of Faith.* London and New York: T&T Clark, 2004.

————. *Paul, Judaism, and the Gentiles: Beyond the New Perspective.* Revised edition. Grand Rapids: Eerdmans, 2007.

————. "'I Received from the Lord . . .': Paul, Jesus, and the Last Supper." Pages 103-24 in *Jesus and Paul Reconnected: Fresh Pathways into an Old Debate.* Edited by Todd D. Still. Grand Rapids: Eerdmans, 2007.

————. "By Faith (of Christ): An Exegetical Dilemma and Its Scriptural Solution." Pages 147-63 in *The Faith of Jesus Christ: Exegetical, Biblical, and Theological Studies.* Edited by Michael F. Bird and Preston M. Sprinkle. Peabody, MA: Hendrickson, 2009.

————. "Mistranslation and the Death of Christ: Isaiah 53 LXX and Its Pauline Reception." Pages 215-50 in *Translating the New Testament: Text, Translation, Theology.* Edited by Stanley E. Porter and Mark J. Boda. Grand Rapids: Eerdmans, 2009.

Webster, John. *Barth's Ethics of Reconciliation.* Cambridge: Cambridge University Press, 1995.

————. "Incarnation." Pages 113-50 in *Word and Church: Essays in Christian Dogmatics.* Edinburgh and New York: T&T Clark, 2001.

Wedderburn, A. J. M. "Some Observations on Paul's Use of the Phrases 'in Christ' and 'with Christ.'" *JSNT* 25 (1985): 83-97.

Weinandy, Thomas. *The Father's Spirit of Sonship: Reconceiving the Trinity.* Edinburgh: T&T Clark, 1995.

Weiss, J. *Der erste Korintherbrief.* Revised edition. Göttingen: Vandenhoeck & Ruprecht, 1977 (1910).

————. "Die Bedeutung des Paulus für den modernen Christ." *ZNW* 19 (1919/20): 127-42.

Welch, Claude. *The Trinity in Contemporary Theology.* London: SCM, 1953.

————. *God and Incarnation in Mid-Nineteenth Century German Theology: G. Thomasius, I. A. Dorner, A. E. Biedermann.* New York: Oxford University Press, 1965.

Wengst, Klaus. *Christologische Formeln und Lieder des Urchristentums.* StNT 7. Gütersloh: Mohn, 1972.

Westerholm, Stephen. *Perspectives Old and New on Paul: The "Lutheran" Paul and His Critics.* Grand Rapids: Eerdmans, 2004.

White, Thomas Joseph, O.P. "Review of Gilles Emery, O.P., *Trinity, Church, and the Human Person.*" *Pro Ecclesia* 18/4 (2009): 474-77.

Wilckens, Ulrich. *Der Brief an die Römer.* 3rd edition. 3 volumes. EKKNT 6. Zurich: Benziger, 1997.

Williams, Rowan. "*Sapientia* and the Trinity: Reflections on the *De Trinitate.*" Pages 317-32 in *Collectanea Augustiana.* Volume 1. Edited by B. Bruning. Leuven: Leuven University Press, 1990.

Wilson, Todd A. "Wilderness Apostasy and Paul's Portrayal of the Crisis in Galatians." *NTS* 50 (2004): 550-71.

Winter, Bruce W. "Religious Curses and Christian Vindictiveness (1 Corinthians

12-14)." Pages 164-83 in *After Paul Left Corinth: The Influence of Secular Ethics and Social Change*. Grand Rapids: Eerdmans, 2001.

Witherington, Ben, III, and Laura M. Ice. *The Shadow of the Almighty: Father, Son, and Spirit in Biblical Perspective*. Grand Rapids: Eerdmans, 2002.

Wolff, C. *Der erste Brief des Paulus an die Korinther*. THKNT 7. Leipzig: Evangelische Verlagsanstalt, 1996.

Wrede, William. "The Task and Methods of 'New Testament Theology.'" Pages 68-116 in *The Nature of New Testament Theology*. Edited and translated by Robert Morgan. Naperville, IL: Alec R. Allenson, 1973.

Wright, N. T. "Adam, Israel and the Messiah." Pages 18-40 in *The Climax of the Covenant: Christ and the Law in Pauline Theology*. London: T&T Clark, 1991.

———. "Jesus Christ is Lord: Philippians 2.5-11." Pages 56-98 in *The Climax of the Covenant: Christ and the Law in Pauline Theology*. London: T&T Clark, 1991.

———. "Poetry and Theology in Colossians 1.15-20." Pages 99-119 in *The Climax of the Covenant: Christ and the Law in Pauline Theology*. London: T&T Clark, 1991.

———. "Monotheism, Christology and Ethics: 1 Corinthians 8." Pages 120-36 in *The Climax of the Covenant: Christ and the Law in Pauline Theology*. London: T&T Clark, 1991.

———. "The Seed and the Mediator: Galatians 3.15-20." Pages 157-74 in *The Climax of the Covenant: Christ and the Law in Pauline Theology*. London: T&T Clark, 1991.

———. *The New Testament and the People of God*. Christian Origins and the Question of God 1. Minneapolis: Fortress, 1992.

———. "The Letter to the Romans: Introduction, Commentary, and Reflections." Pages 393-770 in *NIB* 10. Edited by Leander Keck. Nashville: Abingdon, 2002.

———. *The Resurrection of the Son of God*. Christian Origins and the Question of God 3. Minneapolis: Fortress, 2003.

Yates, John W. *The Spirit and Creation in Paul*. WUNT 2/251. Tübingen: Mohr Siebeck, 2008.

Yeago, David S. "The New Testament and the Nicene Dogma: A Contribution to the Recovery of Theological Exegesis." *Pro Ecclesia* 3/2 (1994): 152-64.

Ziegler, J. *Isaias*. 2nd edition. Septuaginta 14. Göttingen: Vandenhoeck & Ruprecht, 1967.

Ziesler, John. *Paul's Letter to the Romans*. TPINTC. Philadelphia: Trinity Press International, 1989.

Zimmermann, Christiane. "Leben aus dem Tod. Ein Spezifikum in der Gottesrede des Römerbriefs." Pages 503-20 in *The Letter to the Romans*. Edited by Udo Schnelle. BETL 226. Leuven: Peeters, 2009.

Zizioulas, John D. *Being as Communion: Studies in Personhood and the Church*. Crestwood, NY: St. Vladimir's Seminary Press, 2002 (1985).

Index of Subjects and Names

Telos: christological, 64, 67-68, 72, 75,
124-25; God as creation's, 116
Theology: christology as aspect of, 6, 9,
10, 12, 49, 58-59, 71, 169; and exegesis,
21-22, 21n.76, 46-47, 171-72; in New
Testament, 27
Thiselton, Anthony, 128
Time and timelessness, 56, 67, 69,
74n.62, 75
Torrance, Thomas, 43n.156
Trinitarian hermeneutics, 19n.70, 31,
72-75, 132-33, 144, 149-53, 170-71. *See
also* Redoublement; methodology of,
43-47; suspicion of, 21-22
Trinitarianism: defining, 45-46, 46n.159;
terminology of, 19n.70, 22n.78; and
"trinitarian monotheism," 19; and
trinitarian renewal, 36-43
Trinitarian model, 1n.1, 21-22, 36-43;
distinct from christological model, 1,
18-20, 23-25
Trinity. *See also* Binitarianism; Persons
of Trinity: eastern understanding of,
38, 39; economic and immanent, 37,
165n.80; irreducibility of, 43, 44; and
Scripture, 21-22, 41-42, 62, 73n.61,
121n.22, 170-71; terms for persons of,
2n.2, 34
True vs. false, discernment of,
140nn.11-12

Vanhoozer, Kevin, 36n.123, 101, 103n.88
Veil, 145, 146, 148, 149
Vertical axis, Jesus plotted on, 2-5, 24-25,
28, 43-44, 80, 164, 168

Volf, Miroslav, 130n.59

Waaler, Erik, 115
Wanamaker, C. A., 120, 121, 122n.28,
131
Watson, Francis, 6n.11, 29, 31, 60, 73,
92n.52, 125n.40, 145n.25
Web metaphor, 25, 167, 168-69
Wedderburn, Alexander, 151n.47
Weinandy, Thomas, 165n.80
Wilckens, Ulrich, 161n.74
Williams, Rowan, 103n.89
Winter, Bruce, 138
Wisdom: christology, 8-9; as
mediator, 8
Witherington, Ben, III, 65n.44
Worship of Jesus, 9-10, 14-15, 17; in ear-
liest strands of New Testament, 18; as
honoring God, 17
Worship vs. veneration, 14n.53
Wrede, William, 21n.76
Wright, N. T., 8n.17, 30n.101, 68n.51, 91,
110n.102, 129
Writing on believers' hearts, 146

Yahoel, 11, 94-95
Yates, John, 162n.75
Yeago, David, 96
YHWH, 16, 84, 93, 145, 148-49; Jesus as,
94, 95-96, 109n.101, 144, 147; speaking
from within the cloud, 151n.45; Spirit
as, 153
Young, Frances, 43n.156

Zizioulas, John, 39, 40

Index of Scripture and Other Ancient Writings

Index of Greek Words